Military Recruiting in the United States

by Pat Elder

St. Mary's City, MD
First Edition-2016

Praise for *Military Recruiting in the United States*

"Books like this are critical to understanding the methodology of militarism. The growing intervention by the armed forces in our educational system is not solely for the purpose of recruiting bodies to fight our wars–it is also about recruiting minds. With a strategic focus on children, programs like the Young Marines, Starbase and JROTC are all mechanisms for embedding the values of militarism in a broader segment of the population. The implications of allowing this to continue are frightening to consider, yet civilians are failing to grasp the dangerous nature of the problem. Hopefully, coverage of the issue in this book will lead to increased awareness of the issue and, most importantly, stimulate greater activism to confront it."
~ *Rick Jahnkow, Program Coordinator of the Project on Youth and Non-Military Opportunities (YANO)*

"Aggressive military recruitment in our schools is a dark and dirty secret, ensnaring some of our most vulnerable students in a web of high pressure sales tactics to compel them to join the military. But communities can and should stand up for their students. Start by reading this book."
~ *Sue Udry, Executive Director, Defending Rights & Dissent*

"Pat Elder's knowledge and passion in protecting students from the predatory tactics of military recruiters is long and consistent. He led the effort in Maryland to pass a law regarding the administration of the Armed Serves Vocational Aptitude Battery, (ASVAB) in the state's schools. The law provides for parental consent for the military to use test results for recruiting purposes. Additionally, his work has caused schools across the country to take steps to protect student privacy from the military. Having Pat's wisdom and expertise in one book is welcome."
~*Lynn and Stephen Newsom, Directors, Quaker House Military Counseling Center*

"*Military Recruiting in the United States* details the need for countering the military's presence in schools. The book brings the aggressive role of military recruiters to light. As a guidebook, it is written for those of us who desire a peaceful future for our children without military influence in their lives. With careful research and extensive experience, Pat Elder details step by step actions to counter the hype and methods of military recruiters."
~*Barbara Harris, New York Coalition to Protect Student Privacy*

"Militarism, like racism, is more dangerous when hidden behind patriotism and policy. Pat Elder exposes the many ways our public schools and the Department of Education collaborate to serve the needs of the Department of Defense and suggests ways to prevent the predatory quest for students to fight wars."
~*Kathy Barker, Assistant Professor of Health Services, University of Washington*

"Pat Elder has been one of the leading antiwar voices in the United States for many years. His new book spells out in one resource how military service can be disastrous for a soldier's mental and physical health. Elder argues that 'cigarette packages come with warning labels; so too, should military recruitment pitches.' Elder's book should be required reading in all America's high schools."
~ *Mark Goldstone, a noted First Amendment lawyer who defended Pat Elder following his antiwar civil disobedience arrests.*

"Long-time counter-recruitment activist, Pat Elder's *Military Recruiting in the United States*, provides an important resource to educate the broader activist community and general public on the need to become involved in the efforts to demilitarize our public schools."
~ The National Network Opposing the Militarization of Youth

"If our culture better understood the truths that are in this book, we at the GI Rights Hotline would get fewer calls from military personnel in crisis."
~ Bill Galvin, Counseling Coordinator, Center on Conscience & War and counselor and board member, the GI Rights Hotline

©2016 Pat Elder

All rights reserved. No part of this book may be reproduced or transmitted in any form or by any means, including mechanical, electric, photocopying, recording, or otherwise, without the prior written permission of the publisher.

Elder, Pat, 1955, Aug. 16

Military Recruiting in the United States

Book design by Nell Elder
Printed in the USA
First Edition / December 2016

ISBN 13:978-1540353757
10:1540353753

www.counter-recruit.org

Contents

Introduction 8
Foreword by David Swanson 9
1. Military Enlistment Ruins Lives 15
2. The Military Enlistment Document Is Fraudulent 27
3. Recruiting Is Psy Ops at Home 34
4. Should Recruiters "Own" Our Schools? 44
5. Love Our Enemies? Or Kill Them? 65
6. Hollywood Pledges Allegiance to the Dollar 79
7. Madison Avenue Joins the Army. 96
8. Video Games Recruit & Train Killers 117
9. Schools Teach Reading, Writing, & Marksmanship 131
10. The Pentagon Is Tracking Our Kids 159
11. "Career Program" Is Enlistment Tool in Camo 175
12. JROTC Militarizes American Youth 205
13. U.S. Flouts U.N. Protocol on Child Soldiers 227
14. Conclusion 237
Further Research 249
Acknowledgments 250
About the Author 251
Index 252

Introduction
By Pat Elder

In 2014 researchers surveyed people from 65 nations and found that the United States topped the list as "the greatest threat to peace in the world today." It's not surprising. Although Americans see their military as defenders of freedom and democracy, much of the world views it as a ruthless projection of American power.

The U.S. has 800 foreign military bases while the rest of the world combined has 30. The U.S. has killed more than 10 million people in 35 nations since the end of World War II while none of the generally accepted Christian notions of a "Just War" have been present. We start the wars and we kill indiscriminately. The U.S. is the world's judge, jury, and executioner.

This is the backdrop for resisting the military's stated goal of the ownership of our high schools. No one in good conscience should join the U.S. military unless it is to alter or abolish it. It is a myth to suggest that America has a volunteer military force. Instead, it is a recruited force whose members are criminally conned into signing an enlistment document that forces pitiful souls to relinquish all of their rights to the military.

Two out of every five Army recruits never complete their first term. 17 and 18-year-olds are rushed into making decisions to enlist against their will, like you'd twist someone's arm behind their back right out of its socket. Hundreds of thousands of soldiers say they hate their jobs and several thousand desert their posts yearly, while the military barely pursues them. It's easier, the Pentagon reasons, to find more recruits in the high schools.

World domination starts in high school cafeterias and parking lots where recruiters increasingly enjoy unfettered access to our children. This book describes how the Pentagon manages to fill its ranks and it provides resources for resistance. This resistance is tempered and strengthened by our love and compassion. After all, our brothers, and sisters, friends, and neighbors serve in the U.S. military.

The peaceful revolution we struggle to birth can only draw breath if substantially more of us direct our creative energies toward the battle raging over the minds of America's school children. This book should aid in that struggle.

FOREWORD
By David Swanson

Most people in the United States are far from aware of the full extent of military marketing, advertising, and recruitment efforts. We run into movies and comic books and video games and toys and school worksheets and science fairs and television shows and websites all the time that have been funded by and created in collaboration with the U.S. military. But we don't know it. Or we know it, but we have so internalized the idea that the most expensive and extensive military the earth has ever known is simply normal, that we don't think of its role in our educational and entertainment systems as in any way questionable. We don't even think of the military's marketing as being aimed at recruitment, much less ask each other whether that's a good thing or being done in a proper way, or whether we ourselves should be forking over some $600 million a year just for the military's advertising budget.

Even more people are unaware of the work of counter-recruiters, of individuals and organizations that work to increase awareness of military recruitment and to counter it with inconvenient information — that is, information that may be inconvenient to recruiters but highly useful to potential recruits. Counter-recruiters bring veterans into schools to talk about their regrets. Counter-recruiters warn young people of the dangers of false promises and of contracts that will be binding only on them, not on the military. Counter recruiters lobby for policy changes that prevent the military from obtaining information on students without parental consent.

Sometimes – very rarely – counter-recruiters write outstanding books that inform us of the current state of affairs and guide us toward paths for engagement with their work. Pat Elder is a counter-recruiter turned author, and we are all in his debt. This book makes clear the need for counter-recruitment, and it provides the tools to expand it.

Why is counter-recruitment appropriate even when there is no draft, the military is all volunteer, and many people reading this book have never been pressured to enlist at all? Well, 99% of us in the United States are asked only to pay taxes for wars, vote for war architects for public office, tell pollsters we support wars, and tolerate war promotion throughout our culture. Nothing more is asked of us. But what about that other one percent? Our tax dollars don't fund a dime's worth of pro-peace propaganda for them. Despite warnings of health threats from the American Medical Association, military recruiters do not, like cigarette or alcohol marketers, have to provide the slightest shred of warning regarding the risks involved. They also are permitted to market to younger people than are the marketers of cigarettes and alcohol. As Elder points out, in most U.S. states you must be 21 to drink alcohol and 25 to rent a car, but at 18 you can kill or die in war.

Explaining the heavy, one-sided push experienced by targeted young men and women, disproportionately in low-income communities, to those who haven't experienced it, is like trying to explain predatory mortgage loans that push the borrower to default in order to collect more fees to someone who's only ever encountered banks that hoped their loans would be paid back. If you doubt the reality of aggressive recruitment, that's not your fault. But you won't doubt it after you read this book.

Counter-recruiters don't make any promises to anyone, though they may try to help young people find peaceful careers. They don't ask anyone to sign a contract to remain peaceful for six or eight or an infinite number of years. They don't secretly receive detailed data on students without their knowledge in order to better target them for counter recruitment. If we are to truly think of those who enlist in the U.S. military as volunteers, we are required to make sure they have accurate information. Volunteering on the basis of insufficient or misleading knowledge is not volunteering at all. Counter-recruitment, then, is not something to tolerate, but something to insist upon.

One of the first things a counter-recruiter, and this book, will make clear, is that even a well-informed volunteer in the U.S. military, unlike any other volunteer in any other enterprise, is not permitted to cease volunteering. Even when a contract expires, the military can extend it indefinitely. Before it expires, the recruit cannot end it without risk of a dishonorable discharge and/or prison, and the recruit— by the terms of the contract—lacks basic Constitutional rights that he or she is often told the wars are fought to somehow defend. The risks haven't stopped tens of thousands of people from deserting the U.S. military in recent years as soon as they discovered that, like most things, the military does not really resemble its television commercials.

War participation, unlike in the movies, does not come easily in real life. It takes intense conditioning to get most people to kill other human beings, and most people have a hard time recovering from having done so. This is great news for humanity, but bad news for veterans. The top cause of death in the U.S. military is suicide, and the suicide rates far exceed those for civilians. As Elder reports, some 45% of U.S. veterans of Iraq and Afghanistan have filed injury claims, and some 25% have sought mental health treatment through the Veterans Administration. About 26,000 sexual assaults occurred within the U.S. military in 2012. Some states are working to eliminate veteran homelessness. This is an indication of the normalization of war in a society in which at some point in the future all homeless people could be non-veterans. It is also an indication of the fact that veterans for many years have been far more likely than non-veterans to lose all means of subsistence. "Support the troops" bumper stickers don't actually pay anybody's rent.

On June 12, 2016, the *New York Times* ran an article that reported that "modern warfare destroys your brain." This was a reference to newly understood physical evidence of the damage done by being near explosions. If this were the National Football League you might expect a movie like Concussion to dramatize the problem. This being the military, which— by the way— pays the NFL with our money for most of the war hype at football games, one must rely on counter-recruiters to spread the word.

There are two major ways in which war destroys your brain, one of them long predating modernity, and both of them serious, real, and tragic whether neuroscientists have figured out what they look like under a microscope or not. In addition to the trauma of explosions, a participant in war faces the trauma of morality, the pain of facing hatred and violence, the agony of threatening and inflicting hatred and violence — aggravated in many cases by the weakness of belief in the cause. Once you join up, you're not asked to kill in only the wars you believe in. You're asked to obey without thinking at all.

In an end-of-year worldwide poll in 2014, Gallup asked people in dozens of countries whether they would be willing to fight in a war for their country. The results were encouraging, with some countries listed at only 10% or 20% willing to join in a war. The United States, at 44% willing to fight in a war, was quite high— though not the highest—by comparison. But people surveyed by Gallup covered the full age range of adults, and most of those years are above recruitment age. Most of those years are years in which you cannot enlist even if you want to.

This poll was conducted at a time when the United States had multiple wars underway and had for many years. Why would people claim that they "would" fight in a war, when clearly they would not? Why would the National Rifle Association produce a video with an elderly musician, Charlie Daniels, encouraging warmongering toward Iran? I think a lot of people like to imagine themselves at war from the safety of their backyards. But in doing so, they fuel a culture that encourages young people to sign up without thinking it through. In the words of Phil Ochs:

> It's always the old to lead us to the war
> It's always the young to fall
> Now look at all we've won
> With the saber and the gun.
> Tell me, is it worth it all?

I've met many veterans who signed up imagining they'd be global policemen and rescue workers, who discovered they were global pirates and snipers. Many of the most dedicated peace activists in the United States were once among the most enthusiastic recruits in the military. Many of them would not have been recruited had they had more information and other options. Many would not have been as attracted to Donald Trump's "steal their oil!" and "kill their families!" as they were to pretenses of defense or humanitarianism.

Polls have found that a majority of recruits say the lack of other career options was a major factor in their joining up. This is why one of the most indirect but powerful means of countering recruitment is to increase access to jobs or college. A "volunteer" military in a full-employment society with free college and job training would be far more significantly volunteer.

There are, of course, many sorts of peace activism, including education, demonstrations, protests, civil disobedience, citizen diplomacy, and so on. I engage in all of these and support them. But one major form of peace activism in need of expansion is counter-recruitment. It's a means of working locally, something that has greatly benefitted the environmental movement. It's a means of working face-to-face with people. It's a means of achieving immediate personal successes. When you help one young person stay out of the military, you know that you have done good work.

And don't imagine that every person you keep out will be replaced by someone else going in. And don't imagine the military does not need people now that it has robots. The military is having a heck of a time recruiting enough people to manage its robots. Even drone pilots have suffered PTSD and suicide. It's struggling with recruitment, while counter-recruiters are piling up successes they can point to. Elder points to some of them in this book and advises on how to achieve more—how to limit the use of military tests to collect data from students, how to counter recruitment pitches.

The military not only wants more recruits than it is getting right now, it wants the ability to use the draft again if desired. Bills have made significant progress in Congress this year to require that young women register for the draft just like young men, and to abolish the Selective Service entirely. The liberal progressive position has been in favor of keeping the Selective Service in place while adding women to it. That's how deeply war has been normalized. Some peace activists even want a draft because they think it would enlarge the peace movement. They claim the peace movement has never been as large as during the Vietnam War era when there was a draft. But there also has not been a U.S. war that killed anywhere close to as many people since that war. Imagining that we need a worse war in order to halt war requires that we fail to know our strength. We actually have the potential to end the draft forever and to deny the military the "volunteers" it wants as well.

People as smart as Tolstoy and Einstein thought we would end war only when individuals refused to take part. Ninety-nine percent of us are not asked to take part, but we have a role to play in protecting that other one percent. Of course the harm that U.S. wars inflict is overwhelmingly on the people who live where the wars are fought. The harm to U.S. troops is a drop in the bucket. But much of that harm is the moral injury that follows the infliction of harm on others. The experience of killing and injuring is traumatic for adults and even more so for kids. The United Nations, as Elder details, has sought to hold the United States accountable for its violation of a treaty in its recruitment of 17-year-olds. The United States is also now the only country on earth that has not ratified the Convention on the Rights of the Child. It's hard to dismiss the suspicion that military recruitment plays a role in the decision to remain outside that otherwise universal treaty and basic standard of modern civilization. •

A group of recruits take the oath of enlistment in New York City in April 2009.
D. MYLES CULLEN/US ARMY

Chapter One

MILITARY ENLISTMENT RUINS LIVES

The military is a scourge on the American experience

Our military is a scourge on the American experience. Forty percent of those recruited every year drop out in the first term. Musculoskeletal injuries alone account for 2 million medical encounters yearly. Desertions are rampant. Nearly half of all veterans who get out have filed injury claims with the U.S. Department of Veterans Affairs, whose waiting list still stands at a half million. Suicide is at or near record levels, and so are rapes and assaults. It's a monstrous institution in desperate need of reform, but the public fails to hold it responsible for the staggering level of human suffering it causes.

Harsh criticism of every major American governmental institution, including all of the executive departments, is a deeply ingrained part of the American experience, but criticism of the military is off limits. We are conditioned to "support the troops" and every aspect of American militarism. Evidence of the destructive role the military plays in the life of the country is overwhelming, yet when Gallup asks Americans to rate their most trusted institutions, the military consistently ranks at the top of the list. Gallup's poll of June 2016 showed that 73% of Americans had either a great deal or quite a lot of confidence in the institution. Another 19% of Americans have "some" confidence in the military. The military has ranked at the top of the list all but one year since 1989. The current 73% confidence level is significantly higher than the average 67% rating given the military since it was first measured in 1975. Disturbingly, the same poll showed that an all-time low, just 9% of Americans, have confidence in the US Congress.[1]

In September of 2016, Gallup asked Americans about their confidence in the media's ability to report "the news fully, accurately, and fairly" and only 32% thought it did—also an all-time low.[2]

Americans don't trust Congress, the very institution that is charged with representing their interests and guaranteeing their rights. They are also losing their faith in the media, leaving them rudderless in a hostile and rising tide of corporate ascendancy. In this environment, it is frightening to witness blind faith in the military, among the country's least democratic and least transparent institutions.

In the words of the great peace and justice advocate Medea Benjamin,

> Obsessed with maintaining access to power, the mainstream media just keeps handing their megaphone to the powerful and self-interested. Rarely do we hear from people who opposed the disastrous 2003 invasion of Iraq or rightly predicted the chaos that would result from NATO intervention in Libya. The few anti-war voices who manage to slip into the dialogue are marginalized and later silenced. Let's face it: fear sells, violence sells, war sells.[3]

Perhaps Orwell's description of "DOUBLETHINK" in *Nineteen Eighty-Four* can help to put this into perspective:

> The subtlest practitioners of DOUBLETHINK are those who invented DOUBLETHINK and know that it is a vast system of mental cheating. In our society, those who have the best knowledge of what is happening are also those who are furthest from seeing the world as it is. In general, the greater the understanding, the greater the delusion; the more intelligent, the less sane. One clear illustration of this is the fact that war hysteria increases in intensity as one rises in the social scale. - *George Orwell, 1984*[4]

Orwell's quote provides an excellent segue. The American people are duped. They've been deceived, tricked, and defrauded, but on a different level, they know the score. The military is the nation's most trusted institution because militarism and war are marketed like other consumable American commodities. The military defends our freedoms and Huggies Little Movers Camo Diapers "go on the march," exclusively at Walmart. But, our boy, who spent two tours in Iraq, is losing his mind, drinking himself to death while the VA continues to deny his disability compensation benefits. Orwell's doublethink pervades the public's attitudes concerning the military. Consider the issue of military desertions.

Eddie Slovik was the last American service member to be executed for desertion. Researcher Karen Mercury tells Slovik's story,

> The execution was carried out in France on January 31, 1945. Eddie

told his commander he was too scared to serve in a rifle company, asking to be assigned to a rear area unit. He told the commander he'd run away if sent to the front. Eddie was denied his request and sent to the front. He was immediately arrested. Shortly thereafter, soldiers strapped him to a post with belts and the chaplain said to him, "Eddie, when you get up there, say a little prayer for me." Slovik said, "Okay, Father. I'll pray that you don't follow me too soon." And Slovik was slammed with eleven bullets.[5]

Most Americans know death is the penalty for desertion, but they probably don't know when the last execution for this "crime" occurred or have any clue regarding the numbers of desertions in today's military. Certainly, they must think, it has to be a very low number! Actually, there were more than 20,000 deserters from the Army alone during the period from 2006 to 2014. Desertion is so common the military often looks the other way. The Army has pursued just 1,900 cases of desertion since 2001, and most of these prosecutions have resulted in little more than a slap on the wrist.[6]

Desertions are just one manifestation of a dysfunctional American military. The overwhelming majority of Americans who would qualify for military service aren't interested. The recruiting command is experiencing its greatest crisis since the end of the draft in 1973, although most Americans are oblivious.

For instance, click on www.goarmy.com/about and this is what you'll see:

> The U.S. Army is made up of the most dedicated, most respected Soldiers in the world. These Soldiers protect America's freedoms while serving at home and abroad, and they are always prepared to defend the nation in times of need.

Click on *Soldier Life* and the disconnection with reality becomes even more apparent, "You'll spend your days training, working and serving together to protect America's freedoms. You'll also have time after work for family, friends and personal interests. From recruitment to retirement, the U.S. Army provides a unique lifestyle."

It all sounds pretty enticing, but 15% of all enlistees don't make it through initial-entry training, and another 25% leave during their first permanent duty assignment in the operational Army. That means nearly 40% of all Army enlistees never complete their first term.[7]

The recruiting command is headed for a calamity on many fronts, notwithstanding the sophisticated marketing campaign that suggests otherwise. Not only do nearly half leave right off the bat, but the pool of potential recruits continues to shrink. Over 75% of the 30.6 million Americans between ages 17 and 24 can't become soldiers due to four main factors: inability to pass the enlistment test, criminal records, obesity, and other health issues.8

There is, however, no valid data for the generalizations the military circulates about failure rates for the enlistment test. These estimates misrepresent the capacity of the general population to pass the ASVAB. The military-misinformation machine making these misrepresentations doesn't want to admit that intelligent people are more likely to make a non-military choice, so they use statistics that filter them out. This trick helps them justify greater militarization of our schools.

Each year less than 400,000 young people become truly eligible for military service, but across all the services, around 200,000 are "needed". Each Army recruiter averages just 10 contracts a year. The numbers are similar for the Navy and the Marine Corps. The Army alone initiates 16,000,000 contacts a year—in the hopes of signing up 68,000 recruits for active duty.9

We can see why so many youth report being hounded by recruiters from all branches.

Obviously, one way to deal with the dropouts and desertions is to allow more recruits in by easing the requirements. For instance, the leading factor prohibiting enlistment is obesity, causing approximately 20% of ineligibilities.10

Throughout its history the Army has always demanded that all recruits meet the same rigorous physical requirements, but the top command is considering relaxing these requirements for Military Occupational Specialties (MOS's) that don't require a great deal of physical stamina. This might free leaner recruits for more rigorous duty. From Military.com,

> Today, we need cyber warriors, so we're starting to recruit for Army Cyber," Maj. Gen. Allen Batschelet said. "One of the things we're considering is that your [mission] as a cyber warrior is different." Maybe you're not the Ranger who can do 100 pushups, 100 sit-ups and run the 2-mile inside of 10 minutes, but you can crack a data system of an enemy. "But you're physically fit, you're a healthy person and maintain your professional appearance, but we don't make you have the same physical standards as someone who's in

the Ranger Battalion.[11]

Reportedly, recruits' scores on the Armed Services Vocational Aptitude Battery (ASVAB) have plummeted in recent years, making even fewer eligible to enlist. Batschelet, the Army's top recruiter, says the inability of potential recruits to clear the ASVAB test is of more concern than obesity. It's easier to help a soldier make weight than improve his smarts, he says.[12] But this doesn't apply to the vast majority of high school seniors who are heading to college and better employment opportunities. They have the smarts to pass the simple enlistment test. They're just not interested in the military. They've got better options.

The Army is considering relaxing minimal ASVAB scores to allow the lowest echelon recruits to enlist. Army regulations allow for 4% of enlistees to score in Category IV (10th to 30th percentile) and no more than 40% to score lower than Category IIIA (50th percentile or higher). Relaxing this criterion or substituting a non-academic personality test may open the floodgates to recruits who have hitherto been locked out. They may not be the brightest soldiers to join the ranks but, the Army reasons, some may have a greater propensity to stick it out.

The Army is toying with the idea of dispensing with the ASVAB in some cases if a candidate demonstrates a propensity to stick with the program. The Tailored Adaptive Personality Assessment System, or TAPAS, is being given at Military Entrance Processing Stations to 'screen in' candidates who are adaptive, resilient and have dedication, but perhaps scored only marginally on the ASVAB. According to Lt. Gen. James C. McConville, Lieutenant General Deputy Chief of Staff, G-1, "It's not necessarily SAT scores, it's not necessarily GPAs, it's people who have grit. And so how do you define grit -- how do you measure that?"[13]

It may be tough to measure *grit*, but it'll probably involve soldiers who are barely literate if they can't score at least above the 31% threshold on the Armed Forces Qualification Test, or AFQT.

Rick Jahnkow of the San Diego-based Project on Youth & Non-Military Opportunities (YANO) explains,

> They will have to stop having recruiters initially promise a particular MOS. In the past they have traditionally elected to allow recruiters to offer some degree of job guarantee. While this benefits recruiting, it also reduces the military's post-basic training assignment flexibility. If there is going to be an increase in recruits who score

marginally on the ASVAB and are accepted because of their "grit," they will need more flexibility for job assignments after basic. So stopping the practice of recruiters offering an MOS guarantee would become necessary, even if it would require recruiters to work harder to sell enlistment.[14]

The average recruit is in terrible shape, compared to his predecessors, and not simply in terms of weight. He is much more prone to being injured, leaving the ranks even further depleted. The statistics are mind-boggling because we're conditioned to think of the Army in terms of being an invincible force.

It takes much longer today for the military to transform civilians into traditionally "qualified service members," while the amount of time allotted to basic training and the overall rigor of the program hasn't changed much from the days when youth were in much better shape. The process is excruciating for tens of thousands who must endure it annually. Something has to give, and it is typically not the drill sergeant.

The Army could stretch out the boot camp and start soldiers off by walking and doing very light calisthenics for a few weeks, but that would require a degree of humanism and common sense generally lacking in the chain of command. Instead, new soldiers are breaking bones and wreaking havoc on their bodies in record numbers.

According to a 2013 article by Dr. Bradley Nindl, science advisor for the U.S. Army Institute of Public Health, musculoskeletal injuries (MSI) represented the leading cause of medical care visits across the military services resulting in almost 2,200,000 medical encounters in 2012 alone.

> Many of the injury-related musculoskeletal conditions are due to the cumulative effects of repetitive microtrauma forces: overreaching/training, overuse, overexertion, and repetitive movements experienced during both occupational duties and physical training. Overuse injuries are an indicator that a unit is overtraining. Of the almost 750,000 MSIs reported in 2006 in military medical surveillance data on active duty, nondeployed service members, 82% were classified as overuse.[15]

According to the article the Army's deployment readiness was at just 85% for active duty and only 70% for Guard and Reserve forces because of the MSI problem.

Tens of thousands of soldiers desert their posts. 40% drop out in the first few months, thousands fail an elementary-level entrance test, and three-quarters of a million who aren't even deployed sustain musculo-skeletal injuries every year.

It gets worse.

USA Today reported in April of 2015 that nearly half of the 770,000 soldiers polled in 2014 "have little satisfaction in or commitment to their jobs," according to resiliency assessments soldiers are required to take every year. "The effort produced startlingly negative results. In addition to low optimism and job satisfaction, more than half reported poor nutrition and sleep, and only 14% said they are eating right and getting enough rest."[16]

Taken all together the reality of military life and the squeaky clean marketing image just doesn't jibe. Factor in the abysmal treatment offered by the Veterans Affairs Administration and the entire military conflagration looks like a major train wreck.

Forty-five percent of the 1.6 million veterans of the U.S. wars in Iraq and Afghanistan have filed injury claims with the Department of Veterans Affairs. Furthermore, the veterans are claiming an average of 8-9 physical or mental injuries each. (For comparison, only 21% of veterans filed injury claims after the 1991 Gulf War.)[17]

The following numbers were supplied by the DOD in 2012 for various injuries claimed by Iraq and Afghanistan veterans:

- More than 1,600 of them lost a limb; many others lost fingers or toes.
- At least 156 are blind, and thousands of others have impaired vision.
- More than 177,000 have hearing loss, and more than 350,000 report tinnitus (noise or ringing in the ears).
- Thousands are disfigured, as many as 200 of them so badly that they may need face transplants. One-quarter of battlefield injuries requiring evacuation included wounds to the face or jaw, one study found.
- More than 400,000 of them have been treated by the VA for mental health problems, most commonly PTSD.

Nearly half of all the soldiers sent to a combat zone suffer a serious injury that could forever limit their ability to get a job, go to college, get married, or have a normal personal life. Enlisting is like playing Russian roulette with half the chambers loaded with bullets. The recruiting command never includes this information in their marketing campaigns. Care to hop on the bus to basic training?

Soldiers kill people. It is their raison d'etre. When they return home many obsess on their crimes. They grovel in their shame; their anxiety, guilt, and anger. They often feel alienated and without meaning. They experience withdrawal and self-hatred and as a response they harm themselves and the people they love the most. They're taking their own lives in record numbers and the systems we've established to help them are failing miserably. But only a few American can connect the dots.

When the military is through with many soldiers they're no longer Army Strong nor can they be all they can be, although they may feel like an Army of One, left alone, considering their treatment by the Veterans Administration. The number of veterans waiting more than a month for care at Department of Veterans Affairs hospitals climbed well over half a million at the start of October, 2016.[18]

There's more horror. In 2013 The Citizens Commission on Human Rights reported the following:

> In 2013 the Pentagon announced the startling statistic that the number of military suicides in 2012 had far exceeded the total of those killed in battle—an average of nearly one a day. A month later came an even more sobering statistic from the U.S. Department of Veterans Affairs: veteran suicide was running at 22 a day—about 8,000 a year.[19]

Military service can be disastrous for a soldier's mental health. Cigarette packages come with warning labels; so too, should the way the military packages its recruitment pitch. It's just not clear to the American people. Take, for instance, an *LA Times* story by Alan Zarembo that ran on March 3, 2014. Nearly 1 in 5 had mental illness before enlisting in the Army, one study says. Zarembo cites studies published in the *Journal of the American Medical Association* finding that "despite screening, pre-enlistment rates of depression, anxiety, bipolar disorder and substance abuse were on par with civilian rates. Rates of suicidal ideation, planning and attempts were lower than in the general population but still significant, given the military's practice of excluding recruits with a known suicidal history."

This is hardly newsworthy, although the editors allowed the lead to be buried in the story:

> During their military service, the soldiers' rates of most psychiatric disorders climbed well past civilian levels, several times the rate for some disorders. A quarter of soldiers were deemed to be suffering from a mental illness — almost 5% with depression, nearly 6%

with anxiety disorder and nearly 9% with PTSD. The percentage of soldiers who had attempted suicide rose from 1.1% to 2.4%."[20]

Apparently, military children are more likely to have a history of suicide attempts than their civilian counterparts. The findings are based on a survey of 9th and 11th graders at 261 schools across California in 2012 and 2013. Of 2,409 students with a parent in the military, 11.7% answered yes when asked if they had attempted suicide in the previous year. For the 21,274 students with civilian parents, that figure was 7.3%.[21]

The researchers said the stresses of more than a decade of war—parents away on long deployments or back home dealing with physical and mental health problems—had trickled down to children in military families.

Sexual assaults against women and men are at record levels in the military. An estimated 26,000 sexual assaults took place in the military in 2012, the last year that statistic is available; only 1 in 7 victims reported their attacks, and just 1 in 10 of those cases went to trial.[22]

Military sexual trauma (MST) is devastating. It includes depression, substance abuse, and paranoia. It's certainly not the stuff of recruitment brochures. Attempts to address the epidemic by U.S. Senators Kirsten Gillibrand (D-N.Y.) and Barbara Boxer (D-Calif.) were defeated in 2014. From Senator Gillibrand's website:

> The Military Justice Improvement Act would have moved the decision whether to prosecute any crime punishable by one year or more in confinement outside of the chain of command to independent, trained, professional military prosecutors. 50% of female victims stated they did not report the crime because they believed that nothing would be done with their report. Commandant of the Marine Corps General James F. Amos said victims do not come forward because "they don't trust the chain of command."[23]

John McCain, typically a poster boy for all things military, told the top U.S. military chiefs in 2013 he could not advise women to join the service with a sexual-assault scourge the military has not contained.

> Just last night, a woman came to me and said her daughter wanted to join the military and could I give my unqualified support for her doing so. I could not," the Arizona Republican, a Vietnam veteran and ex-prisoner of war, told the uniformed chiefs of the Army,

Navy, Air Force, Marine Corps and Coast Guard at a Senate Armed Services Committee hearing.[24]

The record presented here is extraordinarily damning to the Pentagon; nonetheless, they still manage to meet most of their annual recruiting goals, though barely. This Teflon-clad institution has built a recruiting system upon a slippery bedrock of deception and obfuscation.

Exposing the lies and countering recruitment is fundamentally revolutionary. Resisting the unprecedented and relentless militarization of American youth transcends the current US-sponsored wars du jour. Countering military recruitment confronts an ugly mix of a distinctively American brand of institutionalized violence, racism, militarism, nationalism, classism, and sexism.

The Department of Defense and a misguided American foreign policy have become destructive of life, liberty, and the pursuit of happiness. Meanwhile, the military, paradoxically, enjoys the consent of the people. The nation is victimized by a brutal military machine and its malicious, criminal propaganda campaign. It is one of the greatest tragedies of the American experience.

Notes to Chapter 1

1. "Confidence in Institutions." Gallup.com 5, June 2016. Web 3 Dec. 2016.http://bit.ly/K86edV

2. Swift, Art. "Americans' Trust in Mass Media Sinks to New Low" Gallup.com 16 Sept. 2016 Web 3 Dec. 2016 Americans' Trust in Mass Media Sinks to New Low.

3. Benjamin, Medea. "The Fourth Estate in Flames: On the US Media's Award-Winning War Propaganda." Common Dreams. 10 Oct. 2014. Web. 8 July 2015. http://bit.ly/2eZoBTf.

4. Orwell, George, Nineteen Eighty-Four, Penguin Books, 1956, p. 169.

5. Mercury, Karen. "Unusual Historicals." Cowards: The Execution of Private Slovik. 11 Apr. 2011. Web. 8 July 2015. http://bit.ly/2dZ26ep.

6. Associated Press. "Army Data Shows Rarity of Desertion Prosecutions." The New York Times, 24 Dec. 2014. Web. 9 July 2015. http://nyti.ms/2dROuq4.

7. Sheftick, Gary. "Army considering Major Changes for Recruiting." ARMY.MIL, The Official Homepage of the United States Army. U.S. Army, 23 Oct. 2014. Web. 9 July 2015. http://bit.ly/1HGaMzw.

8. "About Us." Mission Readiness - Military Leaders for Kids. Web. 9 July 2015. http://www.missionreadiness.org/about-us/.

9. Lopez, C. Todd. "To Become ' Force of Future,' Army Must Fix Personnel Churn." ARMY.MIL, The Official Homepage of the United States Army. U.S. Army, 26 June 2015. Web. 9 July 2015. http://bit.ly/1Jt27Fo.

10. "ARMY.MIL, The Official Homepage of the United States Army. Forum Studies Bleak Recruiting Future of the All-volunteer Army." U.S. Army, 20 Oct. 2014. Web. 9 July 2015. http://bit.ly/1sIkYS6.

11. Davis, Clifford. "Army Says Only 30% of Americans Could Join." Military.com. 24 Oct. 2014. Web. 9 July 2015. http://bit.ly/2eHA9vO.

12. Jahner, Kyle. "Lower Test Scores Hurting Army Recruitment Efforts." Military Times. 4 Dec. 2014. Web. 9 July 2015. http://bit.ly/2eZqGP9.

13. Sheftick, Gary. "Army considering Major Changes for Recruiting."

14. R. Jahnkow Counter-Recruitment Activists, Yahoo Groups, October 26, 2015, https://yhoo.it/2dRNfYa.

15. Lindl, PhD, Bradley. "Strategies for Optimizing Military Physical Readiness and Preventing Musculoskeletal Injuries in the 21st Century." The U.S. Army Medical Department Medical Journal. Web. 1 Oct. 2014. http://bit.ly/JuPCw0.

16. Zoroya, Gregg. "Army Morale Low despite 6-year, $287M Optimism Program." USA Today. Gannett, 16 Apr. 2015. Web. 9 July 2015. http://usat.ly/1aBELxD.

17. Marchione, Marilynne. "U.S. Vets' Disability Filings Reach Historic Rate." USATODAY.COM. 28 May 2012. Web. 9 July 2015. http://usat.ly/1OFZPnb.

18. Chalfant, Morgan. "Half a Million Vets Waiting Over 30 Days for VA Care" Washington Free Beacon, 18 Oct. 2016 Web. 3 Dec. 2016. http://bit.ly/2fTBhy1

19. Sexton, Connie Cone. The Arizona Republic. "As Suicides Rise among Veterans, Outreach Increases." USA Today. Gannett, 19 Mar. 2013. Web. 9 July 2015. http://usat.ly/2fiiXyW.

20. Zarembo, Alan. "Nearly 1 in 5 Had Mental Illness before Enlisting in Army, Study Says." Los Angeles Times, 3 Mar. 2014. Web. 9 July 2015. http://lat.ms/2frLIZf.

21. Zarembo, Alan. "Military Children More Likely to Have a History of Suicide Attempts." Los Angeles Times, 19 Mar. 2015. Web. 9 July 2015. http://lat.ms/1MRFQho.

22. Calvert, Mary F. "Photos: Women Who Risked Everything to Expose Sexual Assault in the Military." Mother Jones, 8 Sept. 2014. Web. 9 July 2015.

http://bit.ly/1oiHuwu.

23. "Comprehensive Resource Center for the Military Justice Improvement Act." Sen. Kirsten Gillibrand. Web. 9 July 2015. http://www.gillibrand.senate.gov/mjia.

24. Dietsch, Kevin. "McCain: Sex Assaults so Bad I Advise Women to Avoid Military." UPI, 5 June 2013. Web. 9 July 2015. http://bit.ly/2eUqimF.

SGT. ABE THE HONEST RECRUITER

EXPLAINS THE ENLISTMENT/REENLISTMENT DOCUMENT
OF THE ARMED FORCES OF THE UNITED STATES

By Chuck Fager &
John Stephens
Sgt. Abe images by:
Max Miller Dowdle
www.Artagem.com

Sgt. Abe: So, you're looking for **ADVENTURE, JOB TRAINING,** and **MONEY FOR COLLEGE?**

If you join the military, you'll fill out a 4-page from just like this. But **BEFORE YOU SIGN IT,** there are some **VERY IMPORTANT** things you need to know!

Sgt. Abe: On the first page, things seem pretty solid. But *nothing* is as simple as it looks.

Take the length of enlistment, for instance. Here, it looks definite & limited. But in fact it's **NOT**. The military can make it longer. If you don't believe me, turn the page!

Sgt. Abe: In this section recruiters make a lot of *sweet* promises. They might attach extra pages with even more promises.
But **GET THIS—**
THE MILITARY can **BREAK ALL OF THEM!**

NOTICE: if you change your mind about **DEP**, you can get out easily. If a recruiter says you can't, **THAT'S NOT TRUE**. Details on page 4.

Chapter Two

THE MILITARY ENLISTMENT DOCUMENT IS FRAUDULENT

Enlistment agreement is binding upon the recruit but not binding upon the military

The Enlistment/Reenlistment Document, DD FORM 4, amounts to an unconscionable sucker punch that lays out the woefully unsophisticated and uneducated recruit. It is reprehensible and entirely unacceptable that the United States of America, a nation with a rich tradition of constitutionally guaranteed civil liberties, should resort to proffering this charade of an "agreement" to the vulnerable young. This document is an imprisoning, one-sided, legally obligating miscarriage of justice.

Every year American high schools produce hundreds of thousands of semi-literate youth who are routinely devoured by the vultures of American capitalism through extraordinarily complex multi-page contracts that represent corporate interests in every sector of the American marketplace. Twenty-page cell phone and credit card agreements are written in complex terms in very fine print, although these are relatively simple instruments compared to most finance and insurance contracts. High school graduates might study Chaucer and Algebra but they're functionally illiterate and woefully unprepared for the American marketplace. They can't comprehend the contracts that govern their lives because they don't teach that stuff in American high schools– and they're not likely to any time soon. The handful of corporate behemoths that control the lion's share of the US economy prefers ignorant consumers in this regard.

These contractual entanglements produce a tyranny of the corporate elite, but they stop short of exercising the all-encompassing and incarcerating power of the military Enlistment/Reenlistment Document, DD FORM 4.

Its unlikely many military recruits read and fully comprehend the fine print in the enlistment document, although they'd be well advised to pay attention to Page 2, Sec 9. 5(b), which states:

> **Laws and regulations that govern military personnel may change without notice to me. Such changes may affect my status, pay, allowances, benefits, and responsibilities as a member of the Armed Forces REGARDLESS of the provisions of this enlistment/ reenlistment document.**[1]

This is tantamount to a credit card agreement that says cardholders are locked in for a minimum of 8 years or a maximum of eternity with the possibility of interest rates reaching 100% or more without notice.

The enlistment/reenlistment document is not a contract. It is a one-way arrangement that is binding upon the recruit but not the military. The document is like the indentured servant agreement executed during the colonial period in many of the American colonies, except that the indentured servant contract typically lasted seven years, whereas the military enlistment contract lasts longer and may be renewed indefinitely.

Section 10 a. requires recruits to serve for eight (8) years. While soldiers may only serve four years of active duty, they are legally contracted, and may be called up any time, during those eight years. Too often, new recruits think they've signed up for four years of active duty only to find later they may be required to serve for four additional years – and longer.

During a time of "war" soldiers might be required to serve indefinitely. Section 10 c. addresses "Stop-Loss":

> As a member of a Reserve Component of an Armed Force, in time of war or of national emergency declared by the Congress, I may, without my consent, be ordered to serve on active duty, for the entire period of the war or emergency and for six (6) months after its end (10 U.S.C. 12301(a)). My enlistment may be extended during this period without my consent (10 U.S.C. 12103(c)).

Unfortunately, most high school youth are not afforded the opportunity to study constitutional law. If they did, they'd learn the crucial importance of cases like Wallace v. Chafee, the litigation of a military enlistment contract in which the Court of Appeals for the Ninth Circuit held, "One who enters a contract is on notice of the provisions of the contract. If he assents voluntarily to those provisions after notice, he should be presumed, in the absence of ambiguity, to have understood and agreed to comply with the provisions as written."

The recruiting command doesn't want potential recruits to spend a great deal of time thinking about the most important decision most have ever made up to this point in their lives. Consider this outrageous excerpt from the Army's Recruiter Handbook, USAREC Manual 3-01, which gives advice to recruiters who must fill a monthly quota;

> Even though face-to-face isn't the most efficient means of prospecting, it is the most effective if excessive travel is not required. With the lowest contact to contract ratio, face-to-face prospecting should be your method of choice when you need a quick contract. Simply make a list of people you haven't been able to contact, grab some RPIs (recruiting publicity items), and knock on some doors.[2]

It doesn't have to be this way. In many European nations, where youth are much better educated in the public high schools, soldiers are allowed and encouraged to join either a professional association or a trade union representing their interests. European national forces are prohibited from victimizing individual members of the armed forces for participation in unions.

In the United States, Title 10 U.S. Code § 976 specifically prohibits soldiers from organizing or joining military unions. Military labor organizations are illegal. Collective bargaining is illegal. Soldiers who attempt to address their grievances against the military by striking, picketing, marching, or demonstrating risk arrest.[3]

The law is unconscionable. Eighteen-year-olds can't be expected to possess the skills to fully understand and negotiate the military enlistment/reenlistment agreement nor are they able to advocate for themselves once they're subjected to the chain of command.

Too often parents are exasperated and disheartened when their rebellious teen is befriended by recruiters at school and enlists without their knowledge or approval. Imagine a mother's fear and her feelings of remorse and guilt and betrayal when she realizes her only son is joining the Army largely to spite her. It happens all too frequently.

But the Army is pretty cool because it lets you blow stuff up and the Staff Sergeant at school is a great guy and a bus ride to boot camp is a ticket out of the basement at home. Mom and dad are furious when they discover their boy and the recruiter have become fast friends and they've been playing one-on-one basketball in the gym after school since spring break. They're shocked when they discover that their 18-year-old child has already signed an enlistment contract and has been placed into the Delayed Entry Program (DEP).

For many parents it's the powerlessness and sense of betrayal that cuts most deeply. The high school, which is supposed to be a safe place for kids, encouraged the staff sergeant to ensnare their child. In a few dizzying days, mom and dad have learned about the enlistment process and the DEP and have spoken to counselors with the GI Rights Hotline, who explain there's really not much they can do other than attempt to persuade their son not to report to basic training.

It is instructive to examine the illogical treatment of 18-year-olds in American society. Eighteen-year-olds are not allowed to drink alcoholic beverages anywhere in the U.S.; they have to wait until they're 21, and most states set the legal age for gambling at 21. Hawaii requires residents to be 21 to purchase cigarettes. Most rental car agencies set a minimum age requirement of 25.

A 20-year-old Army Specialist, returning from Afghanistan after a tour as a military police officer, wouldn't be allowed to serve in most municipal or state police forces. Nonetheless, federal law allows 17 year-olds to enlist with parental O.K.

Almost all of the 17- and 18-year-olds recruited through their high schools are placed into the Delayed Entry Program or DEP;

The GI Rights Hotline is an excellent source on the DEP.

> The DEP is pushed hard by recruiters to high school seniors who are unsure what to do after graduation. A lot can happen in a year, and many people change their minds about what they want to do with their lives. Also, more and more people are realizing that recruiters misrepresent military life and lie to them. The promises made by recruiters about money for college and job skills are not really what the military is about, and many realize they don't want to go to war for a cause they may be opposed to, have questions about, or feel is not really their concern.
>
> Others have talked to people who have been to Iraq, and who may have been wounded or traumatized by their participation in the war. Still others are concerned about the open-ended nature of military enlistment, and have heard of soldiers being Stop-Lossed beyond the time they were supposed to get out. In the case of Sgt. Emiliano Santiago, a federal Circuit Court in April, 2005 upheld the government's right to hold him until the year 2031, even though Santiago had already finished his eight-year commitment!

For whatever reasons, many people who have enlisted through the DEP change their minds before their ship date. They have the right to do this and do not have to go.[4]

The bottom line deserves repeating. Anyone in the DEP who changes their mind about joining the military can make the nightmare go away by not reporting to basic training.

Hotlines and counseling centers have logged thousands of calls from helpless and frustrated parents who've lost control of their children. Trained counselors explain that their son or daughter can get out of the Delayed Entry Program (DEP) by simply not showing up for boot camp and that they might be verbally threatened, but in the end there's nothing the recruiter or anyone in the chain of command can do and they're out. It sounds too easy, but it's true.

In 2015, the Army managed to meet its recruiting goal of 59,000 new soldiers only because it depleted its pool of recruits in the DEP.[5]

What happens if the youth reports to boot camp? Is there any way out then? It's the stuff of thousands of conversations across the country between parents and trained counselors. Mom is absolutely convinced her son won't make it. She cites a litany of reasons: hyperactivity, bouts of depression, anxiety disorder, poor executive functioning skills, poor work ethic, etc. She's convinced he'll join the 40% who drop out by the end of their first term. She's written letters to her boy's recruiter and even the commander at the local military entrance processing station but she's not getting any response.

Hotline counselors explain that if he hasn't adapted to military life within his first 180 days he may be eligible for an Entry Level Performance and Conduct Discharge. Mom is advised that her son may consider seeking such a discharge if he:
- believes he made a mistake enlisting in the military,
- is not willing or able to complete his training,
- experiences emotional distress, or
- has difficulty coping with military life.

This is a command-initiated discharge, which means there is no application procedure and no one has a "right" to this discharge. Visit girightshotline.org/ or call 1- 877-447-4487 for more information.

In January of 2001 the American Friends Service Committee published a brilliant brochure that is still widely distributed today. "Ten

Points to Consider Before You Sign a Military Enlistment Agreement" offers compelling advice for youth who are considering enlistment.

1. Do not make a quick decision by enlisting the first time you see a recruiter or when you are upset.
2. Take a witness with you when you speak with a recruiter.
3. Talk to veterans.
4. Consider your moral feelings about going to war.
5. Get a copy of the enlistment agreement.
6. There is no period of adjustment during which you may request and receive an immediate honorable discharge.
7. Get all your recruiter's promises in writing.
8. There are no job guarantees in the military.
9. Military personnel may not exercise all of the civil liberties enjoyed by civilians.
10. You will not have the same constitutional rights.

It's not a rose garden. If you report to basic and you refuse to obey orders, you roll the dice. You could be harshly disciplined, imprisoned, and perhaps receive a dishonorable discharge. A dishonorable discharge might prevent you from working for or receiving funding from the state or federal government. It never goes away.

This sober appeal is directed toward all adolescents, including those who refuse to clean their room, take out the trash, or do the dishes.

Notes - Chapter 2

1. "Enlistment/Reenlistment Document - Armed Forces of the United States." Defense Technical Information Center. 1 Oct. 2007. Web. 16 July 2015. http://bit.ly/2emLoqp.

2. See Sec. 10-19 Face to Face Prospecting "Recruiter Handbook USAREC 3-01." U.S. Army Recruiting. 22 Nov. 2011. Web. 16 July 2015. http://bit.ly/2f47G04 3. "10 U.S. Code § 976 - Membership in Military Unions, Organizing of Military Unions, and Recognition of Military Unions Prohibited." 10 U.S. Code § 976. Legal Information Institute, Cornell University Law School. Web. 16 July 2015. https://www.law.cornell.edu/uscode/text/10/976.

4. "Delayed Entry Program Discharge Fact Sheet." GI Rights Hotline. Web. 16 July 2015. http://bit.ly/2eQlxYK.

5. V, T., & Brook, E. (2015, December 24). Defense Secretary Ash Carter's historic personnel changes irk generals. Retrieved December 26, 2015, from http://usat.ly/1YynPQl.

AMERICAN PUBLIC HEALTH ASSOCIATION
For science. For action. For health.

Cessation of Military Recruiting in Public Elementary and Secondary Schools

"Military recruiters engage in aggressive behaviors to gain the trust of youth that are inappropriate, according to psychologists. For example, recruiting behaviors observed in schools can be characterized as "the process by which a child is befriended…in an attempt to gain the child's confidence and trust, enabling [the recruiter] to get the child to acquiesce."

Chapter Three

RECRUITING IS PSY OPS AT HOME
Leading health organization calls for ending school recruiting

In 2012 the American Public Health Association, (APHA), one of the country's foremost health organizations and publisher of the influential *American Journal of Public Health*, adopted a policy statement calling for the cessation of military recruiting in public elementary and secondary schools.

> APHA demands the elimination of the No Child Left Behind Act requirement that high schools both be open to military recruiters and turn over contact information on all students to recruiters and eliminating practices that encourage military recruiters to approach adolescents in US public high schools to enlist in the military services.1

APHA identifies several compelling public health reasons in calling for the cessation of military recruiting in the public schools. Most importantly, they argue that adolescents experience limitations in judging risk at this stage in life and they are unable to fully evaluate the consequences of making a choice to enter the military. The pre-eminent health organization points to the greater likelihood that the youngest soldiers will experience increased mental health risks, including stress, substance abuse, anxiety syndromes, depression, posttraumatic stress disorder, and suicide.

According to APHA,

> Military recruiters engage in aggressive behaviors to gain the trust of youth that are inappropriate, according to psychologists. For example, recruiting behaviors observed in schools can be characterized as "the process by which a child is befriended...in an attempt to gain the child's confidence and trust, enabling [the recruiter] to get the child to acquiesce." Another definition notes the importance of being "exceptionally

charming and/or helpful" while "failing to honor clear boundaries."

Youth are more likely to heed the overtures of these uniformed predators during difficult economic times. Conversely, it's a lot tougher for recruiters to parlay their psychological advantage into enlistment agreements when the US economy, especially the employment picture, is doing well.

Falling unemployment rates translate to tough times for military recruiting, although we rarely hear the recruiting command acknowledge the impact of economic conditions on their trade. This would imply that youth choose the military as a last resort when they feel they have no other options. Instead, Pentagon spin masters cite a litany of reasons why Johnny isn't signing up.

```
===========================
```

U.S. Unemployment Rate by Year

January 1, 2010	9.8%
January 1, 2011	9.2%
January 1, 2012	8.3%
January 1, 2013	8.0%
January 1, 2014	6.6%
January 1, 2015	5.7%
January 1, 2016	4.9%

- Source: Bureau of Labor Statistics [2]

```
===========================
```

According to Maj. Gen. Allen Batschelet, Commanding General of the U.S. Army Recruiting Command at Fort Knox, Kentucky from 2013 to 2015, all military services have seen an "erosion of willingness" from schools to let military recruiters in to talk to young people. It's a claim that can't be substantiated by press reports and it's eerily reminiscent of the year 2000 when similar economic conditions were prevalent and the recruiting command made the same kind of largely unfounded accusations. Batschelet's calculated rhetoric is directed to bolster congressional support for the continued militarization of the public schools and a lessening of restrictions placed on the movements of recruiters. It is reprehensible.

In a sense, the Army Recruiting Commander had been crying uncle. For instance, during the Recruiting 2020 Forum at RAND Corporation in September, 2014, top Defense officials and civilian professionals discussed the challenges facing Army recruiting. An exasperated Batschelet remarked, "The supply of qualified men and women who are inclined to serve in the Army continues to decline. I believe supply is inadequate to demand and we must change our national strategy to maintain an all-volunteer force."3

These are tough times for the recruiting command.

For the first 10 months of fiscal year 2015, the Army was down by 14% in the number of recruits compared to the year before. During that period recruiters made more than 415,000 appointments with young men and women interested in the Army. Those resulted in just over 50,000 signing up to serve. For the same period in 2014, they made 371,000 appointments and had signed up 52,000 soldiers.4

A two-day 'Wargames' event in Northern Virginia held in June of 2015 brought together Silicon Valley experts and Pentagon officials to address DoD worries regarding recruiting and retention. Not only is the Pentagon grappling to address projected overall shortages in manpower, but the advancements in technology and the way wars are expected to be fought are revolutionizing the demands of the job and necessitating the recruitment of higher skilled soldiers or at least those who can be more easily trained to perform high tech tasks. Brad Carson, Undersecretary for Personnel and Readiness, told *Military Times*,

> We don't know who the most talented officers and enlisted personnel are. We don't track them over time. We don't make any special effort to retain them. And we don't ensure that for every job in the military or on the civilian side, that we understand what talents are necessary for success.5

The Pentagon recognizes the demand for tech-savvy soldiers but it's heading in the opposite direction by relaxing its adherence to minimum scores on the Armed Forces Qualification Test. Incredibly, it fails to find, train, and keep the best man for each job. It's deeply ironic that the thrust of the Army's recruitment pitch promises training in more than 150 different career paths. "As an active duty soldier, you will have access to all of them. Choose from jobs in art, science, intelligence, combat, aviation, engineering, law and more. There is no limit to what you can achieve."6

The same problems occur in the Navy which has a kind of "conveyor belt" approach to promotions rather than tracking individual skill sets to match the right sailor to an appropriate occupation. The Navy says it is pursuing a new approach.7

Of course, you'll never hear recruiters tell a potential recruit that the military won't value his individual talents nor will it challenge him to perform to the extent of his abilities. It's the antithesis of being all you can be. Instead, the Army Recruiter Handbook lists several ways for recruiters to apply pressure on high school seniors, including this suggestion, "John, the career field you're looking for isn't always open. I think there are a few slots left. Why don't we schedule you for your physical on Thursday or Friday?"8

The military must move to a system that rewards talent with promotions rather than relying on 'time-in-grade requirements' as Carson puts it. Soldiers are bored. They're suffering -- and their message of misery is filtering to potential recruits: "Don't do it."

Just 1% of young people are both "eligible and inclined to have conversation" with the military about possible service, according to the Defense Department.9

All of the military branches together enlist about 200,000 into the active forces yearly. There are 34 million Americans in the 17 to 24 age bracket, considered to be prime recruiting age by the Pentagon so one out of every 189 in that age bracket joins.

When military recruiting gets tough the brass prefers to blame a host of familiar scapegoats. The schools are unfriendly. Parents are unsupportive. There is an increasing number of youth who have tattoos on the neck or head above the lines of T-shirt. They have ear gauges. Too many are addicted to prescription drugs. They're obese in record numbers. They can't pass a simple enlistment test. Graduation rates are declining. Too many have criminal arrest records. The 17 to 24 age group is a shrinking population pool. etc., etc.

The recruiting command has its lackeys who throw out terribly misleading information to explain why the military can't find enough recruits. For instance, Lt. Gen. Jerry Boykin (USAF-Ret.), executive vice president of the rabidly right wing Family Research Council says all the services are struggling.

> [But] what has happened since 2008 are the radical programs that have been implemented by this administration – to include the repeal of 'don't ask, don't tell,' women in front-line units, transgender [policies], budget cuts," he cited." Boykin thinks religious liberty is

the number-one factor for why recruitment is down. [10]

The U.S. Military Entrance Processing Command has always preferred to steer the conversation away from the obvious -- that fewer want to join because they have better options that don't carry the risk of getting killed or disabled for life. Meanwhile, increasingly attractive civilian options allow youth to retain their personal freedom. This generation of potential recruits is less likely to want to endure the physical

PHOTO BY THOMAS R MACHNITZKI - WIKIMEDIA COMMONS

and mental hardships required of soldiers.

Meanwhile, the Army is likely to shrink to its smallest numbers since before WWII. Already, the Army has reduced its FY 2016 active-duty recruiting goal to 62,000, down from about 80,000 per year during the height of the Iraq War. [11] Nonetheless, it's still a tough sell for recruiters.

The Army may be needing fewer recruits because it expects to draw down in size from 490,000 to 450,000 by the end of fiscal 2018. If sequestration continues, the Army is expected to shrink further to about 420,000 Soldiers.[12] With all of this in play the Army still has difficulty filling its ranks.

On April 17, 2014, after years of economic stagnation, about when the US economy began showing real growth, the *New York Times* ran a story, "Industrial Output Climbs, and New-Home Starts Tick Up" that documented a robust American economy. The article cited stronger than anticipated industrial production and increased output at the nation's factories, mines and utilities. The story reported positive figures on retail sales and employment in painting an upbeat picture of the economy at the end of the first quarter.[13]

On the same day, in an uncharacteristically candid statement, Jessica Wright, Acting Undersecretary of Defense for Personnel and Readiness told the Senate Armed Services Committee, "Generally, a slow economy makes recruiting less challenging, and operates to the advantage of those who are hiring, including the U.S. military." The positive recruiting environment could be coming to an end, she said, if the economy demonstrates "signs of economic improvement."[14]

Two years later, signs of economic improvement have continued, raising fears the Pentagon will mislead Congress and national and local education officials in an effort to further open the high schools to a military presence.

Keep in mind, too, that the Pentagon faces deeply entrenched cultural barriers. According to the recruiting command, most parents, teachers, counselors, and similar authority figures who influence decisions about enlisting in the military generally don't recommend military service.[15]

Of course, economic activity is cyclical in nature, as are the Pentagon's policy machinations reacting to deteriorating or improving recruiting conditions. A positive economic climate is likely to cause the recruiting command to turn to more non-HS diploma "Tier II" enlistments and increased waivers for criminal history. A better economy may cause the military to resort to healthy signing bonuses, an increased number of medical waivers, and an uptick in fraudulent enlistments.

The pressures to rely on substandard recruits to fill the ranks is somewhat relieved by the largely unfettered access to children recruiters enjoy in the nation's high schools. Access to the high schools represents the ultimate treasure trove of potential recruits. Whether the pressures on the recruiting command deteriorate during robust economic periods or they improve due to lessened manpower needs, the military always seeks greater access to the schools.

On January 1, 2000, the seasonally adjusted unemployment rate as reported by the US Bureau of Labor Statistics stood at 4.00%, the lowest figure since 1971. It has never been that low since. These were extraordinarily lean days for recruiters. 9/11 hadn't happened and military spending had been flat for most of the 1990's. Discussions of a "Peace Dividend" still reverberated throughout academic circles.

The Pentagon fixed its crosshairs on the high schools, either fabricating statistics or embracing data they knew was faulty to justify unprecedented recruiter access to high school children.

In 2000 Congress passed a law requiring high schools to guarantee physical recruiter access to children and to provide directory information. If a request for this access were denied by school officials, the law directed branches to send an official to meet with the representatives from the school district. If, after a meeting, such access continued to be denied, the services were to notify state officials and request access. Should the denial of access continue, the Secretary of Defense was instructed to notify the Secretary of Education. If the Secretary of Defense determined that that access was denied to at least two of the military services Congress would be notified.[16]

The implementation of these draconian policies followed a bogus claim from the Pentagon that recruiters across the country had been routinely and systematically refused access to high school students. According to a story on July 6, 2000 in the *Tampa Tribune*, a mouthpiece for the Pentagon, "Easier Access for Military Recruiters," "Approximately 2,000 public high schools have policies that bar military recruiters from one or more services, and high schools barred recruiters more than 19,000 times last year."[17]

The Pentagon has never released data to substantiate this outrageous claim and it cannot be verified by the public record. Based largely on these assertions, Congress amended the Elementary and Secondary Education Act (ESEA) in 2001 to require local educational institutions, upon request, to provide physical recruiter access to children, along with their names, addresses, and phone numbers. During floor debate in the House, Rep. David Vitter (R-Louisiana) repeated the claim of the Pentagon that 2,000 schools nationally ban recruiters from school grounds. When such figures were thrown out to House committee members no one present challenged them and no documentation was provided. It had also been claimed that 25% of all high schools refused to provide student directory information to recruiters, yet when the military was trying to regain access to student lists in the 1990's in San Diego, recruiters claimed that only two school districts west of the Mississippi wouldn't release the lists.[18]

In June of 2001, The Palm Center, a public policy group "in the areas of gender, sexuality, and the military", attempted to exploit the claim that 2,000 high schools closed their doors to military recruiters, arguing that the "gay ban" was detrimental to recruitment efforts because "many high schools refuse to cooperate with the military as long as the Pentagon continues to fire gay and lesbian service members."

According to a June 1, 2001 press release by the Palm Center, "Alan Dowd, former Associate Editor of *The American Legion Magazine*, says high schools denied military recruiters access to their campuses on 19,228 separate occasions in 1999 (the last year for which figures were available), in part as an effort to "challenge the Pentagon's policy on homosexuals in the military." A professional staff member of the House Armed Services Committee, which recently conducted a nationwide review of school recruitment efforts, confirmed that each service of the military maintains its own list of roughly two to three thousand schools that limit or prohibit access to recruiters on campus."[19]

It's inconceivable that 2,000 American high schools closed their doors to military recruiters in 1999.

In reality, military recruiters have always enjoyed tremendous access to high school kids and even more so since the passage of the No Child Left Behind Act in 2001. The law provides that "Each local educational agency receiving assistance under this Act shall provide military recruiters the same access to secondary school students as is provided generally to post-secondary educational institutions or to prospective employers of those students."[20] Fourteen years later the military enjoys unprecedented access to high school youth that far exceeds the "same access" mandated in the law.

Notes - Chapter 3

1. Hagopian, Amy, and Kathy Barker. "Cessation of Military Recruiting in Public Elementary and Secondary Schools." Policy Statements and Advocacy. American Public Health Association, 30 Oct. 2012. Web. 16 July 2015. http://bit.ly/18Kz8MX.
2. "Databases, Tables & Calculators by Subject." Bureau of Labor Statistics Data. Web. 4 Dec. 2015. <http://data.bls.gov/timeseries/LNS14000000>.
3. "ARMY.MIL, The Official Homepage of the United States Army." Forum Studies Bleak Recruiting Future of the All-volunteer Army. The United States Army, 20 Oct. 2014. Web. 16 July 2015. http://bit.ly/1sIkYS6.
4. Vanden Brook, T. (2015, July 30). Army faces recruit deficit, may miss '15 goal. Retrieved August 1, 2015, from http://usat.ly/2fgjUDz/.
5. Tilghman, Andrew. "DoD Wargames' Look at the Future of Recruiting, Retention Challenges." MilitaryTimes. Tegna Co., 28 June 2015. Web. 16 July 2015. http://bit.ly/2eZXrK1.
6. "Browse Army Jobs and Careers." Goarmy.com. U.S. Army. Web. 16 July 2015. http://www.goarmy.com/careers-and-jobs.html.
7. Seck, H. (2015, December 11). Navy Personnel Chief: Service may Face Recruiting, Reten-

tion Drop-Off. Retrieved December 12, 2015, from http://bit.ly/1jTGPpa.

8. "Army Recruiter Handbook." U.S. Army Recruiting Command, 22 Nov. 2011. Web. 18 July 2015.

9. Feeney, Nolan. "Pentagon: 7 in 10 Youths Would Fail to Qualify for Military Service." Time - U.S. Military. Time, 29 June 2014. Web. 16 July 2015.

10. Woodward, C. (2015, August 5). Boykin: Obama policies = shortage of military recruits. Retrieved August 6, 2015, from http://bit.ly/2ggGa4Y.

11. Tice, Jim. "Army recruiting market tightens but service expects make 2016 goal." Army Times. 23 Feb. 2016. Web. 27 Nov. 2016. http://bit.ly/2cYT6ZL

12. Lopez, C. Todd. "ARMY.MIL, The Official Homepage of the United States Army." Army to Realign Brigades, Cut 40,000 Soldiers, 17,000 Civilians. The United States Army, 9 July 2015. Web. 16 July 2015. http://bit.ly/2fV3hhx.

13. "Industrial Output Climbs, and New-Home Starts Tick Up." The New York Times. The New York Times, 16 Apr. 2014. Web. 17 July 2015.

14. Maze, Rick. "Services Prepare for Scant Recruiting Year." Military Times. Gannett, 2 May 2013. Web. 17 July 2015. http://bit.ly/2fggqRu.

15. Ibid.

16. Burrelli, David, and Jody Feder. "Military Recruitment on High School and College Campuses: A Policy and Legal Analysis." Federal Publications. Cornell University, 22 Sept. 2009. Web. 17 July 2015. http://bit.ly/2fwPKyG.

17. Easier Access for Military Recruiters, Tampa Tribune, July 6, 2000

18. Jahnkow, Rick. "COMD: Committee Opposed to Militarism and the Draft." COMD: Committee Opposed to Militarism and the Draft. 1 May 2001. Web. 17 July 2015.

19. "Pentagon's Recruiting Shortfalls Seen as Self-Inflicted." Pentagon's Recruiting Shortfalls Seen as Self-Inflicted. Palm Center, 1 June 2001. Web. 17 July 2015. http://bit.ly/2fHDuMq.

20. "Other Provisions – Sec. 9528" Elementary and Secondary Education Act - Subpart 2. U.S. Department of Education. Web. 17 July 2015. http://bit.ly/2fX62RU

Headquarters   ***USAREC Pamphlet 350-13**
United States Army Recruiting Command
1307 3rd Avenue
Fort Knox, Kentucky 40121-2726
1 September 2004

Training
School Recruiting Program Handbook

1-4. School Recruiting Program

    c. The objective of the School Recruiting Program is to assist recruiters with programs and services so they can effectively penetrate the school market. The goal is school ownership that can only lead to a greater number of Army enlistments

Chapter Four

SHOULD RECRUITERS OWN OUR SCHOOLS?

Military's goal is school ownership; communities push back

Throughout the country military recruiters are increasingly allowed to casually share lunch in high school cafeterias and interact freely with high school youth in hallways and classrooms. Military recruiters are on campus so frequently in many schools that they get to know kids on a first-name basis. They "chill" in the locker room and hang out in the parking lot and they play one-on-one basketball with kids after school. Meanwhile, college recruiters are typically required to meet with students by appointment in the guidance office. It's not the "same" access called for in the federal Every Student Succeeds Act (ESSA). Forget the old adage that familiarity breeds contempt. With vulnerable 16 and 17 year olds, familiarity breeds trust and trust produces enlistment agreements.

The military is secretive concerning the amount of time its recruiters and civilian employees spend in the nation's public schools. Researchers must file Freedom of Information Act (FOIA) requests to receive empirical evidence documenting the military's presence. Data from Massachusetts and Connecticut shed light on the extent of their presence in the high schools in these states.

The three most heavily recruited schools in Massachusetts, according to data obtained through the Freedom of Information Act by Seth Kershner, a researcher and co-author of *Counter-Recruitment and the Campaign to Demilitarize Public Schools*, are Fitchburg High School, Roger L. Putnam Vocational Technical Academy, and Springfield Central High School.[1]

During the 2012-2013 school year Fitchburg received 121 separate daily visits from Army recruiters, the most of any school in the state.

Military Recruitment in Western Massachusetts High Schools

First Edition
March, 2015

Andrea McCarron and Jeff Napolitano

The school has a student population that is 50% minority with 49% of students eligible for the free lunch program. Putnam Vocational (87% minority; 80% free lunch) allowed 102 visits, and Springfield Central High School (78% minority; 57% free lunch) was visited 97 times by Army recruiters. Navy, Marine, and Air Force recruiters also make regular visits to these high school campuses, competing with the Army for the same students.

In March of 2015 the American Friends Service Committee Western Massachusetts Program published "Military Recruitment in Western Massachusetts High Schools."[2] The study reports on the findings of a survey sent to officials in 38 high schools in Western Massachusetts regarding military recruitment. From July 2012 to the winter of 2013, AFSC staff submitted public records requests to all public high schools within the four counties of Western Massachusetts: Hampshire, Hampden, Franklin, and Berkshire. Among other questions, the survey asked administrators how often recruiters visit, where they set up, and who (if anyone) supervises them.

From the study:

> Many schools do not consistently monitor the presence of recruiters, or the content brought by visiting recruiters. There do not appear to

be standards for what recruiters are allowed to do, say, or distribute. Of the thirty-eight schools in Western Massachusetts, most schools (twenty-two) required more than one request for AFSC to receive public information on recruiter policies. Five did not respond until the request was made via certified mail. Even then, three did not respond or rejected our request.

The study awarded schools a letter grade, from A to F. An A meant the school did everything possible to minimize the military's interaction with students. An F grade meant the school was in violation of the law. A school's failure to alert parents of their right to opt out merited an automatic F. A failure to respond to the Massachusetts Public Records Act request merited an automatic F unless clarification was obtained through other means. There were 5 A's, 10 B's, 11 C's, 6 D's, and 6 F's.

Roger L. Putnam Vocational Technical Academy in Springfield received an F because it failed to respond to four requests. Apparently, Putnam officials didn't want to share their open-door policy regarding military recruiters. Additionally, 83 students took the ASVAB during the same school year, with all results being forwarded to recruiters without parental consent.[3]

In Connecticut it's pretty much the same story. Crosby High School (76% minority, 71% free lunch) was visited 73 times by Army recruiters during the 2012 - 2013 school year. On October 18, 2011 the recruiter made the following notes, "Great day at Crosby made 36 appointments. A lot of positive staff and kids. We will be conducting all appts this week."[4]

At Bloomfield High School, northwest of Hartford (97% minority, 34% free lunch) Army recruiters visited on 62 separate days. Recruiters use the JROTC Program as a base within the school. They routinely assist in physical training exercises with the kids.

In September of 2012 the recruiter at Hartford Public High School reported, "I gave a presentation in English class and they had lots of questions... gave a ppt presentation. On the way out met _____ (redacted) and he was interested in having me come in during class and talk about the Middle East at some point in the future."

Throughout the country non-degreed recruiters befriend supportive teachers to gain access to children. They complement thousands of JROTC instructors, who are typically the only non-degreed, non-certified "teachers" in American classrooms.

Not all schools in Massachusetts and Connecticut are as friendly to the recruiting command as the schools discussed above. Consider the notes the recruiter made regarding his experiences with Classical Magnet School in Hartford on March 12, 2012.

> Dropped off request to _____ (redacted) she stated that their school does not release school lists. When asked about table days and presentations she said, we really don't do that. trouble school will not release directory info. receives federal funds. also limits access to recruiters. Forwarding school info to explore possibility of Battalion intervention to release list or begin the Recruiter Access to High Schools Database Process In accordance with Elementary and Secondary Education Act of 2002.

Withholding directory information or disallowing recruiter access may result in a suspension of federal funding to schools. It is the military's trump card. The "Every Student Succeeds Act" (ESSA), the re-written 2015 version of the No Child Left Behind Act, maintains this provision regarding military access to schools.

Robert E. Lee High School in Staunton, Virginia provides a typical scenario regarding recruiter visits. Military recruiters are allowed to have lunch in the cafeteria with all of the students in the school. Army recruiters visit on the first and third Thursdays throughout the school year, while Navy recruiters visit on the second Tuesday of every month. Marine and Air Force recruiters also show up for the lunch periods in the cafeteria. Meanwhile, college recruiters are required to make appointments to meet with students in the counseling office.[5]

According to the Army's *School Recruiting Program Handbook*, "The objective of the Army's school recruiting program is to assist recruiters with programs and services so they can effectively penetrate the school market. The goal is school ownership that can only lead to a greater number of Army enlistments." [6]

The following roles military recruiters perform in thousands of high schools across the country illustrate exactly how the Army is attaining school ownership:
- Football conditioning coach
- Career Day Counselor
- Interactive recruiting vans with simulators
- Presentations to the Student Government

- Presentations to the PTA
- Presentations to the School Board
- Training the school color guard
- Facilitating flag raising/Pledge of Allegiance
- Helping with school registration
- Regularly delivering donuts to faculty meetings
- Placing advertisements in the student newspaper
- Assuming a leading role in the homecoming parade
- Chaperoning at homecoming dance and other dances throughout the year
- Regular presentations to history and government classes
- Basketball conditioning coach
- Coin toss at football games
- Attendance at all home football games
- Halftime football ceremonies
- Timekeeper
- Recruiter v. Faculty basketball games
- Track and Field Assistant
- Baseball assistant coach
- On stage at graduation

Ironically, the Army has developed an anti-bullying campaign to further "penetrate" the middle and high school "markets." The issue of bullying has captured an extraordinary amount of attention nationwide, while the nation has witnessed a proliferation of anti-bullying programs in schools. The Army has produced a video, *Be a leader against bullying*, that provides additional license for recruiters to be on campus. Consider this piece, "Army Recruiter Works to Prevent Bullying," that appeared on the Army's homepage in 2013:

> The Army's Anti-Bullying Campaign is making an impact one family, one school and one community at a time. Sgt. 1st Class Jeremy Athy of the Asheville, North Carolina Recruiting Center discovered his own daughter was being picked on and bullied for being overweight after he had an at-home viewing and discussion of the anti-bullying campaign video with his family.
>
> "As a father it broke my heart that this was going on and I couldn't protect my daughter," said Athy. Then his son began asking questions, as well, after a student at his middle school committed suicide

because of bullying. "After that, I thought I have to find a way to help and maybe even change some things," said Athy. He introduced members of the Buncombe County Board of Education to the Army's campaign explaining how he wanted to help and was welcomed with open arms.

Athy conducted anti-bullying presentations at four schools this past school year and plans to conduct presentations in all of the area middle and high schools in the coming school year." 7

From the Army's perspective, it's a win-win situation. The video is professionally produced and does a good job framing the issue, while recruiters gain access to the entire student body. Realizing the public relations bonanza, the Army has commissioned interactive tractor trailers to crisscross the country showing the anti-bullying video in a mobile theatre to the middle and high school crowd. The Army's website says the massive trucks require four recruiters to provide "support assistance".8

Army Recruiting Van - U.S. Army Mission Support Battalion BY ARMAND PEREZ, DEFENSE VIDEO IMAGERY DISTRIBUTION SYSTEM

The Pentagon puts up a great front. In fact, though, the DOD has the worst record of all American institutions regarding the acceptance of violence within its ranks. Assault and bullying in the military occur at alarming rates. Rather than making revolutionary changes to radically alter chronic abuse in the chain of command, the Pentagon relies on sophisticated marketing campaigns to make it all go away—at least in the public's eye. Their anti-bullying campaign kills two pesky birds with one stone.

Sen. Kirsten Gillibrand (D-NY) addressed the Senate in 2014 regarding violence in the chain of command. Gillibrand has also led the fight in Congress to remove sexual assault cases from military jurisdiction.

She hit upon the term *toxic leadership* in the Army's own materials, and described it as a main cause of bullying and suicides in the military. According to Army Doctrine Publication 6-22 (September, 2012), "The toxic leader operates with an inflated sense of self-worth and from acute self-interest. Toxic leaders consistently use dysfunctional behaviors to deceive, intimidate, coerce, or unfairly punish others to get what they want for themselves."[9]

According to Col. George Reed, former director of Command and Leadership Studies at the War College, 20% of the American military force is victimized by toxic leadership, intimidating, hostile, aggressive, and frightening behavior directed by officers toward enlisted soldiers.[10] The officers call it "smoking" a soldier. This behavior is a contributing factor in the skyrocketing number of suicides in the military.

The Army knows a lot about bullying.

Troops to Teachers

The DOD established Troops to Teachers (TTT) in 1994. Today it is funded by the U.S. Department of Education but run by the DOD through Defense Activity for Non-Traditional Education Support (DANTES), in Pensacola, Florida.

DANTES has established a network of state TTT offices to provide separating soldiers with counseling and assistance regarding certification requirements, routes to state certification, and employment leads. The TTT homepage provides information and resource links, including links to state departments of education, state certification offices, and other job listing sites in public education.

Troops to Teachers candidates must meet all state teacher certification requirements for the state where they desire to teach, although every state has implemented alternative licensing programs that make it a lot easier for soldiers and others to begin immediately teaching while licensure without a bachelor's degree is worked out over the course of several years.

Some states, like Texas, make it relatively easy for non-degreed soldiers to find work as teachers. Soldiers often leave the military with skills in areas where the high schools offer technical education to their students. In Texas and elsewhere, the process for certification in a technical field like shop or auto mechanics is distinct from standard subject area certification and may be accomplished without a bachelor's degree.

Separating soldiers in Texas are instructed through the Troops to Teachers program to contact an authorized state college or university, like the Wayland Baptist University, which offers an On-Line Certification Program, to evaluate their experience as a first step in applying to teach in Career and Technical Education (CTE) programs throughout the state. The soldier files his DD 214 discharge papers and completes the Texas Education Agency Statement of Qualifications form detailing his or her military technical experience.

Once the educational brokers evaluate the documentation, they issue a deficiency plan, which details the courses that a soldier must eventually take to complete certification. The plan often involves up to 18 semester hours of CTE courses, plus a course in the US/Texas Constitution or government. Depending on how many credits are required, soldiers are given between one and three years to complete course work.[11]

When the deficiency plan is created, departing soldiers may apply to school districts to teach with full pay and benefits on a probationary certificate for up to three years. Before certification is authorized, the veteran must pass the applicable Texas Examination of Education Standards (TExES).

Troops to Teachers provides a pipeline of high school-educated soldiers who fill technical teaching jobs in high schools across the country.

Eligible military veterans may receive a federally funded stipend of up to $5,000 to help them pay for state teacher certification and a one-time bonus of up to $10,000 for agreeing to teach in a high-poverty school. The stipend and bonus combined cannot exceed a total of $10,000.

In the Houston Independent School District (ISD), the largest school district in Texas, TTT members may pursue certifications in areas such as welding, automotive technicians, diesel mechanics, culinary arts, and many more. In fact, there are 153 skills in Houston ISD that Service members could qualify to teach using their military experience.[12]

Army propagandists are quick to note the beneficial impact TTT has on recruiting. According to a 2014 story, "Troops to Teachers program offers post-Army careers" on www.army.mil, the official homepage of the U.S. Army, Troops to Teachers helps the Army "because it puts people into the classrooms that are going to be preparing future Soldiers for service."

The piece continues:

> Today, discipline in the classroom comes into question, and that's where their military training comes into play. Army values really help create people that would be wonderful teachers. And Soldiers can instill the Army values into their students and can be great role models along with appropriate disciplinarians.[13]

Some of these Army values will have to change to be successful in the classroom. Perhaps the "mission" in the Army is clearly defined, but it won't be so cut and dry in a high-poverty area 9th grade classroom where some students won't take orders.

Great teachers don't rely on fear and discipline. Soldier/teachers will be forced to ignore the *Soldier's Creed* and admit defeat, often daily. They may be professional soldiers but they aren't professional teachers. Their "proficiency in warrior tasks" and drills won't help them in classes with a dozen students carrying Individualized Educational Plans. Can these battle-tested soldiers cope with children on the Asperger's scale, with Attention Deficit Hyperactivity Disorder, and with undiagnosed anxiety disorders? This is the reality in many American classrooms today.

Are these soldiers willing and able to devise diversified classroom instructional plans while being mindful of strategies to employ with divergent learners? Will they devise several plans for one lesson that reach children with different learning styles such as visual-spatial, bodily-kinesthetic, linguistic or logical, to name a few?

Saltman and Gabbard, in the introduction to their edited book, *Education as Enforcement - The Militarization and Corporatization of Schools*, put the TTT program into perspective, referring to it as part of military education,

> Military education refers to explicit efforts to expand and legitimate military training in public schooling. These sorts of programs are exemplified by JROTC (Junior Reserve Officer Training Corps) programs, the Troops to Teachers program that places retired soldiers in schools, the trend of military generals hired as school superintendents or CEOs, the uniform movement, the Lockheed Martin corporation's public school in Georgia, and the army's development of the biggest online education program in the world as a

recruiting inducement. 14

It is alarming to witness the rapid proliferation of programs that contribute to the militarization of American youth.

Col. John Box, Commander of the U.S. Army Recruiting 3rd Brigade, wrote a revealing article that provides a glimpse into the mentality of the recruiting command. The piece pits the recruiters against youth in a demented kind of surveillance-based guerilla warfare scenario. The disturbing commentary, "A guide to intelligence driven prospecting," dated December 18, 2013, appeared on the Army's homepage, www.arm.mil. In Box's military mind the high schools provide the brick and mortar where the "enemy or target" is confined to meet the "challenge of the counterinsurgency fight."[1]

Col. Box readies for the counterinsurgency fight. - www.army.mil
BY ARMAND PEREZ, DEFENSE VIDEO IMAGERY DISTRIBUTION SYSTEM

Box's analogy is particularly chilling now that the Pentagon allows recruiters to carry loaded and concealed automatic weapons into the schools. You'd have to be familiar with a boatload of acronyms to decode the colonel's message. These acronyms all appear in Box's 1,100-word piece, which is meant for public consumption:

FOB	Forward Operations Base
IPB	Intelligence Preparation of the Battlefield
SUR	Small Unit Recruiting
ET	Engagement Team
RST	Recruiting Support Team

FSL	Future Soldier Leader
CC	Center Commander
ACC	Assistant Center Commander
OPS	Operations
NCOIC	Non-Commissioned Officer in Charge
S2	Intelligence
3-01	Recruiting Manual
3-06	Recruiting Manual
AAR	After Action Review
TPU's	Troop Program Units
HPTL	High Payoff Target List
APL	Automated Processing List
SASVAB	Student Armed Services Vocational Aptitude Battery
TNEL	Tested Not Enlisted List
ALRL	Automated Lead Refinement List (from the high schools)
SUR	Surveillance

Sample a taste of recruiting brigade culture from Box's piece.

> The RST's role is to process applicants after handoff has occurred from the CC, ET, or FSL. Similar to the roles of an S2 in any maneuver unit using IPB, the RST considers market intelligence, prospecting analysis, and creates a high payoff target list (HPTL) for the CC, ET, and FSL. This HPTL is created from the automated processing list (APL), Student Armed Services Vocational Aptitude Battery (SASVAB) test list, tested not enlisted (TNE) list, or the National Advertising (ADHQ) leads when formulating prospecting plans for the ET, CC, and FSL.

Colonel Box treats teenagers and the local high school like the enemy on a battlefield. He writes,

> In the 3rd brigade we, The Marauders, use an operational mindset and treat every recruiting center like a forward operations base (FOB). In the operational Army, a Soldier would never engage the enemy or a target without having the proper intelligence preparation of the battlefield (IPB) and target information prior to departing the FOB; so why should our recruiters be any different?

To answer the colonel's question, recruiters should be different because they operate in our home towns and their prospects are our children. They're tender and they're vulnerable, and although they often think otherwise, the kids don't know much about the world.

An American community is not a battlefield, although understandable public resentment in some schools and towns may make it seem that way to the colonel.

The brigade commander's battlefield analogy continues,

> Just as Soldiers in a combat environment have to change, adapt and become more innovative, we must do the same in Recruiting Command. A key challenge of the counterinsurgency fight in both Iraq and Afghanistan are reflected in Sun Tzu's adage that the enemy "Swims in the sea of the people." I would offer that our prospects swim in the sea of high schools, colleges, and the communities at large.

While Box's troops are pinning down the "enemy" in our schools they're also involved in a kind of *virtual* counterinsurgency. The command realizes kids are glued to their smartphones, so they've created an impressive, virtual presence. Recruiters lurk on social media sites to determine where youth might congregate over the weekend. Is it the parking lot behind Appleby's? Is it the food court at the mall, or is everyone heading to the pond to ice skate?

Recruiters also pose online as potential recruits sharing their frustrations or asking for advice regarding the military's entrance exam, the ASVAB. They try to drum up interest in the test, which is offered at 12,000 high schools across the country. The Army requires a minimum test score of 31 to qualify for enlistment. (See the chapter on ASVAB Testing.) Although it's tough to gauge, a 31 on the ASVAB is roughly equivalent to low 8th grade level, if that. A score of 17 translates to functional illiteracy, perhaps a 2nd to 4th grade level. The item below was posted by "Leticia." Leticia only capitalizes half of her I's and never uses an apostrophe. Other than that, her grammar and spelling are stellar, suggesting a much higher level than a 17 for the writer.

> ASVAB HELP! NEED TO SCORE A 50 but i got a 17 :(?Okay, so i got a 17 on my ASVAB score. What can i do to improve? I need a 50 or higher. I can retake in one month. School ends in two weeks and ill have enough time to study. PLEASE HELP ME OUT! I really am interested in this. Im working really hard for it. I dont want to give up. How can i aim for that 50 or higher? I dont understand how i got a 17.[16]

There are thousands of posts like this in dozens of chat rooms. They're written by deceptive, sucker-punching recruiters looking for their next lead.

Here's an obvious one:

> Im a category 4 asvab wavier for the marines how will this effect my career am i in for horrible time or will i be ok im not nerves of leaven?
>
> **Best Answer:** once your in the marines, your asvab score doesn't matter it will effect what mos you can do when you enlist and it will effect trying to get into things like recon in the future but other than that, no one ever looks at your asvab score
>
> **Henry:** Marines aren't taking people below a 50 last I heard.
>
> **Wine Wine:** U Dirty Skunk: No way! Someone with your obvious mastery of the written language a CAT IV?!?! Get out of here.[17]

CAT IV means a potential recruit scored between 10 and 30 on the AFQT, the Armed Forces Qualification Test. Recruits must score at least a 32 to join the Marine Corps. A few exceptions are created for extraordinarily talented recruits that have exceptional skills. This post is very likely engineered by the recruiting command to give hope to the lowest echelon of recruits, if they can read it.

The "Best Answer" is likely from the same recruiter and is posted to reassure academically challenged potential recruits. The responses by Henry and Wine are obviously not sanctioned by the military entrance processing command.

Here's another:

> I GOT A 26 ON MY ASVAB?
>
> I saw a job ad for a "linguist" on monster.com and it was for the U.S military. I'm an interpreter already and always looking for new work. I signed up and got an interview. I had NO IDEA, what to expect. I was just looking for more work. I got there, and was blown away. First off, they had me take the ASVAB which I was NOT prepared for. I didn't think I would ACTUALLY be joining the military if I was gonna work as an interpreter for them. So I took the test, I had no idea what to expect, I thought it was gonna be really easy. I didn't think I had an issue on the language portion (English and Reading Comprehension) but I hadn't taken a math class for four years and it's always been my toughest subject, and I am AWFUL at problem solving, I was never good at it, so I'm pretty sure that had

a lot to do with my low score. Does a 26 practically mean I could be mildly retarded? [18]

What we see here is a tendency to suggest that jobs requiring advanced degrees might be within the realm of possibility for someone who operates at an elementary school level. Imposters say they're struggling to score a 31 and are looking for high paying jobs. Readers can dream of being all they can be, but infantry is typically the reality for enlistees who barely score a 31.

The military is still largely an archaic institution, a throwback to the 19th century with an antiquated, authoritarian structure and mindset. Sometimes, however, it can be surprisingly forthright. Sometimes, though rarely, it demonstrates the honesty and transparency that are appropriate for a responsive governmental institution in a 21st century democratic republic. A case in point is an article by Lance Corporal David Flynn, "A Snapshot of a Recruiter's World," which appeared in *Marine Corps News* in June of 2011.[19] Flynn tracks Staff Sgt. Michael Hauck, Recruiting Station Baltimore, as he makes the rounds between two Maryland high schools,

> I go to Duval High School every Thursday and Friday," said Hauck. "On Monday and Tuesday I go to Bowie High School. I spend so much time at the schools that they've given me offices at both where I can meet with students." Hauck tutors students on the ASVAB in his offices.

It's not uncommon for recruiters to have offices in schools across the country. They're often regarded as supplemental guidance counselors, although most are staff sergeants with little or no college. JROTC instructors teach credited courses without degrees.

The American School Counselor Association (ASCA) urges guidance counselors to steer "at risk" youth toward the Army's "Planning for Life" (PFL) program, ostensibly designed to help students further their education and plan for life. The ASCA claims "at-risk" youth receive motivational messages and tools to strengthen "mind, body and soul" during half-day workshops co-hosted by the Army and community groups.[20]

The article on the Maryland recruiter describes how Staff Sgt. Hauck brought Duval history teacher Brent Sullivan to Parris Island earlier that year to attend the Educators Workshop and experience recruit training first hand. Each year, from October through May, Marine

Corps recruiters invite high school educators, counselors, coaches, and other influencers to visit Marine Corps Recruit Depot, Parris Island, S.C. There, they witness firsthand the Marine Corps' recruit-training program.[21] Teachers get to shoot weapons and pretend to be a recruit. They even get yelled at by drill instructors. "We're an all-recruited force," said Hauck. "Of course we all volunteered, but someone had to find those volunteers."

Is it a recruited force or a volunteer force? Is it fair to say impressionable teens "volunteer" for military service when so much institutional coercion is involved?

The access military recruiters enjoy on a given high school campus is largely determined by the principal. If the principals of Bowie and Duval high schools in Maryland didn't want recruiters to use office space to regularly prepare youth for the military's enlistment test, that would be the end of it. Although the military is chipping away at its goal of school ownership, local communities are legally empowered to exercise day-to-day control over their schools.

The office of a public high school principal occupies a unique position in American society. A retired U.S. Marine Commander and a pacifist Quaker may be principals in neighboring high schools under the nominal jurisdiction of a school board, each exercising a remarkable degree of autonomy. There are few institutions in America where one individual exerts such direct, unfettered control over the daily lives of so many.

As we've seen, the access granted to military recruiters on high school campuses is a function of the culture of an individual school, but it is also determined by the geographical region of the country and the particular recruiting brigade and battalion.

The relatively progressive New England states of Connecticut, Rhode Island, Massachusetts, and Vermont have military enlistment rates of 1.48, 1.26, 1.43, and 1.63 recruits respectively per 1,000 youth aged 18-24. Meanwhile, South Carolina, Georgia, Florida, and Alabama have rates of 3.45, 3.46, 3.25, and 3.15.[22] It's not a shocker that young men and women from states of the old confederacy are twice as likely to join the military as youth from New England states. Generally, southern states appear most likely to have an open-door policy regarding military recruiters, followed by schools from the Midwest, West, and Northeast. Of the top 10 states that select ASVAB Option 8 to protect student privacy (*See the Chapter on Military Testing*) five are from the Northeast and the rest are from the West, with the exception of Minnesota and Nebraska, where robust citizen activism has pressured school authorities to take steps to seek parental consent when children are tested by the recruiting command.

We also see variations in the ASVAB data that correlate closely to the high schools covered by particular Recruiting Brigades. High schools in the 3rd Recruiting Brigade in Fort Knox, Kentucky, which encompasses Recruiting Battalions in Chicago, Cleveland, Columbus, Indianapolis, Great Lakes, Milwaukee, Minneapolis, and Nashville, are much more likely to require ASVAB testing than schools in the 1st Recruiting Brigade, headquartered in Fort Meade, Maryland, which recruits from high schools in the Northeast.

To put this discussion into context, consider the rebellious, obstinate, contrarian 17- year-old who is not getting along with his parents, who are frightened by his stated intentions to join the military. Consider the recruiting command that gathers a virtual portrait of the youth for its targeted, sophisticated pitch and consider the school that allows recruiters to "chill" with students in the cafeteria during lunch.

In addition to the presence of military recruiters in our schools, the military also manages to "penetrate the school market" through the following DOD-supported programs operating in the nation's public schools:

- 4-H Tech Wizards
- Adopt a School Program
- Armed Services Vocational Aptitude Battery
- Army Junior Reserve Officer Training Corps Program
- Air Force Junior Reserve Officer Training Corps
- Army Educational Outreach Program
- Army Junior Reserve Officer Training Corps, Battlefrog
- Building Engineering and Science Talent
- Camp Invention
- Career Exploration Program
- Civil Air Patrol
- Civilian Marksmanship Program
- Computers for Learning Program
- Cyberpatriot
- ECybermission
- Expanding Your Horizons
- FIRST Lego

- FIRST Robotics Competition
- FIRST Tech Challenge
- Gains in the Education of Mathematics and Science
- Internship Programs for High School Students through the Army Educational Outreach Program
- Iridescent
- Junior First Lego League
- Junior Science and Humanities Symposia Program
- Junior Solar Sprint
- March to Success
- Marine Corps Junior Reserve Officer Training Corps
- Mathcounts
- Math Video Challenge
- Mobile Discovery Center
- National Guard Youth ChalleNGe Program
- Naval High School Science Awards Program
- Navy Junior Reserve Officer Training Corps
- Navy Seal Fitness Challenge
- Navy STEM
- Project Partnership for All Students' Success
- Remotely Operated Vehicle Program
- Research & Engineering Apprenticeship Program
- School Challenge
- Science and Engineering Apprenticeship Program, SEAP
- Sea Perch
- Starbase Program
- Students Taking Active Roles
- Summer Engineering Experience for Kids
- Ten80 Education
- US First Robotics
- US Navy Music for Recruiting Program
- UNITE
- U.S. Army Reserve National Scholar/ Athlete Award Program
- U.S. Naval Sea Cadet Corps
- We the People: The Citizen and the Constitution
- West Point Bridge Design Contest
- Young Marines.

Counter-recruiters have legal rights to access schools

Rick Jahnkow with the Project on Youth & Military Opportunities (Project YANO) is widely regarded as the ultimate source for a range of counter-recruitment issues, particularly the access activists have to the nation's high schools to counter the message of recruiters.

In Jahnkow's words:

> For anyone who might be seeking school access, it's useful to know that there are solid legal arguments in favor of allowing groups to disseminate negative factual information on military enlistment in schools. While it would not be wise to litigate the issue in the current judicial climate—with a very conservative, pro-military Supreme Court—it's good to know what the lower courts have said on the topic so we can thoughtfully bring it up when necessary.

Jahnkow outlines a host of lower court rulings, including the 9th Circuit Appellate Court's decision, which says,

> "[I]t has long been recognized that the subject of military service is controversial and political in nature." The court went on to say that if a school has created a forum for advocates of military service, "the Board cannot allow the presentation of one side of an issue, but prohibit the presentation of the other side." (San Diego CARD v. Grossmont Union H.S. District, 1986)

> These rulings make it clear that along with presenting positive alternatives to the military in schools, counter-recruitment groups have a legal right to present negative facts to help students fully evaluate the military as a career option.[23]

Notes – Chapter 4

1. Data received through a Freedom of Information Act Request; Database documenting U.S. Army recruiter visits to Massachusetts schools in the Springfield Company from October 1, 2012 to September 30, 2013. USAREC Albany Recruiting Battalion.

2. Military Recruitment in Western Massachusetts High Schools. (2015, March 1). Retrieved August 8, 2015, from http://bit.ly/2fFfjv9.

3. The state data was created from the national database received on December 18, 2013 from Yasmeen Hargis, FOIA Analyst For Suzanne Council, Senior Advisor on behalf of Paul J. Jacobsmeyer, Chief, Freedom of Information Office of the Secretary of Defense and Joint

Staff FOIA Request Service Center http://www.dod.mil/pubs/foi/ 1155 Defense Pentagon Washington, DC 20301-1155. http://www.studentprivacy.org/state-data.html.

4. FOIA Data

5. "Robert E. Lee High School." School Counseling Home / Military Recruiters. Staunton, VA Public Schools. Web. 20 July 2015. http://staunton.k12.va.us/Page/918.

6. 1-4 (c) USAREC Pamphlet 350-13 School Recruiting Program Handbook Headquarters, United States Army Recruiting Command September 1, 2004 http://www.grassrootspeace.org/army_recruiter_hdbk.pdf.

7. Garcia, V. (2013, August 1). ARMY.MIL, The Official Homepage of the United States Army. Retrieved August 11, 2015, from < http://bit.ly/2fVKX6X >

8. Mobile Exhibit Company's Interactive Semis. (n.d.). Retrieved August 11, 2015, from http://www.usarec.army.mil/MSBn/Pages/IS.htm.

9. ADP 622 - Army Leadership. (2012, August 1). Retrieved December 24, 2015, from http://bit.ly/2ggVDSv.

10. Zwerdling, D. (2014, January 6). Army Takes On Its Own Toxic Leaders. Retrieved August 11, 2015, from http://n.pr/1hrqJjC.

11. Troops to Teachers Proud to Serve Again." Texas Troops to Teachers. Web. 07 Mar. 2016. http://bit.ly/2fV5Joy.

12. Nenetsky, Dr. Christene. "Texas TTT Partners with Houston School District." Military. com. 4 Aug. 2015. Web. 07 Mar. 2016. http://bit.ly/2frRhDA.

13. Martin, Sarah. "Troops to Teachers program offers post-Army careers."

7 April. 2014. Web 07 Mar. 2016 http://bit.ly/2f47FMJ.

14. Saltman, Kenneth J. and Gabbard, David A. "Education as Enforcement: The Militarization and Corporatization of Schools." Routledge, 2011 – 320 pages

15. Box, Col. John. "ARMY.MIL, The Official Homepage of the United States Army." A Guide to Intelligence Driven Prospecting. The United States Army, 18 Dec. 2013. Web. 20 July 2015. http://bit.ly/2fYyiBG.

16. "ASVAB HELP! NEED TO SCORE A 50 but I Got a 17 :(?" Yahoo! Answers. Yahoo!, 2013. Web. 20 July 2015. https://yhoo.it/2ggvZwq.

17. "Im a category 4 asvab wavier" Yahoo! Answers. Yahoo! 2016. Web. 22 April 2016, https://yhoo.it/2fFevGu.

18. I got a 26 on my ASVAB? Yahoo Answers. Yahoo! 2013. Web. 20 July 2015 https://yhoo.it/2fwSw7b.

19. David Flynn, Lance Corporal. "Marine Corps Recruiting Command." A Snapshot of a Recruiter's World News Article Display. The United States Marine Corps, 30 June 2011. Web. 20 July 2015.

20. Dahir, Carol, E.D. Planning for Life: Developing and Recognizing Exemplary Career Planning Programs. A Resource Guide for Counselors. American School Counselor Association, Alexandria, VA. Army Recruiting Command, Fort Knox, KY. 2001-00-00 72 p. http://

files.eric.ed.gov/fulltext/ED463467.pdf.

21. "4th Marine Corps District." Resources Educator Resources. United States Marine Corps. Web. 20 July 2015. http://bit.ly/2eFzyMc.

22. "Military Recruitment 2010." National Priorities Project. 30 June 2011. Web. 21 July 2015. http://bit.ly/2f4a5ed.

23. Jahnkow, R. (2011, April 30). Antiwar group claims message stifled. Retrieved December 29, 2015, from https://yhoo.it/2fV4GEN.

Soldiers at prayer. PHOTOGRAPH FROM DEFENSE IMAGERY.MIL

Chapter 5

LOVE OUR ENEMIES? OR KILL THEM?

*Catholic military schools mold young men
into "soldiers of Christ"*

The March 2010 edition of Richmond's Benedictine College Preparatory student newspaper, *The New Chevron*, carried two articles on the Iraq War exploits of the school's newly-hired headmaster, Jesse A. Grapes. During the 2nd Battle of Fallujah in November of 2004, 1st Lieutenant Grapes saved the lives of three Marines in his platoon. The newspaper reports:

> Jesse A. Grapes, only three words can describe this man, patriotic war hero. He consistently showed unyielding bearing, fortitude, intuition, and courage while serving his country in war. The Marines who served under him said, "He is a hard-charging small unit tactician who literally wrote a book about modern urban warfare following his ferocious experience in Fallujah."
>
> 1st Lieutenant Grapes led 3rd platoon into the chaos of Fallujah, in which he furthered his heroism with his actions of saving three wounded marines at the "infamous Hell House." To accomplish this feat, he tore off his body armor, forced his body through a window of a burning house, which enabled him to encounter the enemy soldier who had been firing at his troops.
>
> Following this act of heroism, he was accused of the capture, murder, and torture of several prisoners of war. To this he said, "I know nothing about the alleged capture or order to kill the prisoners. If I had heard such a thing I would have immediately stopped it." Grapes also refused a polygraph examination saying that no machine can trump his honor. "If my word isn't good enough, nothing would be."[1]

Grapes' word was "good enough" to lead the Catholic military school.

Three Marines under the command of 1st Lt. Jesse Grapes shot four defenseless prisoners during the Battle of Fallujah. When the crime came to light a few years later, it made front-page news across the country as the first war crimes charges against service members prosecuted in federal (civilian) court. Naval Criminal Investigative Services, a federal grand jury, and court witnesses documented the events of November 9, 2004, in Fallujah. Grapes' platoon had been taking fire from a house. After the troops entered the building and captured the insurgents, Sergeant Jose Nazario, Jr. used a radio to call for orders on what to do next.

This is according to the testimony of Marines Weemer, Nelson, and Prentice, who say they were in the room with Mr. Nazario at the time. The instructions, Mr. Nazario told them, were to kill the prisoners. "We argued about it, and argued about it, and we had to move, we had to get out, and our unit was moving down the street," Mr. Weemer says in the transcript of his testimony.[2]

Weemer said he shot the insurgent twice in the chest and instantly felt remorseful.[3] During the polygraph examination, Weemer alluded to similar atrocities that had occurred on other occasions, indicating his unit did not take prisoners.[4]

Nazario testified that he was asked over the radio, "Are they dead yet?" When Nazario responded that the captives were still alive, he was told by the Marine on the radio to "make it happen."[5]

Prentice said Nazario exchanged radio messages with higher-ups. "Spartan Three, this is Spartan Three-Three," Prentice claimed Nazario said over his radio. "We have four MAMs (Military-aged males), found AK47s in the house." "Then Nazario says negative," Prentice said. "Then Nazario says affirmative."

Marine Corps records show that at Fallujah "Spartan Three" was 1st Lt. Jesse Grapes, the 3rd Platoon commander. Grapes was not called as a witness.[6]

Grapes told investigators he had no recollection of hearing about captured enemy combatants on his radio. He was discharged from the Marines after refusing to talk to government investigators about his role at Fallujah. He exercised his Fifth Amendment right against self-incrimination and also refused to testify at the Federal Grand Jury hearing.[7]

In the end, all criminal charges were dropped when the Marines refused to testify against each other or their commander. It's quite a lesson for the students at Benedictine College Prep.

The Benedictine website contains the following segment entitled "Why Catholic?" that quotes a selection from the Bible, 1 Peter 3:15,

> Today, Benedictine College Preparatory continues to glorify God and mold young men into soldiers of Christ. In the world, these men will be ready to fulfill St. Peter's command: 'always be prepared to make a defense to anyone who calls you to account for the hope that is in you.' "8

Appearing in the same edition that welcomes the warfighter accused of murder as the new headmaster, this verse is taken out of context and is terribly misleading, bringing to mind the haunting biblical exhortation in Matthew 18:6: "Whoever causes one of these little ones who believe in me to sin, it would be better for him to have a great millstone fastened round his neck and to be drowned in the depth of the sea."

Examine this verse in context in 1 Peter 3:13-16,

> Now who is there to harm you if you are zealous for what is right? But even if you do suffer for righteousness' sake, you will be blessed. Have no fear of them, nor be troubled, but in your hearts reverence Christ as Lord. Always be prepared to make a defense to anyone who calls you to account for the hope that is in you, yet do it with gentleness and reverence; and keep your conscience clear, so that, when you are abused, those who revile your good behavior in Christ may be put to shame.

This is a different message, and it reflects the true gospel message.

The school also has an annual Boxing Smoker in coordination with the Georgetown University Boxing Team. Would Jesus have a front row seat?

Benedictine is a kind of poster child for the militarized Catholic school. Every year the school requires all juniors to take the military's enlistment exam. The school operates an Army JROTC program and teaches small arms practice. Of course, these are expected activities in a military school. The question is whether these activities are appropriate in a **Catholic** school.

The *National Catholic Reporter* put it this way in 2003:

> Long overdue in the American church is a reasoned and deep discussion of U.S. militarism, the proper use of force, the state's responsibility to protect and defend, and the role of people of faith in all of this. To this point, Catholic teaching has had little effect in distinguishing us from any other segment of society when it comes to participation in wars and militarism.

The church has chosen to antagonize the state on issues related to abortion, homosexuality, and contraception, but this peripheral resistance provides a relatively minor irritation to the comfortable, contemporary church-state relationship. A rejection of war and violence, however, carries with it a repudiation of nationalism and patriotism, unthinkable in today's church-state nexus.

The Benedictine website says the work of the school is to mold young men into soldiers of Christ. Did Jesus institute a militant faith?

Military recruiters typically don't frequent Benedictine in search of enlisted men because schools like Benedictine do the work for them, in this case, providing the military with young men who become officers. Many Benedictine Cadets pursue their college education at the service academies or schools like VMI or the Citadel.

Catholics and the military share a tight bond. About 10% of all Catholic priests have a military background, and 20% grew up in military families. Three years ago every member of the Joint Chiefs except for Marine Corps Commandant Gen. John Amos was a practicing Catholic, according to the Archdiocese for Military Services. [9]

Catholic high schools across the country encourage regular visits by military recruiters and sponsor dozens of military programs that entice youth to enlist, often without full disclosure of the true intent of the programs.

Catholics, including youth and priests, enlist in a military that requires the subordination of Catholic doctrine to the military command. For many students, the vestiges of 12 years of Catholic education are largely erased in a few weeks of basic training. Catholic high school students who enlist take an oath that requires obedience to Army regulations, including the Army Field Manual, which states,

> "Your personal values may and probably do extend beyond the Army values, to include such things as political, cultural, or religious beliefs. However, if you're to be an Army leader and a person of integrity, these values must reinforce not contradict,

Army values." 10

Jesus said no one could serve two masters.

The U.S. Military Entrance Processing Command (USMEPCOM) is poised to exploit the dichotomy. For example, the 3rd Recruiting Brigade headquartered in Fort Knox, Kentucky encourages Catholic recruiters to request permission from school officials "to attend Mass in their dress uniform." The Brigade says Catholic high schools would be honored to have recruiters join students at Mass and that attendance should improve relations with administrators.11

Catholic Schools have done a poor job, compared to many of their public school counterparts, in protecting children from the military's predatory practices. In some cases, the recruiting command couldn't be more effective than the Catholic command. For instance, hundreds of Chaminade Catholic High School graduates from Mineola, New York have entered military service upon graduating from the school. Sadly, 55 Chaminade graduates have been killed in combat, at least since the 1960's.12

Like Chaminade, St. Pius X High School in Lincoln, Nebraska acts as a proxy for the Recruiting Command. In 2015 the school apparently required 247 students to take the military's enlistment exam, known as the ASVAB or Armed Services Vocational Aptitude Battery, without providing for parental consent. The school sent test results, along with social security numbers and sensitive demographic information, to the Pentagon without parents specifically saying it was OK. Although military regulations clearly identify the testing regime as a recruiting device, few, if any Catholic schools notify parents of the true nature of the program.13

Catholic schools that receive funds under the Elementary and Secondary Education Act (ESEA) must provide military recruiters, upon request, the names, addresses and phone numbers of children. The law gives parents the right to "opt out" from lists including their children's names being forwarded to the DoD by notifying the school of their intention. Often, Catholic school students or teachers receive services under ESEA programs, but the schools themselves do not receive any ESEA funds.14 Many schools release records nonetheless.

Catholic Schools are a notoriously independent bunch, unlike state and local schools operating under boards that may regulate hundreds of institutions. For instance, Maryland requires all parents to complete a form specifically asking if they want to remove their child's name from lists being sent to recruiters. Catholic schools have no supra-school authority like this (certainly not the National Catholic Education Association), and the military prefers it this way.

The law exempts private schools that maintain a religious objection to service in the Armed Forces. Although this applies to schools affiliated with traditional Christian peace churches like the Church of the Brethren, Quakers, or Mennonites, it does not apply to the military-friendly Catholic Schools.

Instead, schools like St. Louis Catholic High School in Lake Charles, LA apparently require parents to sign a form that releases directory information, along with transcripts, grade point averages, and class rankings to the recruiting command.[15]

In the 2009-2010 school year, one Milwaukee recruiter was able to use his 15-hour-per-week job as a volunteer coach to mentor—and eventually, enlist—five football players from Pius XI High School. Pope Pius XI, the "peace and justice pope" of the 1930s, would have been appalled.[16]

We've seen how the Army calls for school ownership, and it is apparent at Greensburg Central Catholic High School in Greensburg, Pennsylvania, where the U.S. Military Entrance Processing Command presents awards to recruiters and holds regular change of command ceremonies.[17]

Recruiters are intent on getting inside the heads of all high school students, including Catholic school students. During the 2012-2013 school year, the military managed to administer its enlistment test, the Armed Services Vocational Aptitude Battery Career Exploration Program (ASVAB-CEP) to 11,000 students in 113 Catholic High Schools.[18]

An examination of the websites of nearly 100 such schools reveals that no sites clearly identified the ASVAB-CEP as a recruitment tool or mentioned that student data would be transferred to military recruiters. Instead, these websites carried upbeat promotional messages often lifted verbatim from Pentagon sources.

For instance, Mount St. Mary Catholic High School in Oklahoma City encourages students to take the ASVAB. Rather than accurately describing test proctors as military recruiters or Department of Defense employees, Mount St. Mary's officials refer to them as "test administrators from the Federal Government."[19]

Throughout the country, counselors include language provided by recruiters in their school's promotional materials. At Newport Central Catholic in Newport, Kentucky, the test is given to juniors in November. In 2013, 95 students took the test and had their test data forwarded to recruiters without parental consent.[20]

Some schools have gotten the message, though. For example, when Bishop Hartley High School in Columbus, Ohio required its junior class to take the test in 2013, it prohibited the release of student data to recruiters. A notice on the school's website correctly states that data would be kept with the school. However, Bishop Hartley is in the minority. Nationally, just 19.6% of all parochial and religious school students taking the test in 2012-2013 had their results withheld from recruiters.

The Junior Reserve Officer Training Corps (JROTC) program is the military's most effective indoctrination tool in the high schools. JROTC operates in scores of Catholic and religious high schools and teaches military culture and a dangerous, reactionary version of US History and Government. Although many Catholic high schools have embraced anti-violence and anti-gun programs, the JROTC program brings guns and military personnel into these religious schools and teaches students to use them.

Good guns and bad guns?

Army values taught in the four-year JROTC curriculum differ from the Christian message in a host of ways, but most importantly, regarding the 5th Commandment, "You shall not kill." Army values stress killing. The Army Creed has soldiers recite, "I am an American Soldier. I stand ready to deploy, engage, and destroy the enemies of the United States of America in close combat."

Colman McCarthy, the Washington DC-based peace activist, framed the military program this way:

> The first and most fundamental objection to ROTC based on Catholic thought appeals to what is described as the basic contradiction between a religion that teaches peace and institutions that train for and make war. John Dear, a Jesuit priest formerly on the faculty at Fordham University, asks, "How can we teach peace and uphold the peacemaking life of Jesus on the one hand, while on the other support the Pentagon and train our young people to kill in future wars?"[21]

Jesus calls us to love our enemies. The Army calls us to kill them.

Military access to Catholic schools strikes at the core of Catholic identity. For Catholics, it calls to mind the divide between the church as envisioned by Cardinal Francis Spellman, who encouraged Catholic students to join "Christ's war against the Vietcong and the people of North Vietnam"[22] and Bishop Thomas Gumbleton, who urged Catholics not to "unquestioningly accept the war policies of their government."[23]

Furthermore, critical thinking skills—so often hailed by educational progressives—may be undermined by what Protestant theologian Reinhold Niebuhr decried as the "military mind," which "makes unthinking obedience" the greatest good in the "hierarchy of virtues." The seemingly inexorable march to militarize has no about-face.

American Catholic schools are the most military-friendly Catholic schools in the world, based on an exhaustive internet search of military involvement in Catholic schools worldwide. The cultural divide between the American Church and the Vatican was apparent in 2001, when the Vatican ratified the U.N. Optional Protocol to the Convention on the Rights of the Child on the Involvement of Children in Armed Conflict. The treaty required that recruitment practices involving minors must be voluntary and carried out with the informed consent of the child's parents.[24]

It doesn't appear that many of America's Catholic high schools are upholding the Vatican's end of the deal.

The Catholic Catechism teaches war is sanctioned if the following four conditions are met, *at one and the same time*:

- The damage inflicted by the aggressor on the nation or community of nations must be lasting, grave, and certain;
- All other means of putting an end to it must have been shown to be impractical or ineffective;
- There must be serious prospects of success;
- The use of arms must not produce evils and disorders graver than the evil to be eliminated. The power of modem means of destruction weighs very heavily in evaluating this condition.[25]

The totality of the conditions stated above have never been met in post-World War II American military encounters, rendering all American military actions that have resulted in the deaths of enemy combatants, civilians, and Americans since 1945 immoral and unjustified.

The judgment of the souls of the men and women who have participated in these campaigns rests between them and their Creator. Certainly, heaven holds a million soldiers.

Still, we must join a host of saints in questioning the great Doctors of the Church, St. Augustine and St. Thomas Aquinas, who are primarily responsible for the Church's present-day Just War position. They were human, though many regard their teachings as infallible. Pope Francis has challenged the church's 1700-year-old green light for war by stating, "Brothers and sisters, never war, never war! Everything is lost with war; nothing is lost with peace. Never more war." In the U.S., Pax Christi Metro DC – Baltimore has helped to lead the charge to embrace gospel nonviolence as the only stance consistent with Christian discipleship.

Almost every American Catholic classroom prominently displays an American flag and children routinely start their days with a pledge of allegiance to the flag. The practice is rarely questioned. This pledge is an oath to the United States while Jesus condemned making oaths. Consider Matthew 5:33-34, "You have heard that it was said to the people long ago, 'Do not break your oath, but fulfill to the Lord the vows you have made.' But I tell you, do not swear an oath at all."

Nothing in the Gospels calls for Catholics to pledge their loyalty to the state. When Catholics recite, "thy kingdom come, thy will be done," they are giving themselves entirely to God. Their minds should be fixed on establishing God's kingdom on earth, not the violent and sometimes evil American empire. It is an abomination to lead children in pledging allegiance to the American flag. It is the flag of Hiroshima, of Abu Ghraib, and millions dead in Vietnam. It is the flag of several dozen unnecessary and immoral violent conquests in violation of the church's Just War position. We must never consent to pledging allegiance to a flag that symbolizes a political entity whose systems and policies condone killing.

The website of the United States Conference of Catholic Bishops (USCCB) contains the following message regarding the display of American flags in American churches. The USCCB Committee on the Liturgy issued this decision on September 25, 2001, two weeks after the attacks of 9/11,

> Surprisingly to many, there are no regulations of any kind governing the display of flags in Roman Catholic Churches. Neither the Code of Canon Law, nor the liturgical books of the Roman rite comment

on this practice. As a result, the question of whether and how to display the American flag in a Catholic Church is left up to the judgment of the diocesan bishop, who in turn often delegates this to the discretion of the pastor.

The origin of the display of the American flag in many parishes in the United States appears to have its origins in the offering of prayers for those who served during the Second World War (1941-1945). At that time, many bishops and pastors provided a book of remembrance near the American flag, requesting prayers for loved ones – especially those serving their country in the armed forces – as a way of keeping before the attention of the faithful the needs of military families. This practice has since been confirmed in many places during the Korean, Viet Nam and Iraqi conflicts.

The Bishops' Committee on the Liturgy has in the past encouraged pastors not to place the flag within the sanctuary itself, in order to reserve that space for the altar, the ambo, the presidential chair and the tabernacle. Instead, the suggestion has been made that the American flag be placed outside the sanctuary, or in the vestibule of the Church together with a book of prayer requests. It remains, however, for the diocesan bishop to determine regulations in this matter.[26]

Having the American flag in the sanctuary is an outrage. Catholics worship God in this holy place. The U.S. Conference of Catholic Bishops is appeasing the forces of secular correctness. Many Archdioceses throughout the country, like those in Washington, Milwaukee, and Philadelphia, wash their hands of the issue and defer to the USCCB on the flying of the flag in the sanctuary.

Msgr. Charles Pope is the pastor of Holy Comforter-St. Cyprian in Washington, D.C., and writes for the Archdiocese of Washington at the blog.adw.org. Msgr. Pope argues that the practice of displaying the flag in the sanctuary may be theologically justified by considering that patriotism is related to the Fourth Commandment, "Honor thy father and mother." He contends our country nourishes and provides for us as a parent.[27]

Meanwhile, others are adamant that the flag has no permanent place in the sanctuary. The Diocese of Richmond does not allow the flag in the sanctuary. Instead, it says the flag should be relegated to the vestibule, narthex, or commons area.[28] The Archdiocese of Los Angeles calls for the removal of the flag from the main body of its churches. In its statement, "The Display of American Flags in Catholic churches," LA church leaders point to the US Flag Code. The code states, "When displayed from a staff in a church or public auditorium, the flag of the United States of America should hold the position of superior prominence, in advance of the audience..."

According to the Archdiocese,

> Such prominence is not possible in a Catholic church, where the predominant image is that of the crucified Christ. Because of this stipulation, it would be better to give the flag a place of greater prominence outside of the church in a special area, or perhaps in the vestibule or gathering space rather than in the main body of the church.29

The differences between various archdioceses underscore the remarkable autonomy local Catholic districts enjoy on this and other issues. Through its weakness, the USCCB defers decision-making authority to those leaning toward pacifism and militarism alike. It's reminiscent of local school boards that allow high school principals to develop policies and procedures regarding the access military recruiters enjoy to students.

All Catholic churches, however, seem to be in agreement in the case of funerals. In the Order of Christian Funerals, "national flags ... have no place in the funeral liturgy" and thus "are to be removed from the coffin at the entrance of the church."30 The flags of the Knights of Columbus, local sports teams, or the 101st Airborne Division are removed from the casket and replaced by the funeral pall, a reminder of the baptismal garment of the deceased.

For a moment, try to imagine how an eight-year-old 3rd grader in one of the nation's Catholic schools might view the flag and the nation. Every morning the child says the Our Father and recites the Pledge of Allegiance. Both are sacred in her mind. In church, the flag stands on the altar with the crucifix. These stains on the developing political mind last a lifetime and conspire to disable critical, objective thought later in life.

Notes – Chapter 5

1. Holland, Zach, Vol 98, No. 3, March, 2010, The New Chevron, Benedictine High School http://bit.ly/2fXfqFf.

2. Casey, Nicholas. "Civilian Court Tries Case from the Fog of War." Wall Street Journal. 19 Aug. 2008. Web. 10 Mar. 2016. http://www.wsj.com/articles/SB121910667519751613.

3. Ibid.

4. "Nazario v. Riverside NCIS Discovery Outline." Naval Criminal Investigative Service, 17 Mar. 2011. Web. 11 Mar. 2016. http://bit.ly/2fFh0bP.

5. "Fallujah Marine Pleads Not Guilty - USATODAY.com." Fallujah Marine Pleads Not Guilty - USATODAY.com. 12 Sept. 2007. Web. 11 Mar. 2016. http://usat.ly/2fyDLxD.

6. Helms, Nathaniel R. "Fog of War Clouds Recollections 26AUG08." Fog of War Clouds Recollections 26AUG08. 26 Aug. 2008. Web. 11 Mar. 2016. http://bit.ly/2fyFDGE.

7. Helms, Nathaniel R. "Will Marine Show Trials End?" Newsmax. 30 Mar. 2008. Web. 11 Mar. 2016. http://nws.mx/2gf6ysj.

8. "Benedictine College Preparatory - Why Catholic? - About BCP - A Faith-based Education." Benedictine College Preparatory - About BCP - A Faith-based Education. Web. 11 Mar. 2016. http://bit.ly/2fYxqgp.

9. Shinkman, Paul D. "The Catholic Crunch: Inside the Shortage of Catholic Military Priests." US News. U.S.News & World Report, 30 Oct. 2013. Web. 11 Mar. 2016. http://bit.ly/2fIKd8O.

10. "Army Leadership, Be, Know, Do." Army Field Manual 22-100. Web. 12 Mar. 2016. http://bit.ly/2f08liI.

11. Monday, D. Charone. "School Tips from Fellow Recruiters." Recruiter Journal. U.S. Army Recruiting Command, Nov. 2011. Web. 12 Mar. 2016. http://www.usarec.army.mil/hq/apa/download/nov11.pdf.

12. Garamone, Jim. "United States Department of Defense." Defense.gov News Article: Pace Details Lessons He Learned From Young Marines. U.S. Department of Defense, 19 Sept. 2007. Web. 12 Mar. 2016. http://archive.defense.gov/news/newsarticle.aspx?id=47407.

13. Source: through FOIA - SFC Almeter Thompson, USMEPCOM FOIA/PA Officer Headquarters, United States Military Entrance Processing Command

14. "General Issues Frequently Asked Questions Related to Nonpublic Schools - Office of Non-Public Education." U.S. Department of Education. Web. 12 Mar. 2016. http://bit.ly/2fV-92vG.

15. "2014- 2015 ST. LOUIS CATHOLIC HIGH SCHOOL PARENT – STUDENT HANDBOOK." St. Louis Catholic High School. Web. 12 Mar. 2016. http://bit.ly/2fVQF8M.

16. Gomez, Jorge. "Coaching His Way to Success." Recruiter Journal. U.S. Army Recruiting, May 2009. Web. 13 Mar. 2016. http://www.usarec.army.mil/hq/apa/download/RJ/may09.pdf.

17. "Meritorious Service Medal Recipients." Army Strong PA. Cold Steel Penn Press, Harrisburg Recruiting Battalion, Oct. 2010. Web. 12 Mar. 2016. http://bit.ly/2ggH54O.

18. Source: through FOIA - SFC Almeter Thompson, USMEPCOM FOIA/PA Officer Head-

quarters, United States Military Entrance Processing Command

19. Mount St. Mary Student Handbook, 2016-2017. Web 30 Oct. 2016. http://bit.ly/2ggQHgw.

20. Source: through FOIA - SFC Almeter Thompson, USMEPCOM FOIA/PA Officer Headquarters, United States Military Entrance Processing Command

21. Quoted in Colman McCarthy, "Educating Peacemakers," National Catholic Reporter Online, September 29, 2000. http://bit.ly/2f0eBqx.

22. Encyclopedia of War and American Society, Peter Karsten, Editor, MTM Publishing, Inc. New York, NY, 2005. p. 800.

23. "Sermons/Writings." Bishop Thomas Gumbleton. Web. 21 Mar. 2016. http://www.bishopgumbleton.com/sermonswritings.html.

24. "Optional Protocol to the Convention on the Rights of the Child." Optional Protocol to the Convention on the Rights of the Child. Web. 22 Mar. 2016. http://bit.ly/1gT80YF.

25. Pastoral Constitution on the Church in the modern World. Gaudium et Spes, Sec. 79. Promulgated by His Holiness, Pope Paul VI, December 7, 1965 http://bit.ly/1lmUu1K.

26. "Display of Flags in Catholic Churches." Display of Flags in Catholic Churches. U.S. Conference of Catholic Bishops. Web. 28 Mar. 2016. http://bit.ly/2fXLVVf.

27. Pope, Msgr. Charles. "Displaying the Flag." Our Sunday Visitor Catholic Publishing Company. Archdiocese of Washington, 24 Sept. 2014.Web. 28 Mar. 2016. http://bit.ly/2eorlfi.

28. "Diocese of Richmond - The Display of National Flags in Catholic Churches." Diocese of Richmond - Office of Worship, 16 May 2007. Web. 28 Mar. 2016. http://bit.ly/2fyDuel.

29. "The Display of American Flags in Catholic Churches." Archdiocese of Los Angeles. Web. 28 Mar. 2016. http://bit.ly/2ga7soG.

30. "Quick Questions." Must a Pall Replace the Flag at a Funeral Mass? Catholic.com. Web. 28 Mar. 2016. http://bit.ly/2eouGLh.

Marines, sailors man their "battle" stations for the movie, "Battleship."
FROM WIKIMEDIA COMMONS. CREATIVE COMMONS ATTRIBUTION 2.0 GENERIC DVIDSHUB

Chapter 6

HOLLYWOOD PLEDGES ALLEGIANCE TO THE DOLLAR

Censorship is the cost of military access

In July, 2015 the U.S. Army Chief of Public Affairs responded to a Freedom of Information Act (FOIA) request by releasing a massive 1,400-page list of movies and television shows his office had reviewed and influenced from 2010 to 2015.[1] The list provides insight into the murky world of military censorship and sheds light on productions the Pentagon deems helpful to the recruiting effort.

The FOIA request was initiated by Tom Secker, a British-based writer who specializes in security services. The Army's report may be found on Secker's website, spyculture.org. Within a few weeks of Secker's receipt of the data, just a handful of websites had reported on the significant release, including Billboard, Alternet, Salon, Techdirt, and Center for Research and Globalization. No mainstream American newspapers or TV outlets picked up the intriguing story.

The Department of Defense has several offices dedicated to providing "assistance" for a wide variety of entertainment genres. Producers of every stripe who desire military assistance in the production of "feature motion pictures, television shows, documentaries, music videos, commercial advertisements, CD-ROM games, and other audiovisual programs" are directed to contact the military service being portrayed. The Army, Air Force, Navy, and Marines operate liaison offices from four adjacent offices located on Wilshire Blvd in Los Angeles.[2]

Aside from fighting current wars and planning for new ones, the Pentagon spends a lot of time and energy viewing film. Recruiting-age youth increasingly rely on movies, television, YouTube and other video sources to inform and shape their world view. Some 45% of 17-year-olds say

WIKIMEDIA COMMONS

they read for pleasure no more than one to two times a year if that often. The recruiting-age population watches video.[3]

The Pentagon recognizes that film and television deeply influence youth, and all of American society, so military minders regularly edit the scripts for thousands of productions, including "American Idol," "The X-Factor," "Masterchef," "Cupcake Wars," numerous Oprah Winfrey shows, "Ice Road Truckers," "Battlefield Priests," "America's Got Talent," "Hawaii Five-O," lots of BBC, History Channel and National Geographic documentaries, "War Dogs," "Big Kitchens"— the list goes on and on. Alongside these shows are blockbuster movies like *Godzilla, Transformers, and Superman: Man of Steel*.[4]

As unlikely as it sounds, the Air Force has worked with the producers of "Jeopardy," "The Queen Latifah Show," "The Wheel of Fortune," and "The Tonight Show with Jay Leno." When members of the Air Force appear on television, military minders review scripts before airing.

The Army's Office of the Chief of Public Affairs in Los Angeles (OCPA-LA) rates the productions. Although we're familiar with films carrying ratings like G, PG, PG-13, R, or NC-17 from the Motion Picture Association of America, the Army also gives them ratings. They include:
- Supports Building Resiliency,
- Supports Restoring Balance,
- Supports Maintaining Our Combat Edge,
- Supports Adapting Our Institutions,
- Supports Modernizing Our Force.[5]

The Army does not assign negative ratings; instead, it summarily rejects films that it doesn't like. Rejection by OCPA deprives filmmakers of access to military bases, ships, training, maneuvers, etc. Rejection forces filmmakers wanting to tell a story involving the military to potentially spend additional millions in production costs, effectively eliminating low-budget filmmakers not content with toeing the line.

Most of the films on the OCPA-LA list eventually receive a thumbs-up, many after an intensive back-and-forth editorial review process. Films are subsequently categorized, as above, by the way they best support the Army's mission. Producers requesting DoD assistance submit their scripts to the Office of the Assistant to the Secretary of Defense for Public Affairs (OATSD-PA), which authorizes the Military Services to provide suggestions for changes. Refusal on the part of producers regarding any DoD edits results in a rejection of assistance.[6]

The OCPA-LA list of films obtained and released by Secker is prefaced by this disclaimer:

> NOTICE: This report contains information on the development and progress of TV programs, feature films, and other entertainment-oriented and documentary media projects. This information is shared with the Army for the purpose of determining whether the project qualifies for Department of the Army and Department of Defense support. It is pre-decisional information for our Chain-of-Command. **IT IS NOT INTENDED FOR PUBLIC DISSEMINATION.** The information contained in this report, if publicly disclosed, could be financially and professionally detrimental to the entertainment media production entity or individual filmmaker(s) providing the information, and would deter these companies and individuals from seeking Army assistance.

It may be professionally embarrassing to some producers when the public discovers that the financial incentive of working with the DoD entails a substantial degree of restriction and suppression of intellectual independence.

The projects in the recently released OCPA-LA list were governed by the stringent guidelines contained in Defense Instruction 5410.15, dated March 28, 1989. Many productions since 1989 have been edited and subsequently approved with little regard for these guidelines. The release of the information pursuant to the FOIA request may have led the DoD to publish new instructions in an effort to avert embarrassment under the potential spotlight of public scrutiny. The new, more subjective guidelines were made public on July 31, 2015, just three weeks after the OCPA-LA files were released to Secker. The new instructions allow the DoD to approve pretty much anything for any reason and, more importantly, to reject projects using the same fuzzy criteria.

The old policy called for "accuracy in the portrayals of DoD persons, places, equipment, operations, and events." The new policy calls for productions to present "a *reasonably realistic* depiction of the Military Services and the DoD, including Service members, civilian personnel, events, missions, assets, and policies." Reasonably realistic to whom, using what criteria? Do the top brass military censors reject projects if they deem them to be unreasonably realistic? Would scripts based on books by Chalmers Johnson, Howard Zinn, or Noam Chomsky be considered unreasonably realistic? The question penetrates to the heart of the 1st Amendment: "Congress shall make no law… abridging the freedom of speech."

The 1989 guidelines say there should be "no implication or appearance of implication of DoD endorsement or approval of any person, product, partisan or political cause," but the new policy leaves all of this out. It omits words like *endorsement, political,* or *partisan.* Its purposeful vagueness untethers the Pentagon from these intellectual constraints.[7]

Filmmakers and Pentagon brass forge a mutually beneficial partnership. War is profitable to moviemakers and the military is eager to sell its version of it. While Hollywood producers demand access to military bases, ships, planes, and personnel, the Pentagon in return rewrites scripts to enhance the military image and safeguard recruiting and retention numbers. The American public subsidizes the military access provided to filmmakers and is fed the pabulum of homogenized military propaganda while free speech is trampled.

It's like the sanitized version of events produced by embedded American journalists during the Afghanistan and Iraq wars. Those at-

Tareq Ayub was killed in the US bombing of Aljazeera's offices in Baghdad

tempting to gather stories independently were shunned, discredited, and even murdered, like those killed in the US bombings of Aljazeera offices in Kabul in 2001 and in Baghdad in 2003.

By 2010, Reporters Without Borders had recorded the deaths of 230 media professionals, 87% of whom were Iraqis. Many of these deaths were caused by the US military and none have been prosecuted. The Pentagon issued a statement regarding the killing of journalists who were not embedded with US troops, "Baghdad is not a safe place. You should not be there." 8

Moviemakers intent on portraying the military whose scripts don't appeal to Army censors are at a great disadvantage. They're forced to spend millions more than their compliant counterparts to tell their stories with the same degree of military feel. Many can't endure the expense. A 2002 *New York Times* report drives home the point of financial benefits for those surrendering editorial control.

According to the article, "When Hollywood's Big Guns Come Right from the Source," the military "deployed" the following equipment during the filming of *The Sum of All Fears*, based on the 1991 Tom Clancy book about nuclear terrorism:

- 2 B-2 bombers
- 2 F-16 fighter jets
- The National Airborne Operations Center, the highly secure communications aircraft, in a modified 747 jet, reserved for the president and his top staff in case of nuclear attack
- 3 Marine Corps CH-53E helicopters
- 1 UH-60 Army helicopter
- 4 ground vehicles
- 50 Marines and Army troops
- The John Stennis, a 97,000-ton, nuclear-powered aircraft carrier with more than 80 aircraft and a crew of 5,000
- Access to the Central Intelligence Agency's headquarters in Langley, VA

The total charge to Paramount Pictures for use of the equipment came to less than $1 million, a relatively tiny sum.9

Clancy sold the Pentagon's line. His novels turned-to-film caused a cultural about-face after Vietnam, helping to portray the military in a positive light.

The Pentagon is making sure its ships, bombers, and helicopters will never be used to tell a different story. Truth continues to be a casualty in war-making.

The scale of the Pentagon's intrusion and its micromanagement of entertainment projects is disturbing, although we're still largely in the dark regarding the extent of the DOD's editorial tinkering with specific productions in return for cooperation. Specific changes made to movie and TV scripts by the military's public affairs offices are classified information today, whereas the material prior to 2002 has been declassified.[10] Even so, Britain's *Mirror Online* reported in July 2015:

> To keep Pentagon chiefs happy, some Hollywood producers have turned villains into heroes, cut central characters, changed politically sensitive settings – or added military rescue scenes to movies. Having altered scripts to accommodate Pentagon requests, many have in exchange gained inexpensive access to military locations, vehicles and gear they need to make their films. [11]

This Hollywood-military nexus is nothing new. When D. W. Griffith made the silent film *The Birth of a Nation* in 1915, West Point engineers gave him technical advice on his Civil War battle scenes and provided him with artillery. Griffith toed the editorial line.[12]

In his influential 2004 book, *Operation Hollywood: How the Pentagon Shapes and Censors the Movies*, David Robb captures the legal argument that the military is practicing unconstitutional censorship. He writes:

> Many legal experts, including famed First Amendment attorney Floyd Abrams and renowned Constitutional law professor Irwin Chemerinsky, believe that this form of censorship is a blatant violation of the First Amendment.
>
> This sort of viewpoint-based discrimination by the government in which it favors one form of speech over another is flatly inconsistent with the First Amendment," says Abrams, who was co-counsel to the New York Times in the Pentagon Papers case.
>
> Chemerinsky, a professor of constitutional law at the University of Southern California, agrees. The Supreme Court has said that above all, the First Amendment means that the government cannot participate in viewpoint discrimination, Chemerinsky says. "The government cannot favor some speech due to its viewpoint and disfavor others because of its viewpoint. The Court has said that when the government is giving financial benefits, it can't decide who to give to, or not to give to, based on the viewpoint expressed."[13]

During the 1970's the American public soured on war and the military. Public opinion reflected the notion that the country had been misled about Vietnam and the war resulted in the unnecessary deaths of 58,000

American soldiers and *millions* of Vietnamese. Hollywood, through films like *The Deer Hunter* and *Apocalypse Now*, reflected public disgust for the military. The American public was experiencing a kind of a hangover from the unpopular war that made it largely unprofitable for Hollywood to produce big budget films glorifying war.

That changed with the release of *Top Gun* in 1986, and the hangover went away in a hurry. The Pentagon was ecstatic over the level of cooperation with Paramount, the film's producer. Since then, Hollywood has generally increased its output of high-dollar war movies and has cozied up with the Pentagon to use personnel, bases, ships, fighter planes, and other tools of the trade. The offices on Wilshire Blvd. have been humming with activity since, marking up the scripts of thousands of movies.

Top Gun, starring Tom Cruise and Val Kilmer, was the number one film of 1986, grossing $176 million. The movie's hero, Maverick, played by Cruise, helps to shoot down four MIG-28's during a contrived battle over the Indian Ocean. Maverick triumphantly lands his F-14 on the aircraft carrier USS Enterprise and gets the girl at the end. (No offense to women intended). It sounds trivial, but the film is extraordinarily powerful with its portrayal of super-intense, high-speed dogfights between the "good guys" and the "bad guys". Right away, droves of youth lined up to enlist in hopes of becoming fighter pilots.

Paramount Pictures offered to place a 90-second Navy recruiting advertisement at the beginning of the video cassette for *Top Gun*, in exchange for $1 million in credit towards their debt to the Navy for production assistance. An internal memo to the Pentagon from an advertising agency rejected the offer, noting that "Both movies are already wonderful recruiting tools for the military, particularly the Navy, and to add a recruiting commercial onto the head of what is already a two-hour recruiting commercial is redundant."[14]

Lt. Sandy Stairs, the Navy's representative while the film was in production, told the *Los Angeles Times*, "Navy regulations prohibit the service from 'selectively endorsing or appearing to endorse a commercial product.' "[15]

They can say anything they want. Few are paying attention, and the military is still America's most trusted institution.

Paramount, like the rest of Hollywood, isn't wedded to the pro-military narrative. Its allegiance is to profit. The blockbuster *Forrest Gump*, with some unflattering portrayals of the military, was a project of deep-pocketed Paramount Pictures.

Paramount submitted a request to the Pentagon for assistance in filming this great American classic. They wanted to use Chinook helicopters and other Vietnam-era military equipment. The Army had reservations about the film and demanded numerous changes to the script. The brass didn't like the scene when Gump bends over, pulls down his pants, and shows President Johnson the scar on his rear end. They didn't like the way Gump referred to his commanding officer, Lt. Dan Taylor, by his rank and first name. They also didn't appreciate the scene in which Lt. Dan is seen crying after being ordered to send his men on a dangerous mission. In the end, Paramount refused to yield to the Pentagon's censors.[16]

The *Forrest Gump* script runs counter to the military's desire to sanitize films to help with recruiting and retention. Unlike *Top Gun*, it didn't send potential recruits rushing to local recruiting stations.

Consider Forrest's first encounter with the military chain of command as he enters the bus to boot camp, and his descriptions of boot camp and Lt. Dan:

> **Forrest Gump:** Hello. I'm Forrest, Forrest Gump.
>
> **Recruit Officer:** Nobody gives a hunky shit who you are, puss ball. You're not even a low-life, scum-sucking maggot. Get your ass on the bus, you're in the army now!
>
> **Drill Sergeant:** Gump! What's your sole purpose in this army?
>
> **Forrest Gump:** To do whatever you tell me, drill sergeant!
>
> **Drill Sergeant:** God damn it, Gump! You're a goddamn genius! This is the most outstanding answer I have ever heard. You must have a goddamn I.Q. of 160. You are goddamn gifted, Private Gump.
>
> **Forrest Gump:** [narrates] Now for some reason I fit in the army like one of them round pegs. It's not really hard. You just make your bed real neat and remember to stand up straight and always answer every question with "Yes, drill sergeant."
>
> **Drill Sergeant:** ...Is that clear?
>
> **Forrest Gump:** Yes, drill sergeant!
>
> **Forrest Gump:** (Speaking of Lt. Dan) He was from a long great military tradition. Somebody from his family had fought and died

in every single American war. I guess you could say he had a lot to live up to.17

Forrest Gump managed box office success without military cooperation. It was an exception to the rule. Since its release in 1994, no military-related film that has managed to escape censorship has come anywhere close to enjoying Gump's commercial success. The military minders have made sure of it. Films about the military have difficulty surviving without sacrificing editorial control.

The close relationship between the movie industry and the Pentagon was further cemented with the release of *Act of Valor* in 2012. The film was commissioned by the Navy's Special Warfare Command and was produced specifically to "bolster recruiting efforts."18 The film "stars" active-duty Navy SEALs.

In a similar fashion, the Marine Corps Recruiting Command plans to use active duty soldiers for its video advertising campaigns. It held a national casting call at ten military base locations over two weeks in April 2016 to screen interested Marines.19

Only a small number of projects the Army included in its report were turned down in the end. These rejections shed light on the highest level of U.S. government complicity with Hollywood and the philosophical underpinnings of the censorship program.

The entry dated April 30, 2013, from the Army's Office of the Chief of Public Affairs in Los Angeles (OCPA-LA) release regarding *Zero Dark Thirty*, shows the Army was happy to duck the extreme controversy at the highest levels of government involving the movie. From OCPA-LA:

> Representatives from the DoD IG (Inspector general) visited OCPA-LA on 30 April. The purpose of the visit was a spiral increment of the DoD IG investigation into DoD's support of the film titled "Zero Dark Thirty". The US Army did not support the movie "Zero Dark Thirty". Specifically, the DoD IG's focus was on DoD Agencies and Military Services regarding the release of DoD classified and/or sensitive information to the media... OCPA-LA does not have any classified material nor do we have the means to store classified material. The DoD IG team appeared to be satisfied with the procedures and policies implemented by OCPA-LA.20

Apparently, CIA Director Leon Panetta and Under Secretary of Defense for Intelligence Michael Vickers conveyed ultra-sensitive, legally protected information to the makers of *Zero Dark Thirty* regarding the capture of Osama bin Laden. The CIA used White House-approved talking points to brief the filmmakers. That information, according to the CIA and as portrayed in the film, was gained using torture.[21]

In a sense, *Zero Dark Thirty's* Producer Mark Boal and Director Kathryn Bigelow were CIA operatives. The blockbuster film implied that the use of torture led to the discovery of Osama bin Laden. The film actually begins with a statement that the movie is "based on first-hand accounts of actual events." It seems Boal and Bigelow sold a lie to the American people.

In 2014, a Senate Intelligence Committee report on CIA interrogation techniques made it clear that torture did not factor into finding Bin Laden. Regardless, the movie's propaganda achieved its purpose. The public was taught to be tolerant of torture and to applaud those who ordered it.[22]

An OCPA-LA entry regarding the movie *The Hurt Locker*, also produced by Boal and directed by Bigelow, was made available through a FOIA request by Secker and provides insight into the way military censors operate. According to the database, *USA Today* reporter Gregg Zoroya asked an OCPA-LA representative, "LTC," for an explanation of the DOD's decision not to support the movie. Rather than identify specific reasons why the film was rejected, readers were provided the link to Zoroya's February 19, 2010 USA Today piece, "Veterans say 'The Hurt Locker' gets a lot right and wrong".[23]

From the article we can pick out several objections Army censors would have us believe led to a denial of DOD cooperation:
- Filmmakers took enough liberties with war reality to cause those who know better to either grin and bear it or dismiss the movie altogether.
- There were errors in rank, patches, vernacular or procedure.
- The movie is ruined by inaccuracies, ranging from the wrong shade of uniform to a scene in which three soldiers run through Baghdad alleyways alone looking for insurgents.
- "I don't like the way Hollywood cashes in on the troops."
- An Iraqi drives through a military roadblock unharmed during an EOD operation. "They would have killed him, no ifs, ands or buts."

The relative superficiality of these items suggests there were other reasons behind the Army's rejection of the request for assistance. Although the film is largely devoid of political commentary, it is anything but an endorsement of the American war effort. *The Hurt Locker* follows a unit of soldiers whose mission is to defuse and dispose of "IED" bombs. The soldiers appear dispirited and fundamentally shaken by the violence they've been exposed to and the bloodshed they've caused. They seem to care very little about anything but their own survival.

The military censors condemned the film because they found it "fails to build resiliency, restore balance, or maintain our combat edge."

The OCPA-LA list also describes Jason Dutton, a heavy metal guitarist with the band, *Kings of Carnage*, who requested permission to film during their concert at the Fort Irwin Army Base. The request was denied. Apparently, the music was deemed to be suitable for those on base but not suitable to be filmed for a potentially wider audience. Cameras are risky business on army bases.

We can gain a sense of the culture of the active duty crowd at Fort Irwin and the line that separates this cultural identity from that which the Army deems marketable to American society as a whole. The group's debut album shows a kneeling, shackled man being readied for decapitation with a man's head lying nearby.24

Another entry from OCPA-LA concerns a request from independent film producers working for National Geographic to film the story of transplant recipients at Walter Reed Medical Center. The Army censors write:

> They believe transplant recipients are the way to go. They propose the following: 1. Identify four patients who will receive, arm, ear or other transplants who are willing to participate. 2. They obtain the go ahead/funding from National Geographic. 3. They film the patient pre-surgery, surgery and post-surgery. OTSG (Office of the Army Surgeon General) has declined support based on the science today, the only thing they could film would be hand transplants and the command feels that logistically they cannot support. Update: Requesting OTSG to reconsider the project.25

This request must have represented a conundrum for the Army. On the one sutured hand, the Army's medical staff is obviously concerned with the limitations of the available science—they may be leery of the potential for a public relations setback regarding the public's perception of recent medical advances in transplants. On the other prosthetic, the propagandists in Los Angeles see the potential payoff for recruiting. The rationale is that relatively few are killed in combat these days; instead they're losing body parts, and that's OK, because these parts can be re-attached—or reassembled.

Approved films also suggest the political orientation of the censors, at least regarding the nuclear issue. Consider *History and Future of Nuclear Power*, (2013), a documentary film by Robert Stone Productions about the history and future of nuclear power that traces nuclear power development in the United States from the Manhattan Project to the present day. Stone was given the green light to film at the White Sands Missile Range Trinity Site, where the first nuclear weapons test of an atomic bomb occurred. Stone's film was approved by OCPA-LA because it "Supports Broader Understanding and Advocacy."

Stone was the director of *Pandora's Promise*, a 2013 documentary film about nuclear power. The film has been lambasted by the environmental community because it fails to examine the problem of spent nuclear fuel storage, the risk of weapons proliferation, and the likelihood of continued accidents. It also leaves out the exorbitant cost of new reactors. The military is rabidly pro-nuclear and Stone is their man.

OCPA-LA supported the production of Discovery's *Frontline Battle Machines*, an eight-part series covering U.S. operations in Afghanistan.

The host, Mike Brewer, covered U.K. forces in the first season. Mike Brewer returns for a second season to the frontline in Afghanistan to reveal the new technology available to the US Forces in the war against terror. Each of the eight shows will feature key items of equipment from armoured troop carriers to fighter planes, helicopters, light tanks, machine guns and guided missiles. Will meet the Soldiers who operate the equipment, witnesses actual missions and travels with troops to discover how new technology has transformed the modern battlefield. Program aimed at knowledge about the vehicles and equipment that could mean the difference between life and death on the battlefield.[26]

OCPA-LA reported that the U.S. Central Command's Public Affairs Office (USCENTCOM PA) also supported the production of the project. CENTCOM is one of nine unified commands in the United States military, consisting of 20 countries: Afghanistan, Bahrain, Egypt, Iran, Iraq, Jordan, Kazakhstan, Kuwait, Kyrgyzstan, Lebanon, Oman, Pakistan, Qatar, Saudi Arabia, Syria, Tajikistan, Turkmenistan, United Arab Emirates, Uzbekistan, and Yemen.

Brewer's product is unabashed rah-rah over the marvels of technology applied to weapons of mass destruction. It represents the most dangerous, sensationalized brand of propaganda as it endeavors to desensitize a massive world-wide audience to the destructive power of these weapons.

Narrator: Have you ever wondered what we're doing in Afghanistan? We're trying out our new toys.

Narrator: Although these are weapons of death
(*Images of gun-toting armored personnel carriers*)

Narrator: They just somehow make you feel alive.
(*The image is that of a massive, rapidly firing automatic machine gun mounted on a military vehicle.*)

Narrator: Unfortunately, none of them get very good mileage.
(*Now the screen shows stacks of hundred dollar bills.*)

Narrator: Which brings up the second reason we're here.
(*The hundred dollar bills appear to be soaked by a steady stream of thick, black oil.*)

Narrator: Watch Mike Brewer and the newest weapons of technology on Fridays at 10 in Frontline Battle Machines on the Discovery Channel.

(*The next scene shows a jet fighter dropping a guided missile in slow motion. The missile is rotating. A close-up shows it is printed with three lines in succession as it moves menacingly toward its target.*)

COME TO DEMOCRACY
OR DEMOCRACY
WILL COME TO YOU [27]

The show is co-produced by the U.S. Central Command Public Affairs Office and the Discovery Channel. Everything is vetted. This is the image the U.S. wants to project to the world. Mike Brewer is a lackey for the American and British propagandists. He's a dime a dozen. Brewer's website carries this promotion for the film, "Mike was sitting with his wife Michelle one morning reading the newspapers and saw yet another article about how British soldiers' equipment wasn't up to the job."[28]

Meanwhile, multinational corporate sponsors line up for viewers at home to imbibe this British-produced rubbish. It's how propagandists operate.

The PBS *Coming Back* series with Wes Moore was also approved by the censors in the Army's Office of the Chief of Public Affairs in Los Angeles.

The three-part series about returning service members undersells the costs of war, according to a review by the influential A.V. Club. "With the right degree of patient understanding and sweet reason, any subject can be turned into bland mush," writes contributor Phil Dyess-Nugent.

That's his takeaway from the documentary that tracks the lives of 2.5 million Americans who have served in Iraq and Afghanistan and re-enter American society. The piece concludes, "It's just frustrating that the show itself doesn't show a fuller, deeper sense of the cost (of war). Watching it is like seeing someone stick a Band-Aid on a bloody stump."29

One OCPA-LA entry from November 27, 2013, addressed a proposed documentary by NBC Peacock Productions called *On the Trail*, a docu-series about Army Basic Training:

> After more than six months of Peacock Production's unwillingness to sign the DoD Production Assistance Agreement for this project, OCPA-LA and OSD-PA (Public Affairs Office of the Secretary of Defense) are discussing the possibility of terminating negotiations with the production company. This is not a bad project, but the production company's unwillingness to agree to the standard terms of the PAA (Production Assistance Agreement) is cause for concern *about their motivations* and the type of story they want to tell. Our recommendation is that this could be a good story, but perhaps Peacock Productions is not the right production company to make the program.30

From the DoD's perspective, it's time to produce a documentary on basic training. If Peacock drags its feet in signing the production contract on "the type of story they want to tell" the Pentagon will find someone else to produce it.

This homogenizing process works for the Pentagon. Overwhelming numbers of Americans express tremendous confidence in the military.

In the words of David Robb,

> "When the American people are seeing hundreds and hundreds of films and TV shows that have been sanitized by the military to make

the military seem more heroic than it really is, and never wrong and always good, that creates a false image in the American people's minds, and I think it helps to make the American people a more warlike people."31

Many of the productions approved by the four military Entertainment Liaison Offices feed directly into that sewer while the Pentagon promotes a whitewashed version of the military and war. This exploitation is also evident in the world of military marketing, the subject of the next chapter.

Notes – Chapter 6

1. OCPA Weekly Plans & Outreach Summaries; OCPA-LA 4/8/2015
Retrieved from: Spy Culture.com http://bit.ly/2g3jq7O

2. U.S. Military Assistance in Producing Motion Pictures, Television Shows, Music Videos. (n.d.). Retrieved September 3, 2015, from http://bit.ly/2fVhviG

3. National Center for Education Statistics. (2013). The Nation's Report Card: Trends in Academic Progress 2012 (NCES 2013–456). National Center for Education Statistics, Institute of Education Sciences, U.S. Department of Education, Washington, D.C. Retrieved http://nces.ed.gov/nationsreportcard/.

4. Jilani, Z. (2015, July 28). Whoa, Pentagon Influences TV Shows Like 'American Idol'? New Documents Show Scary Collaboration. Retrieved September 29, 2015. http://bit.ly/1U-6R5I6.

5. OCPA West Weekly Reports Dec 10, 2010 FOIA FA-15-0157
Retrieved from: Spy Culture.com: http://bit.ly/2fgClYt.

6. DoD Instruction Number 5410.16 dated July 31, 2015, DoD Assistance to Non-Government, Entertainment-Oriented Media Productions http://www.dtic.mil/whs/directives/corres/pdf/541016p.pdf.

7. Department of Defense Instruction Number 5410.15. (1989, March 28). Retrieved September 29, 2015, from http://www.dtic.mil/whs/directives/corres/pdf/541015p.pdf

8. Jamail, Dahr. "Iraq: The Deadliest War for Journalists." - Al Jazeera English. 11 Apr. 2013. Web. 04 May 2016. http://bit.ly/1y12j8d.

9. When Hollywood's Big Guns Come Right from the Source By KATHARINE Q. SEELYE NY Times June 10, 2002 http://nyti.ms/2fYE46n.

10. July 11, 2015 Janine Yaquoob. The Mirror. Iron Man and Transformers censored by US military for getting too close to the truth http://bit.ly/1Lfk3SV.

11. Ibid.

12. Seeyle, When Hollywood's Big Guns Come Right from the Source.

13. Robb, David (2004). Operation Hollywood: How the Pentagon Shapes and Censors the Movies. New York: Prometheus Books. pp. 47-48.

14. Ibid., 180–182.

15. "'Top Gun' Boosting Service Sign-ups." Los Angeles Times. Los Angeles Times, 5 July 1986. Web. 3 Sept. 2015. < http://lat.ms/2ggMCbc.

16. Robb, Operation Hollywood p. 79

17. Forrest Gump. Dir. Robert Zemeckis. Paramount Pictures, 1994. DVD.

18. Jurgensen, John. "Hollywood Tries a New Battle Plan." Wall Street Journal. 26 Aug. 2011. Web. 11 Apr. 2016. http://lat.ms/2ggMCbc.

19. Bacon, Lance M. "Here's Your Chance to Star in the Marine Corps' next Recruiting Commercial." Marine Corps Times. USMC, 1 Apr. 2016. Web. 11 Apr. 2016. http://bit.ly/2f4kXIZ.

20. OCPA WEEKLY PLANS & OUTREACH SUMMARY 30 April 2013. August 2012 Retrieved from: Spy Culture.com http://bit.ly/2g3jq7O.

21. Zagorin, A. (2015, April 16). Exclusive: New Documents in Zero Dark Thirty Affair Raise Questions of White House-Sanctioned Intelligence Leak and Inspector General Coverup. Retrieved September 29, 2015, from http://bit.ly/2fk2f0k.

22. Apuzzo, M., Park, H., & Buchanan, L. (2014). Does Torture Work? The C.I.A.'s Claims and What the Committee Found. Retrieved October 30, 2016, from http://nyti.ms/1B1tGOu.

23. Zoroya, G. (2010, February 19). Veterans say 'The Hurt Locker' gets a lot right and wrong - USATODAY.com. Retrieved September 29, 2015, fromhttp://usat.ly/2ggGtvJ.

24. Rowe, R. (2014, November 12). Interview: Kings of Carnage Discusses Slipknot, Afghanistan, & Upcoming Album - AlternativeNation.net. Retrieved September 30, 2015, from http://bit.ly/2fXlKg9.

25. OCPA, 47.

26. OCPA, 6.

27. Brewer, M. (2015, January 20). Mike Brewer's Frontline Battle Machines Promo. Retrieved September 30, 2015. https://www.youtube.com/watch?v=xxLFHvdu6Jg.

28. Frontline Battle Machines - Mike Brewer TV. (2015). Retrieved September 30, 2015, from http://mikebrewer.tv/battle-machines/.

29. Dyess-Nugent, P. (2014, May 12). Coming Back With Wes Moore undersells the costs of war. Retrieved September 30, 2015, from http://bit.ly/2fgE8wS.

30. OCPA, 988

31. Military movie censorship 'makes Americans warlike' (2012, June 9). Retrieved September 30, 2015. http://bit.ly/2ggJz2X.

Sergeant 1st Class Don O'Neal prepares for a run in his Army-branded Super Comp dragster during a recent race at the U.S. Nationals. U.S. Army Recruiter Journal November, 2010.

Chapter 7

MADISON AVENUE JOINS THE ARMY

It would not be impossible to prove with sufficient repetition and a psychological understanding of the people concerned - that a square is, in fact, a circle"
—Joseph Goebbels

An 11th grader in a suburban Washington DC classroom is delighted to be excused from Algebra class to spend a half hour shooting a life-like 9 MM pistol and lobbing explosive ordinance from an M1A2 Abrams tank simulator. At the same time, 3,000 miles away in La Habra, California, a 15-year-old girl is released from Biology class to squeeze off rounds from a very real looking M-16 rifle. The kids enjoy the experience, especially the part about getting out of class.

The two students have experienced the Army's Adventure Van, a 60-foot, 30-ton 18-wheeler with several interactive exhibits that bring an adrenaline rush and glorify weaponry and combat. The Army's fleet of vans traveled 635,000 miles and made 2,000 stops in 2013. These visits included 865 high schools, according to the US Army Accessions Support Brigade. The vans drew 308,000 visitors and resulted in 57,000 leads.[1]

In addition to the Adventure Vans, the Army has three other 18-wheelers for recruiting purposes. The Aviation Recruiting Van contains an AH 64 Helicopter flight simulator and an interactive air warrior and weapons display. The Special Ops 18-wheeler has a parachute simulator and a dog tag machine that has proven popular with teen boys.

The Army's STEM Van (That's Science, Technology, Engineering, and Math) is popular among many high school teachers and administrators. According to military manuals, the Army reserves this one for "hard to penetrate" high schools. The hands-on exhibits are "designed to showcase hi-tech capabilities and opportunities within the Army while generating quality leads for local recruiters and ROTC departments."[2]

The Army and the Air Force have their own recruiting motorcycles. The American Soldier Adventure Van has an interactive air/land warrior display and a future warrior display. The Army Marksmanship Trainer has an interactive rifle range.

In addition to the fleet of 18-wheelers, the Army has four Rock-Walls, the climbing walls that are popular with youth. The Army also brings machine gun-toting humvees, tanks, and other military vehicles onto high school campuses to enhance their recruiting efforts. The interactive, theatrical weapons simulators provide a mesmerizing experience for many teens, captivated by the awesome accuracy and power of the Army's killing machines.

The banter between adolescent and Army recruiter is empowering for the LaHabra teenager, as she holds an absolutely frightening replica of the cold, metallic 8.5 pound M-16-A-2. "This is awesome!" The recruiter explains, "The weapon is a 5.56 mm caliber, air-cooled, gas-operated, magazine-fed rifle, with a rotating bolt. It is constructed of steel, aluminum, and composite plastics."

Firing the simulator produces a minor kick to the weapon and a small red dot is projected on a bull's-eye target about 20 feet away. The shooter is accurate from left to right on the target, but she's hitting it a few inches below bull's eye. Her recruiter explains that soldiers shooting the M-16-A-2 might want to aim high in order to place shots on the desired target, especially at close range. "Cool!" is the reply.

The Air Force and the Navy also have fleets of trucks and vans that visit high schools. The Air Force has a Raptor Trailer, with a miniature replica of its newest fighter aircraft and two video game stations that put children behind the joystick, piloting an F-22 fighter that's coming to the aid of a friendly F-4 under attack by hostile Russian MiG-29s. Five Navy Exhibit Centers include a "Nuclear Power Van," and an "America's Sea Power Van."

Recruiting is a psychological game. To be most effective, recruiters must understand the mindset of the recruit. This is evident with the 2014 unveiling of the Army Extreme Truck.[3]

Throughout rural and southern America there is a kind of cult around the pickup truck. Perhaps the word "cult" is too strong, but the pickup is an icon in teen culture. It is revered and idolized. It is a symbol of freedom and independence and its ownership represents a transition to adulthood. For some, it means a 1996 Ford F-150 with a badly rusted bed, a partially rebuilt engine, and an odometer showing 320,000.

For others, it's a 2000 Dodge Dakota, larger than the Ford Ranger and Chevy S-10, with a Dodge 318 engine powerful enough to leave the Ranger and the S-10 in the dust.

Now, if this seems odd, consider your own background and the overall recruitment rates per thousand youth from state to state. Rhode Island, for instance, with an overwhelmingly urban/suburban population, saw just 1.26 per thousand of its 18-24-year-olds enter the Army in 2010. South Carolina and Georgia, with huge rural populations, both saw recruitment rates at 3.45 per thousand.[4] Where do you think high school students are more likely see the Extreme Truck? The kids in Newport or Narragansett, Rhode Island might not be impressed with the Army's Extreme Truck, but the boys of Barnwell County, South Carolina, living along the Savannah River on the border with Georgia, are likely to appreciate it.

This truck's got 47-inch wheels while the standard F-150 has 22-inch wheels. Weighing in at 15,700 pounds, the Army's monster is 11,500 pounds heavier than the F-150. It's 9'4" tall compared to the F-150 at 6'3". You won't find it parading the streets of Brookline, Massachusetts or Palo Alto, California! The Army's Recruiting Journal describes it this way:

> The truck is loaded with features to keep up to 12 people engaged at the same time. Its payload includes two gaming stations with 32-inch flat-screen televisions, an additional 60-inch flat screen, and pull-up and push-up platforms to challenge participants. The Extreme Truck includes a diesel engine producing 900 pound-foot of torque, 325 horsepower and a heavy-duty transmission. It is also equipped with a front mounted winch capable of pulling nine tons. It has two 107-gallon fuel tanks and retractable steps.[5]

According to Army Maj. William Davis. "Attracting young Americans to

The Army Extreme Truck – Army Recruiting Journal

become Soldiers requires ingenuity and faster interaction with our future soldiers and officers. This is where the Extreme Truck will help recruiters and ROTC departments take their interactions to another level."

Some 250 students and their teachers at South Central High School in Winterville, North Carolina were treated to the Army Extreme Truck in April of 2015. They tried out the Army's military tactic video game.

The U.S. Army Chopper is slso a big hit on high school campuses across the country. This 560-pound, 134-horsepower killing machine is a testament to sheer madness, a commodity held in high regard among segments of the teen population.

Consider the listless 17-year-old in the midst of a boring English literature class, pondering the words of Geoffrey Chaucer on the study sheet, "Forbid us something and that thing we desire." The monotonic teacher is droning on about Palamon setting forth for Venus' temple when the announcement comes over the P.A., calling on students to head down to the parking lot to see the Army's Chopper.

The recruiter, a staff sergeant with 22 years of active duty service, is trained in the psychology of his profession. He revs up the engine to ear-shattering decibels. The Staff Sergeant explains that the chopper is equipped with a semi-automatic Colt M-4 carbine that fires the .223 caliber, or 5.56 mm NATO round. The M4, the staff sergeant says, has largely replaced the submachine gun due to increased use of body armor, because submachine guns can't penetrate modern body armor.

There's a discussion as to whether the thing can shoot 45 or 90 rounds per minute, how hot it gets, and how often it jams. A razor-sharp U.S. military M9 bayonet is affixed to the M4. One quick jab brings life to a sudden end.

The recruiter handles the M67 Fragmentation Grenade and explains that the grenade weighs 14 ounces and has a 2.5-inch diameter, compared to a baseball that weighs 5 ounces and has a 2.86-inch diameter. "Twice as heavy but a little smaller."

The Army Chopper comes equipped with an M18 A1 Claymore anti-personnel mine, which is about the size of two elementary school lunch boxes sitting side by side. The military is enjoying unprecedented access to high school kids.

As we've seen, Section 8025 of the Every Student Succeeds Act says military recruiters are to have the same access to high school students as college and career recruiters. The presence of these military vehicles on high school campuses goes far beyond the access college and career recruiters enjoy.

When Maryland parents (including the author) organized a demonstration in 2006 to greet the arrival of the Army's Cinema Van at Montgomery Blair High School, Kelly Rowe, public affairs officer for the Baltimore Recruiting Battalion, compared the Cinema Van visit to efforts by colleges to recruit students. "I don't think it's any different from an athlete who gets 10 letters saying, 'Come play for us,' " Rowe insisted.6

The Pentagon's marketing strategists are apparently convinced that segments of the recruiting-age youth population are enamored of great

The U.S. Army Chopper from the U.S. Army
STEM EXPERIENCE FACEBOOK PAGE

big vehicles that make a lot of noise and go very fast.

The National Hot Rod Association (NHRA) and the U.S. Army have been marketing partners in the NHRA Mello Yello Drag Racing Series since 2000. Mello Yello is the top competition series of the NHRA. There are 24 events held annually across the country.

In 2016 the NHRA Mello Yello Drag Racing Series shifted from ESPN to FOX Sports 1 (FS1) with four events airing on the FOX national broadcast network during each season of the long-term agreement. The deal provided the world's fastest motorsport with live coverage of a majority of its events.7

Dragsters scream down the 1,000-foot track propelled by 8,000 horsepower engines burning nitromethane/methanol fuel at speeds up to 330 miles an hour. The earsplitting sound, the trembling earth, and the odor of the noxious gas produce an overwhelming and sometimes intoxicating high.

The Army leverages its collaboration with the NHRA to offer the Youth & Education Services (Y.E.S.) program, pitching Army careers to 25,000 students a year who attend various hot rod events. The Army's driver, Tony Schumacher, joins soldiers and recruiters to promote enlistment.

Schumacher's Army dragster is a crowd favorite. His race cars have been destroyed in fiery explosions in 2003, 2012, 2015, and 2016, while Schumacher has emerged unscathed.

The Army entertains youth at the racetrack with a variety of interactive exhibits, with a special emphasis on Science, Technology, Engineering and Mathematics (STEM). The kids are solicited for personal information while they're sent home with literature that promotes STEM activities, many of them sponsored by the Department of Defense at middle and high schools across the country.

The racetrack exhibits are nearly identical to those at the "Army Strong Zone," a three-acre sea of interactive displays and exhibits adjacent to the Alamodome in San Antonio, Texas during football bowl games. The Army has generated more than a million leads from this recruiting extravaganza, dating back to 1997.

Even so, the Army appears to be uncomfortable with public perceptions that the Army Strong Zone is about recruiting. "This is not a recruiting event," explained Lt. Col. David Walker, the U.S. Army Accessions operations officer for the Army Strong Zone. Walker sounded a theme that permeates much of the recruiting command. The Army is not groveling for youth with few employment options; it is instead providing a public service by connecting regular Americans with their Army. In 2012, Walker explained to a reporter, "This is a demonstration of changing the perception of the Army and showing that it has moved from the kinetic to a STEM environment and it shows the ability for the Army to interact with the local community and the nation, hence connecting our people with our Army."[8]

The Army has teamed up with the National Hot Rod Association (NHRA) Racing team and a group calling itself Ten80 Education Today to launch the Student Racing Challenge. The Student Racing Challenge uses a STEM curriculum and a racing platform to illustrate various STEM principles.[9]

Events focus on STEM-related military careers while the curriculum targets middle and high school students. Students work together to develop their own racing team. Their race car is one-tenth the size of a typical stock car, powered by electricity. It is driven by remote controls. Middle and high school children meet after school and work with coaches to design and test their race cars.

Ten80 Education Student Racing Challenge Events are sponsored by the Army in various cities throughout the U.S. There's a huge US STEMfest event held annually in a major American city that features Army race team members and well-known entertainers. Ten80 Education also teams up with the Denver Broncos to host the Ten80 STEM Expo sponsored by the U.S. Army at Sports Authority Field, Mile High Stadium.

There may be a lot less connecting people to the Army through NASCAR events going forward. From 2008 through 2012 the National Guard spent $136 million to sponsor Dale Earnhardt Jr.'s #88 Car.[10] According to a stunning May 2014 report in *USA Today*, the Army's NASCAR sponsorship netted NO recruits.[11]

The Guard had always defended its sponsorship of Earnhardt and NASCAR, arguing it would help recruit soldiers, but it didn't take long for so much pressure to build that the Guard announced in August of 2014 it was cutting its ties to NASCAR driver Dale Earnhardt, who drives #88, a favorite of Nazi skinheads.

When the allegations were made public by Sen. Claire McCaskill (D-Mo.), at that time Chairwoman of the Senate Financial and Contracting Oversight Subcommittee, there were few congressional defenders of the program to be found.

One exception was Rep. Richard Hudson (NC-08), who referred to the cutoff of funds to NASCAR and the end of the Guard's partnership as "an irresponsible decision." Despite facts to the contrary, Hudson released a statement to the press saying, "The success of the National Guard using professional motorsports to recruit young men and women has been proven and well-documented."[12]

Hudson represents North Carolina's 8th district, which includes Concord, home of Hendrick Motorsports. Earnhardt is a driver for Hendrick. According to the Center for Responsive Politics, Hendrick Motorsports has contributed $27,150 over the years to Rep. Hudson. Hendrick Motorsports itself did not donate; rather the money came from the organization's PAC, its individual members or employees or owners, and those individuals' immediate families.[13]

Since 2004, when Congress passed a law allowing the DOD to profit from retail sales by issuing licenses and trademarks, the military has also been attempting to connect with the public through a stepped up retail campaign. Go online, visit the Army Strong Zone, or attend a Blue Angels Airshow to see the explosion of retail items.

The DoD Branding and Trademark Licensing Program was established to regulate the sale of military merchandise through third-party vendors. Not surprisingly, the objectives of the program are to enhance the name, reputation, and public goodwill of the military services while "supporting the recruiting and retention efforts of the military departments." There's a rich irony here. The Pentagon profits on selling overpriced, cheaply made merchandise from China, while pitching enlistment to eager consumers. At least one vendor advertised merchandise as having been "Made in America" when it actually originated from China.

WCPO TV in Cincinnati reported in 2014 that a local retired Army officer purchased an Army baseball cap from shopmyexchange.com, one of a multitude of online vendors peddling Pentagon gear. The vet paid $29.95 for the Army cap. The website description says "Made in the USA," but when he received his cap, he was stunned to find a label that said, "Made in China."[14]

No laws were broken. Although the Berry Amendment, passed by Congress in 2006, forbids the DOD from purchasing uniforms from foreign suppliers, this law pertains to soldier uniforms and gear purchased by the government, not merchandise sold at military exchanges.

It's overwhelming to consider the list of "military" merchandise the DOD is aggressively peddling to the public. It seems everything these days carries military insignia, including:

> Banks - Credit Card Companies - Hats - Sportswear - Toys - Models - Games - Clocks - Watches - Jewelry - Coins - Pins - Hats - Clothing - Office Accessories - Software Accessories - Sunglasses - Sporting Goods - Novelty Goods - Furniture - Clocks - Bikes - Autos - Motorcycles - Books - Magazines - Posters - Special Events[15]

Christian Davenport of the *Washington Post* captured the absurdity of the Pentagon's retail market campaign in his brilliant 2011 piece, "The Marine cologne: Strong, with a hint of military spirit."

> Nothing smells quite like a Marine. Pungent with hints of the Parris Island swamp. The unmistakable notes of sweat-soaked combat boots and the earthy musk of a well-dug trench. Isn't that the smell of a Marine? Perhaps. But it's not what the officially licensed Marine Corps cologne smells like. At $45 a bottle, "Devil Dog" is far from eau de grunt. Instead, it boasts a "finely crafted fusion of sandalwood, cedar and citric spices" that "stands as a proud reminder of honor and tradition.[16]

Davenport reported that the Army alone expected to sell $50 million worth of merchandise, generating more than $1.2 million in fees and royalties.

Video games, drag racing, monster pick-up trucks, killer motorcycles, military sportswear; how else can the military get into a potential recruit's head? Comic books, of course! Comichron, a resource for comics research, estimates that the North American comics market, including both print and digital formats, totaled $935 million in 2014.[17]

It's safe to say that several million men and women between 17 and 24, the prime recruiting age, regularly consume digital comic books. With more than 14 million registered users playing the *America's Army* video game, the Army probably realized the potential for mass consumption.[18]

The *America's Army* video game features a conflict between the "bad guys" of Czervenia and the "good guys" of the peaceful nation of Ostregal. The U.N. failed to avert a crisis and failed to provide humanitarian relief, so the government of the good guys has requested help from the United States. The Army has been sent in to "resolve the situation." There's not much else to understand, in terms of the geopolitical complexities of the situation.

The storyline continues in the *America's Army* Comics digital comic book app, available for free on iTunes:

> The App features our first two issues. The first issue, Knowledge is Power, immerses readers in the Ostregal Islands where a humanitarian mission soon turns mysterious and deadly when a Long Range Reconnaissance Team witnesses an ominous scientific discovery deep in an enemy forest - an impending threat that could jeopardize the mission and endanger the entire world.
>
> In the second issue, Rise to the Challenge, Sergeant Roy Lacroix examines his life as he goes from his humble beginnings as a high school student to a Special Forces medic deployed in Czervenia while realizing the value his hard work and determination has meant to the people he's encountered along his journey.
>
> Learn more about the U.S. Army by browsing through the interactive Intel Section that showcases state-of-the-art gear, weapons, aircraft and more!
>
> Experience the official comic book of the United States Army. Download this innovative jump into digital comic technology and

stay tuned for more free exciting issues and updates. HOOAH![19]

There are significant omissions in this brief iTunes introduction to the comics developed by the Army Game Studio at Redstone Arsenal, Alabama. There's no mention of dozens of illegal U.S. military actions in the recent past; no mention of war crimes committed by American soldiers. The reason for the introduction of U.S. military force is that internationally sanctioned multilateral peacekeeping efforts have failed miserably. The comic book leaves out an examination of the American track record in undermining U.N. protocols, particularly those that might challenge the unilateral and aggressive military actions of the U.S. government.

It is the comic book's spy team that uncovers the abominable plans of terrorists deep in the jungle who are hatching a secret plan of nuclear terrorism. There's no discussion of the United States as the nation possessing the largest clandestine apparatus on the earth or the U.S. as the greatest purveyor of nuclear weaponry in the world.

This iTunes summary on behalf of the U.S. Army is outrageously patronizing. Our hero, Sergeant Lacroix, with "his humble beginnings as a high school student," is now an Army medic deployed in Czervenia. He's not an Infantryman or a Cannon Fire Direction Specialist. It's his job to heal, not to kill.

The comic book app has a five-star rating in the Apple App store. Industry critics generally give the Army comic book high ratings, especially for the artwork and the portrayal of Army jargon, acronyms, and combat scenarios. But this is a sterilized glimpse of Army life produced for recruiting purposes.

Apparently, the Pentagon has plenty to spend on half-baked schemes designed to sell the notion of military service to the recruiting-age population. According to a report released by Senators John McCain and Jeff Flake, the DOD spent millions for patriotic tributes at various professional sports events from 2012 to 2015.[20]

From the report, "Tracking Paid Patriotism":

> Altogether, the military services reported $53 million in spending on marketing and advertising contracts with sports teams between 2012 and 2015. More than $10 million of that total was paid to teams in the National Football League, Major League Baseball, National Basketball Association, National Hockey League, and Major

League Soccer. The DOD paid for patriotic tributes at professional football, baseball, basketball, hockey, and soccer games. These paid tributes included on-field color guard, enlistment and reenlistment ceremonies, performances of the national anthem, full-field flag details, ceremonial first pitches and puck drops. The National Guard paid teams for the "opportunity" to sponsor military appreciation nights and to recognize its birthday.

Eighteen teams in the NFL received a total of $5.6 million over the four-year period. For a price, NFL teams provided the military opportunities to perform surprise welcome home promotions for troops returning from deployments and to recognize wounded warriors

The NFL, which spent $1.2 million on Capitol Hill lobbying expenses in 2014 alone, seemed somewhat embarrassed by the findings.[21] Although the football league initially said the McCain-Flake report "paints a completely distorted picture of the relationship between NFL teams and our military," it promised to audit its teams' government contracts and refund any money paid out inappropriately. This contrasts sharply to the reaction of the Pentagon.

McCain said the Pentagon "was unusually and especially aggressive when trying to withhold this information." The report said the DOD "has no measurement on whether the activities paid for are in fact contributing to recruiting" and that the DOD's "lack of internal controls put them at excessive risk for waste, fraud, and abuse."

How else might the Pentagon penetrate the minds of military-aged youth? Maj. Gen. Mark Brilakis, Commanding General of the Marine Corps Recruiting Command, says the Corps will be concentrating on service to nation, a message he said "seems to resound with the current generation of millennials."[22]

The previous recruiting pitch, "Towards the Sounds of Chaos," emphasized service, but it also highlighted combat and crisis response. Perhaps youngsters in their early 20's, still living at home with dreadful employment prospects, are more averse these days to putting their lives on the line to protect their country. Evidently the Marine Corps thinks it makes more sense to sell the Marines as an honorable profession to serve those in need than it does to pitch the thrilling prospect of seeing combat. We can see that very theme in the Army's comic book.

The Army Marketing and Research Group (AMRG), established

in 2012, teamed with New York-based marketing firm McCann Worldgroup to create advertising that presents the Army as an elite team seeking new members because "there is important work to be done."[23]

In 2015, McCann World Group, which has managed the Army account since 2005, was awarded a new one-year $200-million contract to provide the Army with advertising and marketing services for recruitment and retention. McCann is an agency of Interpublic Group of Companies (IPG)[24] That same year the Army changed its recruiting pitch, replacing "Army Strong" with an emphasis on service and sacrifice, and extolling the virtues of joining "the Army team."

The contract is the US government's largest single ad account.[25] The deal is renewable for four years, making it a possible five-year working relationship.[26]

Occasionally, we get a glimpse of what the nation's top advertising minds actually think of their clients and their products. Defense Industry Daily reported in July of 2013 that Mike Hughes, President of Interpublic's subsidiary The Martin Agency, had shared his thoughts about McCann's client, the US Army:

> Are U.S. soldiers heroic in taking on dangerous tasks to help protect us? Are many of the soldiers fine and great men? Yes. Is the Army a prejudiced, misogynistic, self-destructive organization of deeply flawed, violent men and women of low average esteem, suicidal tendencies, and intelligence? Yes, again.

Defense Industry Daily commented:

> The statement in question doesn't come from some random staffer. It comes from a top-level executive of one of IPG's largest subsidiaries – with several direct clients, like Wal-Mart, that are very supportive of the US Army. That an ad agency President, of all people, should see fit to publicly utter such a thing about his group's client, is more than passing strange. That it should come in the form of an evidence-free smear is indefensible.[27]

Of course *Defense Industry Daily* was quick to malign Hughes. Like millions at the Pentagon's teat, they're quick to fall in line. The well-known defense publication failed to mention that Mr. Hughes, who had been diagnosed with lung cancer years before, was in hospice at home when he made the comment. Hughes remained lucid and kept two blogs close to the day of his death. He died on December 15, 2013.

Hughes was one of the country's greatest advertising men, starting at the agency he eventually ran for 20 years as a copywriter in 1978. He was behind Geico's Caveman, the "over the hump" camel, and the brilliant FreeCreditReport.com ads.[28]

The guy was sharp as a tack. He wrote his own obit. He was a word man, like Don Draper of the *Mad Men* series. He knew the value of carefully chosen words. Again, consider the words he used to describe the Army, and keep in mind he knew the Army from a marketing perspective.

- Prejudiced
- Misogynistic
- Self-destructive
- Deeply flawed
- Violent men and women of low average esteem & intelligence
- Suicidal tendencies

It doesn't matter what the ad men think. All that matters are the public's perception of the Army, and that's the job of the Army's propaganda arm, Army Marketing and Research Group (AMRG). The AMRG looked to the advertising gurus at McCann World Group to come up with market-tested strategies to further improve its stellar image. The solution was to use interactive social media to stress the value of Army service. The AMRG describes it this way:

> Historically, the Army's method of marketing and recruiting informs people what benefits a recruit may receive in exchange for his or her service, but not why they should be interested in the first place. *The Enterprise Army Brand* introduces a fundamental shift from promoting the personal benefits of Army service to promoting the value of the Army as an institution. As a cornerstone of the Enterprise Army Brand, AMRG will highlight the stories of soldiers who make significant contributions to their communities and provide a tangible demonstration of the value of the Army to American society.[29]

We can see the strategy at work in high schools across the country. For years, high school students have been routinely indoctrinated by an unconscionable barrage of corporate marketing, state propaganda, and deceptive military recruitment through conventional TV programming in classrooms.

Channel One News loans a school TV equipment in exchange for the school's contractual pledge to show students a daily, 12-minute, highly commercialized TV program. The company claims to reach 5 million students with programming aligned to Common Core State Standards.

Students lose one hour a week of school time, which equates to one lost week of instructional time (32 hours) per year. Not one educational organization endorses the use of Channel One News.[30] The U.S. Army has paid Channel One News to run its recruitment ads and to embed their recruitment pitches into "news" stories.[31]

It's effective, but it doesn't accomplish AMRG's goal of saturating *interactive* media with enticing stories about Army values. Enter SkoolLive.

For years, DOD recruiting commanders have attempted to circumvent student privacy protections designed to shield minors from the wholesale transfer of student information from the nation's high

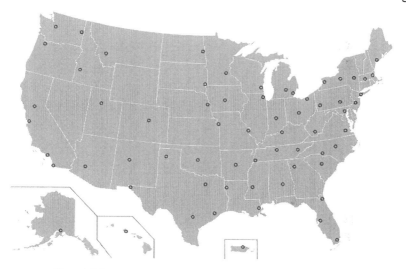

Map of U.S. marked with the locations of all United States Military Entrance Processing Command stations. – WIKIMEDIA COMMONS

schools to the Pentagon's Military Entrance Processing Command.

The DOD markets "career opportunities" through the schools, relying on a variety of methods, from Channel One to posters and announcements touting military service or schemes like STEM Programs and March 2 Success, the free Army test prep software. For the most part, however, these outreach efforts rely on the schools as a third party from which to extract student data. Until now, the DOD's quest for greater access to children has been stymied by pesky state and federal laws that regulate the flow of student information from the schools.

Imagine then, the Pentagon's keen interest in a plan by upstart Skool-Live LLC of Fallbrook, CA to install giant, 6-foot, I-phone-like devices with flashing, screaming, streaming interactive screens in thousands of high school hallways across the country. These life-size digital kiosks allow kids to directly upload their personal information without having to deal with school policies or state and federal laws.

The company says it has agreements with more than 2,000 schools in 27 states and intends to triple that number.[32]

According to SkoolLive, school officials allow the free installation of these devices because they are convinced the gadgets "enrich a student's school experience by replacing mundane printed posters with high-quality digital ads that require less space, reduce visual clutter, move schools into the digital age, and save tons of time, money and trees."[33]

But these officials may not be seeing the entire picture. From the SkoolLive website directed toward potential advertisers:

> The SkoolLive Kiosk screens are touch sensitive. The feature allows us to offer "interactive" ads. With this interactive feature, advertisers are able to conduct student surveys, determine product preferences, enter contests, send text messages containing promo codes, discount coupons, etc. Our proprietary software captures and analyzes this valuable data, providing advertisers the analytics and feedback necessary to effectively measure audience acceptance as well as the effectiveness of their ad.

The placement of these SkoolLive kiosks, however, may circumvent The Family Educational Rights and Privacy Act (FERPA). Generally, the law states that schools may disclose information such as a student's name, address, and telephone number, but are required to allow parents to request that the school not disclose information about children. Many state laws go even further in protecting student rights. By allowing the placement of these giant interactive kiosks, schools may be allowing the transfer of student information without providing for parental consent.

Additionally, SkoolLive's interactive hallway contraptions may be violating the newly enacted Section 8025 of the *Every Student Succeeds Act* (ESSA).

The law says schools shall provide, upon a request made by a military recruiter, access to the name, address, and telephone listing of a high school student, unless the parent submits a written request to the school that the child's information not be released. Schools must notify parents of their right to opt out.34

SkoolLive's kiosks remove the role of the school and allow the military to extract information directly from unassuming minors.

Not only that, but schools stand to make thousands off each kiosk per month, the company claims, depending on the marketing dollars each generates. SkoolLive officials apparently told Chris Marczak, assistant superintendent of Oak Ridge High School in Tennessee, that each kiosk could generate between $2,000 and $5,000 monthly for each of its schools.

Even so, the Tennessee school district stopped the "free" kiosks from being installed. More than 110 students and parents took an online survey about the kiosks and 60% of the respondents were against the proposal. 35

The giant I-pads are sold as a way for students to access information about a particular notice or event. Need to know more about purchasing high school rings or yearbooks? Click here. Want to leave your contact info for an advertiser to get in touch? It's simple!

Want to learn about jobs in the Army, or more specifically, how to take the military's enlistment test, the Armed Services Vocational Aptitude Battery? That information is readily available in a slick, colorful, interactive format in high schools across the country, and it may be coming to a school near you. SkoolLive describes the Army's use of its interactive kiosks this way:

> The Army wanted students to be aware of Army career options while learning student preferences. As a part of their Career Exploration Program, the Army ran a full-screen video interactive career survey. Students entered their grade, selected their career preference and registered to win one of three prizes given away monthly. Winners were showcased in a follow-up ad.36

It seems nothing is sacred, nothing off limits in the overzealous world of military marketing. A case in point is a 2013 posting from the Air Force's Global Strike Team that tries to convince the public that Dr. Martin Luther King would be proud of America's nuclear arsenal.

> Dr. King would be proud to see our Global Strike team - comprised of Airmen, civilians, and contractors from every race, creed, background, and religion - standing side-by-side ensuring the most powerful weapons in the US arsenal remain the credible bedrock

of our national defense. Our team must overlook our differences to ensure perfection as we maintain and operate our weapon systems. Maintaining our commitment to our Global Strike team, our families, and our nation is a fitting tribute to Dr. King as we celebrate his legacy.[37]

The recruiting commands of the various services frequently equate military service with defending freedom and democracy. That ought to net some recruits. Both the St. Louis and San Antonio Army Recruiting Battalions carry this message on their websites: "Our mission is to recruit qualified men and women in order to provide the strength needed to uphold and defend Freedom and Democracy."

In the dominant, secular media marketplace, in our town squares, city streets, and shopping malls, we are immersed in an adoring reverence toward all things military. Nothing else comes close. Less than 1 in 5 Americans actually attend weekly religious worship services, while somewhere between 4,000 and 7,000 churches close their doors every year. If there is near-universal mass worship in America it is a worship of killing institutions and machines.[38]

The National Museum of American History in Washington, D.C. is a great shrine of American military worship. An immensely popular exhibit, "The Price of Freedom: Americans at War" reinforces the pervasive panoply of American military adoration. It is treated as the Gospel truth. The exhibit opens with these words, "Americans have gone to war to win their independence, expand their national boundaries, define their freedoms, and defend their interests around the globe."[39]

This is horrendous propaganda, yet we are so thoroughly seduced that most of us can't see it, not unlike the Israelites of old who worshiped the golden calf.

The prolific antiwar author David Swanson reacted to the exhibit this way:

> The exhibit is an extravaganza of lies and deceptions. The U.S. Civil War is presented as "America's bloodiest conflict." Really? Because Filipinos don't bleed? Vietnamese don't bleed? Iraqis don't bleed? We should not imagine that our children don't learn exactly that lesson. The Spanish American War is presented as an effort to "free Cuba," and so forth. But overwhelmingly the lying is done in this exhibit by omission. Bad past excuses for wars are ignored, the death and destruction is ignored or falsely reduced. Wars that are too recent for many of us to swallow too much B.S. about

are quickly passed over.[40]

The Smithsonian's pro-war propaganda probably wasn't produced with Army recruitment specifically in mind. Rather, it is state-sanctioned pap that accomplishes the same task.

The next chapter expands on the notion of interactive ways to entice the recruitment age population.

Notes – Chapter 7

1. Holiday, Briefer COL. "Accessions Support Brigade Command Brief." U.S. Army Recruiting Command. U.S. Army. Web. 22 Jan. 2016. http://www.usarec.army.mil/asb/branding/ASB_Command_Brief.pdf.

2. "Army STEM Experience with Startup Middle School." Army STEM Experience with Startup Middle School. Eventbrite. Web. 22 Jan. 2016. http://bit.ly/2f0nCjC.

3. Kester, SGT Edward. "Extreme Truck." Recruiter Journal. U.S. Army, 12 May 2014. Web. 22 Jan. 2016. http://bit.ly/2eFTuOZ.

4. "Military Recruitment 2010." National Priorities Project. National Priorities Project, 30 June 2011. Web. 22 Jan. 2016. http://bit.ly/2f4a5ed.

5. Kester, "Extreme Truck."

6. Aratani, Lori. "Military Recruiters Protested At School." Washington Post, 03 Feb. 2006. Web. 22 Jan. 2016. http://wapo.st/2fXjuWb.

7. "NHRA Inks Long-term Deal with FOX Sports." FOX Sports. 14 July 2015. Web. 23 Jan. 2016. http://foxs.pt/1fKkYPW.

8. Hipps, Tim. "ARMY.MIL, The Official Homepage of the United States Army." Army Strong Zone Helps Keep Troops in Touch with Americans. U.S. Army, 12 Jan. 2012. Web. 23 Jan. 2016. http://bit.ly/2fXl8XM.

9. "U.S. Army and Ten80 Education Announce New Student Racing Challenge Events." -- ALEXANDRIA, Va., Sept. 30, 2015 /PRNewswire/ --. Army Marketing and Research Group, 30 Sept. 2015. Web. 23 Jan. 2016. http://prn.to/2fVUYRE.

10. "McCollum: National Guard's $26 Million Sponsoring NASCAR's Dale Earnhardt Jr. Results in ZERO Recruits. 18 May 2012. Web. 23 Jan. 2016. http://bit.ly/2fgCKKM.

11. Vanden Brook, Tom. "National Guard's NASCAR Deal Leads to Virtually No Recruits." USA Today. Gannett, 08 May 2014. Web. 23 Jan. 2016. http://usat.ly/1uCilT4.

12. "Congressman Richard Hudson: Press Releases: Hudson Statement on Political Pressure Ending National Guard Partnership with NASCAR." 7 Aug. 2014. Web. 23 Jan. 2016. http://bit.ly/2fVkpnx.

13. "Rep. Richard Hudson." Opensecrets RSS. Web. 23 Jan. 2016. http://bit.ly/2fx05dX.

14. Matarese, John. "U.S. Army Hats Still Being Made in China." WCPO Cincinnati. 21 July 2014. Web. 23 Jan. 2016. http://bit.ly/UplkzQ.

15. "Army Retired Ball Cap." Shopmyexchange.com. Web. 23 Jan. 2016. <http://bit.ly/2fVn3tu.

16. Davenport, Christian. "The Marine Cologne: Strong, with a Hint of Military Spirit." The Washington Post, 7 Sept. 2011. Web. 25 Jan. 2016. http://wapo.st/2fVVhf1.

17. "Yearly Rankings for Comic Book Sales." Comichron. Web. 23 Jan. 2016. http://www.comichron.com/yearlycomicssales.html.

18. Storey, Deborah. "America's Army Video Game Provides Civilians with inside Perspective of Military Life." AL.com. 26 June 2014. Web. 23 Jan. 2016. http://bit.ly/2eFWafA.

19. "America's Army Comics on the App Store." App Store. Web. 23 Jan. 2016. http://apple.co/1l2CJtr.

20. McCain, Sen. John, and Sen. Jeff Flake. "Tackling Paid Patriotism." McCain.Senate.gov. 15 May 2015. Web. 25 Jan. 2016. http://bit.ly/1iDa8vD.

21. "Recreation/Live Entertainment." Opensecrets RSS. Web. 23 Jan. 2016. http://bit.ly/2f0q2yt.

22. Sanborn, James K. "New Ads, Fresh-looking Football Programs for Recruiting Command." Marine Corps Times. 5 Oct. 2014. Web. 23 Jan. 2016.

23. Lilley, Kevin. "Service Ditches 'Army Strong' for New Branding Strategy." Army Times. 30 Apr. 2015. Web. 23 Jan. 2016. http://bit.ly/1JbIspL.

24. Kyzer, Lindy. "McCann World Group Awarded $200 Million Army Marketing Contract - DoD Daily Contracts - ClearanceJobs." ClearanceJobs. 06 Apr. 2015. Web. 23 Jan. 2016. http://bit.ly/2fx08q7.

25. "IPG Ad Agency President Slanders US Army and Personnel as Prejudiced Deeply Flawed Low Average Esteem, Suicidal Tendencies#8221; " Defense Industry Daily RSS News. 10 July 2013. Web. 23 Jan. 2016. http://bit.ly/2fYI7jh.

26. O'Leary, Noreen. "U.S. Army Is Reaching Out to Agencies Again for $500 Million Account." AdWeek. 14 Nov. 2014. Web. 23 Jan. 2016. <http://bit.ly/1l28R8G.

27. "IPG Ad Agency President Slanders US Army and Personnel as Prejudiced Deeply Flawed Low Average Esteem, Suicidal Tendencies#8221;." Defense Industry Daily RSS News. 10 July 2013. Web. 23 Jan. 2016. http://bit.ly/2fYI7jh.

28. Diaz, Ann Christine. "Martin Agency President Mike Hughes Passes Away." Advertising Age Agency News RSS. 15 Dec. 2013. Web. 23 Jan. 2016. http://bit.ly/2f0i1tK.

29. "Rebranding The Army Stories by Mark S. Davis, Maj. Eric Baiough and Lt. Col. Nick Wittwer" US Army Magazine, June 2014

30. "Houghton Mifflin/Channel One News." Obligation, Inc. Web. 23 Jan. 2016. http://bit.ly/1qq8rmE.

31. Metrock, Jim. "Turning Ads into News: US Army Pays Channel One News for Positive Story." Obligation, Inc. 24 Apr. 2014. Web. 26 Apr. 2016. http://bit.ly/1hqu4OZ.

32. Dale, Mariana. "Schools Open Halls to Electronic Billboards." Arizona Daily Star. 22 Jan. 2015. Web. 23 Jan. 2016. http://bit.ly/1CGqjPq.

33. "Skoollive-kiosks." Skoollive-kiosks. Web. 23 Jan. 2016. http://www.skoollive.com/#!about-us/mainPage.

34. "S.1177 - Every Student Succeeds Act." Congress.gov. 10 Dec. 2015. Web. 23 Jan. 2016. http://bit.ly/1Ldv8Wi.

35. Fowler, Bob. "Digital Kiosks Placed on Oak Ridge Schools' Back Burner." Digital Kiosks Placed on Oak Ridge Schools' Back Burner. 29 Sept. 2015. Web. 26 Apr. 2016. http://bit.ly/2fVm7oX.

36. "Skoollive-kiosks." www.skoollive.com. Web. 26 Apr. 2016. http://www.skoollive.com/#!ad-success/grrko.

37. Greenwald, Glenn. "US Military Says Martin Luther King Would Be Proud of Its Weapons." The Guardian. 22 Jan. 2013. Web. 23 Jan. 2016. http://bit.ly/2ggPF3h.

38. McSwain, Steve. "Why Nobody Wants to Go to Church Anymore." The Huffington Post. TheHuffingtonPost.com, 13 Oct. 2013. Web. 23 Jan. 2016. http://huff.to/1qLakMu.

39. "The Price of Freedom - Americans at War." National Museum of American History. Web. 23 Jan. 2016. http://s.si.edu/2fFrOqD.

40. Swanson, David. "Teach the Children War." Teach the Children War. War Is a Crime.org, 20 Mar. 2013. Web. 23 Jan. 2016. http://warisacrime.org/content/teach-children-war.

Screenshot of *America's Army* Video Game.

Chapter 8

VIDEO GAMES RECRUIT & TRAIN KILLERS

"Where does a 14-year-old boy who never fired a gun before get the skill and the will to kill?

- Video games and media violence"

Violent video games conspire to make Americans warlike, especially extraordinarily graphic games where the player holds a weapon-like game controller. At least that's what about half of the country believes. A 2010 Rasmussen survey finds that 54% of Americans believe violent video games lead to more violence in society.[1]

Some studies link violent video games to aggressive and risky behavior among teens while others show that violent video games may have a calming effect on youth.

Believe what you want to believe.

After all, this is America, where free enterprise creates "research" that substantiates and disseminates pretty much anything for a price. Red meat doesn't lead to heart disease and climate change is not caused by human activity. There's research to "prove" it.

One thing is certain. The military, for its part, believes violent, first person shooter games are an excellent way to recruit youth. The military is looking for killers.

Lt. Col. Dave Grossman offers a chilling indictment of violent video games in a widely circulated and deeply influential article, *A Case Study: Paducah, Kentucky*, published in the fall of 2000. A fourteen-year-old shooter fired eight rounds in fast succession at a high school youth prayer group, killing three and wounding five.

> I train numerous elite military and law enforcement organizations around the world. When I tell them of this achievement, they are stunned. Nowhere in the annals of military or law enforcement history can we find an equivalent "achievement."

> Where does a 14-year-old boy who never fired a gun before get the skill and the will to kill? Video games and media violence.2

Grossman argues that youth who pull the virtual trigger to slaughter thousands become hardened emotionally. He calls these violent military shooting games "Murder Simulators."3

There's an undeniable appeal, an enticement, an attraction to taking virtual human life, and although *America's Army* can't quite match the gore of *Mortal Kombat* or the splattering blood in *Manhunt 2*, it's not bad for free, many adolescents contend.

America's Army is a free online combat game developed by the Pentagon that has helped to recruit youth into the armed forces. The game's technology, and specifically the controls, are strikingly similar to remote-controlled weapons. Actually, it's the other way around! For instance, the controls of the Packbot robot, used extensively in Iraq, and the General Atomics MQ-1 Predator, an unmanned aerial vehicle, are actually modeled after Xbox and PlayStation controllers. Pentagon war planners understand all of this.

The *America's Army* video game has millions of avid fans. It is one of the world's most frequently downloaded games. According to a 2008 study by researchers at the Massachusetts Institute of Technology, "the game had more impact on recruits than all other forms of Army advertising combined."4

Although the Army brushes off claims that violent video games cheapen human life and enhance the appeal to sanctioned killing, the American Academy of Pediatrics recognizes exposure to violence in the media, including television, movies, music, and video games, as a significant risk to the health of children and adolescents. They claim:

> Extensive research evidence indicates that media violence can contribute to aggressive behavior, desensitization to violence, nightmares, and fear of being harmed. Pediatricians should assess their patients' level of media exposure and intervene on media-related health risks. Pediatricians and other child health care providers can advocate for a safer media environment for children by encouraging media literacy, more thoughtful and proactive use of media by children and their parents, more responsible portrayal of violence by media producers, and more useful and effective media ratings.5

America's Army 3, the newest version of the game, is rated "Teen – Blood Violence" by the Entertainment Software Ratings Board. 6

According to americasrmy.com, the official website of the US Army's video game:

> Players have a specific weapon challenge available to every weapon at all times. Players must complete all challenge requirements before moving on to the next challenge and cannot make progress towards a challenge before unlocking said challenge. For example, if a newly unlocked challenge requires a certain number of kills, then kills the player made before unlocking the challenge do not count towards satisfying that challenge's requirements.7

To provide a sense of the degree to which the Army is attempting to replicate taking life in close combat, consider the upgrades to the game published on the America's Army News website in the fall of 2015:

- Weapon sound updates
- Weapon smoke FX no longer move with the weapon
- Bullet impact FX updates
- Tweaks to grenade FX
- Fixed missing shotgun shells ejecting
- M4 and M249 recoil adjustments 8

The game has an ugly and particularly reactionary political message. It rivals the Junior Reserve Officer Training Corps (JROTC) textbooks, in use in thousands of American high school classrooms, in its distorted view of international relations. America's Army is not just a game. Because so many of its players are functionally illiterate, the political messaging amounts to unbridled indoctrination.

From the *America's Army* website:

> Fourteen months ago, the Czervenian government, controlled by the PKC, began expelling civilians from the country by military force. Over 300,000 people have been displaced and those who refused to leave have been executed. Czervenian President Kazimir Adzic and the PKC threaten to destabilize the region. U.N. Security Council resolutions failed to resolve the conflict and U.N. aid workers are overwhelmed. A humanitarian crisis of epic proportions is imminent if decisive action is not taken. The RDO government and the U.N. have requested the help of the United States. The President has sent the U.S. Army to resolve the situation.

Reality check: Although many quasi-literate youth playing these games may believe otherwise, there is no country named Czeverenia; it is a figment of the imagination of U.S. Army war game planners. Kazimir is a Russian name. Adzik is Slavic. In its brief political orientation to the virtual slaughter that makes up the bulk of the *America's Army* game, American youth are instructed that U.N. peacekeeping efforts are a failure. The U.N. and "The RDO government" need the American Army. The PKC is an undefined political entity but we know it "threatens." Apparently, there's nothing more to understand.

The Army understood the visceral appeal of these games and made plans to shift a portion of its nationwide recruiting apparatus to establish gaming centers equipped with X Box 360's running *America's Army*, along with lifelike simulators in shopping malls across the country. The project was launched with the unveiling of the Army Experience Center, (AEC) at Franklin Mills Mall in Philadelphia in August of 2008. The opening was immediately followed by an unprecedented level of organized public indignation and protest that ultimately led the Army to close the operation less than two years after it opened.

In May of 2010, a coalition of about 30 peace groups proved triumphant in its goal of shutting down the AEC. The Army closed the video war game recruitment center, aborting its intention to set up similar stations across the country. The closure of the $13 million, 14,500 square foot AEC was a testament to the steely resolve of a handful of activists from New York to Maryland who were intent on the facility's demise. They organized several protests of hundreds of people that resulted in a dozen arrests, as well as regular vigils and a boycott of mall owner Simon Property Group, Inc.

Witnessing 13-year-old boys giving each other high fives for "blowing away ragheads" while the simulated blood of Afghans poured on their screens provided enough stimulus for these activists to turn outrage to action. The U.S. Army was ultimately forced to retreat.

The AEC boasted dozens of video game computers and X-Box consoles with various interactive, military-style shooting games. The facility had sophisticated Apache helicopter and Humvee simulators that allowed teens to simulate battlefield killing. *Philadelphia Inquirer* reporter Rob Watson compared the Army Experience Center to "a heavy dose of candy cigarettes."

When the center opened, the Army announced it was designed as a pilot program and would decide whether to launch them nationally. In August 2009, Captain Jared Auchey, Company Commander at Franklin Mills, was boasting of the center's success and claiming others were being planned across the country. But the protests escalated. Dozens of local and national peace groups joined the "Shut Down the Army Experience Center" campaign.

Activists infiltrated the AEC's Facebook page, and for days several dozen people opposed to the center dominated a discussion of the ethical implications of recruiting youth using video games. The Army eventually moved to ban many of its new Facebook "friends," but others took their places and the "unwelcome disruptions" continued.

Demonstrators typically cited moral rather than political reasons in their signage and statements to the press. Bill Deckhart, coordinator of BuxMont Coalition for Peace Action, described the AEC as "a monument to dishonesty." He continued, "The AEC teaches children killing without consequence. Real warfare does not have reset buttons or multiple lives. To give this impression to our youth is immoral and must be stopped." It is this burning resolve and strategic messaging that has caused the Army to reconsider its plans to establish video arcade recruiting centers in shopping malls across the country.

Organizers were assisted by St. Luke's United Church of Christ, located adjacent to the mall. When activists asked if the church and its grounds could be used as a staging area for the protests, the pastor responded, "Of course!"

Elaine Brower, who became a leading activist in the campaign to shut down the center and whose son joined the Marines at age 17, was arrested twice. "This is a victory for the entire peace and anti-war movement. The teamwork and coalition building that was accomplished led to our success. We were relentless in our struggle to shut this center down."

The sustained work of committed activists like Brower forced the otherwise complacent mainstream media to take notice. It's difficult to ignore several hundred angry protesters and almost as many police, Army officials, and several dozen pro-military counter-protesters at the local mall. Taking their cues from Gandhi and King, demonstrators held spirited, creative, nonviolent protests — and they worked. No one lost their cool, except for a few Philadelphia police officers, some of whom couldn't differentiate between First Amendment exercise and petty criminal behavior. All of those arrested eventually had their charges dropped.

Military officials were caught off guard by the frequent protests. When asked to comment on the public outcry, Army spokesmen had a variety of responses. Often they tried to isolate the protesters by politicizing the issue. Sometimes they'd question the patriotism of protesters or speak in general terms, defending the necessity of the wars in Afghanistan and Iraq. *Military Times* said the fate of the AEC was attributable to economics rather than protests, even though when it first opened, the Army said it would save money because it replaced five traditional recruiting stations in the suburban Philadelphia area.

The Army's propaganda could never offer an adequate defense of encouraging 13-year-olds to shoot simulated weaponry at life-like targets. Capt. Auchey said the facility was "an innovative way to communicate to society." He often made the point that the same types of combat video games were available just steps away at a mall arcade. Of course, those video games aren't offered for free at taxpayer expense.

When asked why there was so much controversy surrounding the AEC, Program Manager Major Larry Dillard responded, "I think they're terrified it'll work." The major was right.

The Army realizes that sophisticated computer animation that simulates combat is a powerful hook to lure youth. Rather than locate mega-recruiting centers in suburban shopping malls, the Army is now expressing an interest in bringing combat simulations into traditional neighborhood recruiting centers, hoping they will become a cool place for youth to "chill."

According to Gary Evans MD, in his influential piece, *The Pentagon's Child Recruiting Strategy*, "Studies of children exposed to violence have shown that they can become: "immune" or numb to the horror of violence, imitate the violence they see, and show more aggressive behavior with greater exposure to violence."[9]

Brad Bushman and colleagues at Ohio State University conducted a comprehensive review of every study that looked at the effect of violent video games. They examined 381 effects from studies involving 130,000 people, and results showed that playing violent video games increased aggressive thoughts, angry feelings, and physiological arousal.[10]

Jared Lee Loughner killed six and injured 13, including Rep. Gabby Giffords, in a 2011 Arizona shooting. "All he did was play video games and play music," said a friend.[11]

Adam Lanza was the 20-year-old behind the horrendous school shooting in Newtown, Connecticut in 2012, which left 20 children and 6 adults dead. Lanza was an avid player of violent video games. According to the report of the State's Attorney for the Judicial District of Danbury on the Shootings at Sandy Hook Elementary School, the following first person shooter games were seized by police: *Doom, Left for Dead, Metal Gear Solid, Dead Rising, Half Life, Battlefield, Call of Duty, Grand Theft Auto, Shin Megami Tensei, Dynasty Warriors, Vice City,* and *Team Fortress.*

A review of the electronic evidence on Lanza's hard drive showed an infatuation with killing. He had bookmarks pertaining to firearms, military, politics, mass murder, video games, and *Army Ranger.* He had apparently played the computer game titled *School Shooting,* where the player controls a character who enters a school and shoots at students. There were also 172 screen shots of the online game *Combat Arms.*[12]

Lanza and the others mentioned here acquired some of the skill and the will to kill through video games. The Marines' adaptation of *Doom,* a game Lanza played, helped pave the way for the development of *America's Army.*

Although experts disagree over whether there is a direct link between violent video games and violent criminal behavior, a consensus is beginning to develop among the scientific and educational communities that these games lead to increased aggression among players. A 2015 report by the American Psychological Association (APA) summarizes these findings.

> The research demonstrates a consistent relation between violent video game use and increases in aggressive behavior, aggressive cognitions and aggressive affect, and decreases in prosocial behavior, empathy and sensitivity to aggression," says the report of the APA Task Force on Violent Media. The task force's review is the first in this field to examine the breadth of studies included and to undertake multiple approaches to reviewing the literature.
>
> "Scientists have investigated the use of violent video games for more than two decades but to date, there is very limited research addressing whether violent video games cause people to commit acts of criminal violence," said Mark Appelbaum, PhD, task force chair. "However, the link between violence in video games and increased aggression in players is one of the most studied and best established in the field.[13]

The incredibly violent *Doom* video game was released in 1993 by Texas game developer id Software. The game was a revolution of incredible technical innovation coupled with horrendously violent scenes. Doom ushered in the wildly popular first-person-shooter video games that continue to attract the attention of millions of players world-wide. It was an immediate hit among American teens.

Numerous church leaders excoriated *Doom* was for its Satanic themes. Killology Research Group founder David Grossman called it a "mass murder simulator." 14

The U.S. Marines appreciated the extraordinary power of the game.

> The Marine Corps charged its Modeling and Simulation Management Office with finding a commercial product that could be modified for Marine training needs. Lt. Scott Barnett was assigned to play PC games on the market that might fit the bill, and eventually selected *Doom II*. Barnett enlisted the help of Sgt. Dan Snyder to modify the game from its sci-fi Mars terrain to a small desert village, and replace the game's demon enemies with more real-world adversaries.
>
> While "Marine Doom" never became an official training tool, Marines were encouraged to play it, and it was sanctioned to be installed on government PCs. In 1997, Gen. Charles C. Krulak, who was the commandant of the Marine Corps at the time, issued a directive supporting the use of PC games for "Military Thinking and Decision Exercises.15

Screenshot of FreeDoom BY LIFTARN AT ENGLISH WIKIPEDIA

Doom was a source of fascination for Dylan Klebold and Eric Harris, the murderers in the Columbine High School shooting.16

In the video Harris and Klebold made in the basement of Harris' house, Harris says the shooting will "be like [expletive] Doom" and shortly thereafter describes his sawed-off shotgun as being "straight out of Doom." Furthermore, Harris named his 12-gauge pump shotgun "Arlene" after Arlene Sanders of the *Doom* novels.17

Evan Ramsey brought a shotgun into his Alaska high school, where he gunned down a fellow student and the principal, and wounded two others. Ramsey said playing video games warped his sense of reality. He was an avid fan of *Doom*.

Ramsey survived the ordeal. In an interview that aired in 2007 with CNN's Anderson Cooper, Ramsey said, "I based a lot of my knowledge solely on video games. You shoot a guy in *Doom*, and he gets back up. You have got to shoot the things in *Doom* eight or nine times before it dies. And I went with that concept on—with—from the video game and added it to life."[18]

Michael Carneal, the 14-year-old who fired upon a group of classmates at Heath High School in West Paducah, KY in 1997, also loved to play Doom. Authorities noted that his aim was uncannily accurate. He fired just once at each person's head, as one would do to rack up bonus points in the video game.[19]

David Grossman, quoted earlier in this chapter, was astounded by Carneal's "achievement."

In 2003 Devin Moore, an Alabama teen, stole a gun from a police officer and shot three officers, then stole a police cruiser to make his escape. Moore spent much of his life playing single-shooter games. "Life is a video game," he said after his arrest.[20]

Kip Kinkel frequently played violent video games such as *Doom, Counter-Strike*, and *Castle Wolfenstein*. He was the 1998 Thurston High School shooter. Kinkel murdered his parents before opening fire at Thurston High School in Springfield, Oregon, killing 2 and wounding 25.[21]

Norwegian mass murderer Anders Behring Breivik, who killed 77 people in Oslo in 2011, spent countless hours playing violent video games, especially *Call of Duty: Modern Warfare*. Breivik has described how he "trained" for the attacks he carried out in Norway in the summer of 2011 by using the computer game.

Describing the game, he said: "It consists of many hundreds of different tasks and some of these tasks can be compared with an attack, for real. That's why it's used by many armies throughout the world. It's very good for acquiring experience related to sights systems."[22]

In *Call of Duty*, the player controls Pvt. Martin from the 506th Parachute Infantry Regiment, 101st Airborne Division. In *Call of Duty 2*, the player controls Cpl. Bill Taylor from Dog Company. In *Call of Duty 2: Big Red One*, the player takes control of Sgt. Roland Roger of the 1st Infantry Division, 16th Mechanized Infantry Regiment, Fox Company. In *Call of Duty 3*, the player "becomes" Pvt. Nichols from the 29th Infantry Division.[23]

James Holmes killed 12 people and injured 70 others at a Century movie theater in Aurora, Colorado, on July 20, 2012. Holmes loved playing the *World of Warcraft* video game. It's what he did.[24]

The military realizes that the skills in the strategy and tactics used in games like *World of Warcraft* are similar to those commanders on the battlefield use in real combat. With this in mind, the U.S. Army Combined Arms Center-Training has been developing its own Massively Multiplayer Role Playing Games (MMRPGs) to train new recruits. Col. Robert White, the Deputy Commander, U.S. Army Combined Arms Center-Training, has described a gaming system that allows individual soldiers world-wide to log into the Army MMRPG and play as individuals or as units.[25]

A secret NSA document, "Exploiting Terrorist Use of Games & Virtual Environments," disclosed by Edward Snowden in December of 2013, shows that the spy agency and its UK sister agency GCHQ have deployed real-life agents into the virtual *World of Warcraft* and have built mass-collection capabilities against the Xbox Live console network, which has more than 48 million players.[26]

According to the *Guardian* story by James Ball dated December 9, 2013:

> If properly exploited, games could produce vast amounts of intelligence, according to the NSA document. They could be used as a window for hacking attacks, to build pictures of people's social networks through "buddylists and interaction," to make approaches by undercover agents, and to obtain target identifiers (such as profile photos), geolocation, and collection of communications.
>
> The ability to extract communications from talk channels in games would be necessary, the NSA paper argued, because of the potential for them to be used to communicate anonymously: Given that gaming consoles often include voice headsets, video cameras, and other identifiers, the potential for joining together biometric information with activities was also an exciting one.[27]

According to the *Guardian* article, Blizzard Entertainment, the California-based producer of *World of Warcraft*, said neither the NSA nor GCHQ had sought its permission to gather intelligence inside the game. The documents contain no indication that the spying uncovered terrorist activity.

Army Experience Center protesters, cited earlier, alleged that the *America's Army* video game reinforced prejudices and cultural stereotypes. An Army spokesman defended the practice as an innovative way to communicate to society. Paradoxically, the NSA expressed the same concerns, noting that Hezbollah had produced a game called *Special Forces 2* that trained terrorists. The NSA document acknowledges Hezbollah got the idea from the US Army. Similarly, Iraqi gamers modified the game *Battlefield 2*, enabling players to take on the role of extremists whose home village in Iraq suffered collateral damage during a fictional US operation.28

The Army understands the visceral appeal of these games. AS A WORK OF THE U.S. FEDERAL GOVERNMENT, THE IMAGE IS IN THE PUBLIC DOMAIN.

These first-person shooter games have the propensity to attract and nurture killers, especially among those who spend significant portions of their lives immersed in this virtual netherworld. Meanwhile, the real world places a premium on securing the services of those who are wired to kill. These games will continue to play an increasingly important role in recruiting and training soldiers, particularly those willing to put their lives on the line. The communal aspect of these games, along with their relatively porous platforms, allows sophisticated state-supported actors, who understand their transformative power, to infiltrate activities.

Notes – Chapter 8

1. 54% Think Violent Video Games Lead to More Violence in Society. (2010, November 11). Retrieved November 7, 2015, from http://bit.ly/2fx8mym.

2. Lt. Col. Dave Grossman, Phi Kappa Phi National Forum, Fall 2000, A Case Study: Paducah, Kentucky http://www.killology.com/print/print_teachkid.htm.

3. Grossman, L. (2000). Printable Copy of Trained to Kill - Lieutenant Colonel Dave Grossman, Author. Retrieved November 7, 2015, from http://www.killology.com/print/print_teachkid.htm.

4. Holmes, J. (2009, December 28). US military is meeting recruitment goals with video games but at what cost? Retrieved November 7, 2015, from http://bit.ly/2eFVZks.

5. "Media Violence," American Academy of Pediatrics, Policy Statement, Pediatrics, Vol. 108#5, Nov. 2001, pp.1222-1226.

6. Search ESRB Ratings. (n.d.). Retrieved November 7, 2015, from http://www.esrb.org/ratings/search.aspx.

7. America's Army News. (n.d.). Retrieved November 7, 2015, from http://news.americasarmy.com.

8. America's Army News. (n.d.). Retrieved November 7, 2015, from http://news.americasarmy.com/weapon-challenges/.

9. The Pentagon's Child Recruiting Strategy. American Academy of Child & Adolescent Psychiatry. Gary Evans, MD. June 2008 http://www.ringnebula.com/Oil/recruiting-children.htm.

10. Keim, B. (2013, February 28). What Science Knows About Video Games and Violence. Retrieved November 7, 2015, from http://to.pbs.org/1fgh67i.

11. Fudge, J. (2011, January 11). Report: Jared Loughner Called a 'Big Video Gamer' By Former Classmates. Retrieved November 7, 2015, from http://bit.ly/2eFXD5w.

12. Report of the State's Attorney for the Judicial District of Danbury on the Shootings at Sandy Hook Elementary School and 36 Yogananda Street, Newtown, Connecticut on December 14, 2012. http://bit.ly/1vrYZOD.

13. APA Review Confirms Link Between Playing Violent Video Games and Aggression. (2015, August 13). Retrieved November 7, 2015, from http://bit.ly/1TRPnIJ.

14. Irvine, Reed & Kincaid, Cliff (1999). "Video Games Can Kill." Accuracy In Media. Archived from the original on 2007-07-19. Retrieved November 15, 2005.

15. Beekman, C. (2014, November 17). The US Military's Close History With Video Games. Retrieved November 7, 2015, from http://bit.ly/2fYNyP5.

16. Rage: A Look At A Teen Killer. (1997, August 1). Retrieved November 7, 2015, from http://cbsn.ws/2f0qeOf.

17. Langman, P., PhD. (2014, July 29). Transcript of the Columbine Basement Tapes. Retrieved November 7, 2015, from http://bit.ly/2fYQnzK.

18. Anderson Cooper 360 Degrees. (2010, October 10). Retrieved November 7, 2015, from http://www.cnn.com/TRANSCRIPTS/0710/10/acd.01.html.

19. Psychology: Concepts and Connections Spencer Rathus Cengage Learning, Jan 1, 2011 - Psychology.

20. Jaccarino, M. (2013, September 12). 'Training simulation:' Mass killers often share obsession with violent video games | Fox News. Retrieved November 7, 2015, from http://fxn.ws/2f0xSbn.

21. Brown, V. (2007, December 7). The Devil Made Me Do It: Video Games and Violence. Retrieved November 7, 2015, from http://www.psmag.com/business-economics/the-devil-made-me-do-it-video-games-and-violence-4789.

22. Pidd, H. (2012, April 19). Anders Breivik 'trained' for shooting attacks by playing Call of Duty. Retrieved November 7, 2015, from http://bit.ly/1ReYAsv. 23. "Call of Duty." Call of Duty Wiki United States Army. Web. 28 Apr. 2016. http://bit.ly/2fx8GNW.

24. Johnson, T. (2015, July 28). Aurora Theater Shooting Trial: Father of James Holmes Testifies as Jurors Weigh Death Penalty. Retrieved November 7, 2015, from http://bit.ly/2ghn7Yd.

25. Simmins, Charles. "U.S. Army Looks to Harness World of Warcraft Technology - ClearanceJobs." ClearanceJobs. 27 Feb. 2012. Web. 28 Apr. 2016. http://bit.ly/2ggZEFL.

26. Ball, James. "Xbox Live among Game Services Targeted by US and UK Spy Agencies." The Guardian. Guardian News and Media, 09 Dec. 2013. Web. 28 Apr. 2016.

27. Ibid.

28. "Games: A Look at Emerging Trends, Uses, Threats and Opportunities in Influence Activities." National Security Agency. Edward Snowden, 9 Dec. 2013. Web. 28 Apr. 2016. http://bit.ly/2gefJtn.

WIKIMEDIA COMMONS

Chapter 9

THE CIVILIAN MARKSMANSHIP PROGRAM INTRODUCES AMERICAN SCHOOL CHILDREN TO THE INTOXICATING USE OF FIREARMS

While Endangering the Health of the American Public Through Lead Exposure

When I hold you in my arms
And I feel my finger on your trigger
I know nobody can do me no harm
Happiness is a warm gun
Bang bang shoot shoot
- Lennon-McCartney

The public knows it as the Civilian Marksmanship Program (CMP), but since 1996 its legal name has been the Corporation for the Promotion of Rifle Practice and Firearm Safety, Inc. A Congressionally-chartered program, the CMP is a prolific small arms and ammunition dealer. Although more responsible nations prudently destroy their aging, warehoused military rifles, pistols, and ammunition, the U.S. government gives it to this private, non-profit corporation based in Anniston, Alabama, home of the Army weapons depot. In turn, the CMP sells the weaponry and ammo to U.S. citizens at discounted prices. This is irrational public policy.

The CMP, according to its annual report, "promotes firearms safety training and rifle practice for all qualified U.S. citizens with special emphasis on youth." There are 4,664 clubs, teams, and other shooting sports organizations currently affiliated with the CMP, many in the high schools that are associated with Junior Reserve Officer Training Corps (JROTC) programs. The CMP is responsible for training JROTC instructors and certifying JROTC ranges in the nation's high schools. It has trained more than 4,000 JROTC instructors since 2005.[1]

The CMP creates and disseminates curriculum for marksmanship and safety instruction. It also publishes "The Guide to Lead Management for Air Gun Shooting," a widely distributed document that rules out the use of non-lead ammunition and is based on questionable science that purports to minimize exposure to toxic lead. The CMP is best known to the public for organizing the National Air Rifle Championships at Camp Perry in Port Clinton, Ohio.

The Corporation for the Promotion of Rifle Practice and Firearms Safety, Inc. has total net assets of $220.8 million and holds $184.7 million in publicly traded securities. It received more than $17 million from the federal government for 2013. The corporation's 2013 990 states,

> JROTC and active Army programs — at no cost to the government, develops curriculum for marksmanship and safety instruction, trains and certifies JROTC coaches, inspects high school range facilities, organizes, administers, and conducts JROTC Air Rifle competitions for all military services, subsidizes JROTC travel to CMP events, awards significant scholarships to deserving JROTC and other high school marksmanship competitors, provides annual grants to state 4-H shooting programs. At no cost to the government CMP produces and provides marksmanship safety videos and literature, administers Army and USMC rifle competitions.[2]

At no cost to the government? Their 2013 Form 990 reported $17 million in government grants. The corporation spent just $410,000 on the above items, slightly more than the compensation received by its Chairman and CEO, Judith A Legerski.

Air Guns are dangerous weapons

> Ralphie: "I want a Red Ryder carbine action two-hundred shot range model air rifle. Oooooooh!"
>
> Mother: "No, you'll shoot your eye out!"
>
> - A Christmas Story

We laughed, but air guns are no laughing matter. Some air rifles today are capable of routinely hitting a dime at 50 yards and killing rabbits at 100 yards and beyond. Some of the new breeds of air guns shoot pellets at supersonic speeds of 1,500 feet per second (FPS) and are capable of taking coyotes, wild boar, and even bigger game.[3]

The rifle Ralphie got for Christmas, the *Daisy Red Ryder* air gun, shoots a BB, typically made of steel, at 350 FPS and is available online today for $39.

The Daisy Avanti 887 CO2 air rifle, a powerful cousin of Ralphie's Red Ryder, is classified as an Army weapon and is used by Army JROTC Marksmanship programs in high schools across the country. It shoots a .177 caliber flat-nose (wadcutter) air gun pellet at speeds up to 500 feet per second. A .177 caliber pellet has a diameter of .177 inches, just like a "22 rifle" shoots a bullet with a diameter of .22 inches. A .22 pistol, the kind that was used in the attempted assassination of President Reagan, fires at about 900 feet per second. They are both lethal weapons.

The Daisy Avanti 887 Operation Manual carries the following warning:

> **NOT A TOY. THIS AIRGUN IS DESIGNED FOR USE BY EXPERIENCED SHOOTERS AND IS INTENDED FOR MATCH COMPETITION OR TARGET RANGE USE. MISUSE OR CARELESS USE MAY CAUSE SERIOUS INJURY OR DEATH. MAY BE DANGEROUS UP TO 257 YARDS (235 METERS).**
> **THIS IS A SPECIAL CLASS OF NON-POWDERED GUNS AND NOT FOR GENERAL USE. IT IS TO BE USED FOR TRAINING AND TARGET SHOOTING UNDER SUPERVISION. RECOMMENDED FOR USE BY THOSE 16 YEARS OF AGE OR OLDER. THIS GUN SHOOTS PELLETS ONLY. THE PURCHASER AND USER SHOULD CONFORM TO ALL LAWS GOVERNING THE USE AND OWNERSHIP OF AIRGUNS.**[4]

The Daisy Avanti 887 is available online for $450. Although the warning above recommends the use of these rifles for those 16 years of age and older, JROTC Marksmanship Programs include high school freshmen who are usually 13 or 14 years of age.

There are no federal laws regarding air guns, although they are regulated by the Consumer Product Safety Commission (CPSC). Federal law prevents states from prohibiting the sale of traditional BB or pellet guns but *allows* states to prohibit the sale of these weapons to minors.[5]

The CPSC specifically required Daisy Outdoor Products, Inc. to label its air guns as potentially dangerous to children. Like cigarette manufacturers who fought to keep cancer warnings off their cigarette packages, Daisy opposed the measure, not wanting to give Ralphie's dad and others a reason to think twice before buying the gun.[6]

Twelve states and the District of Columbia impose age restrictions on the possession, use, or transfer of air guns like the Red Ryder, the Daisy Avanti 887, or the Boar-killing weapon described above: California, Delaware, Florida, Illinois, Maine, Massachusetts, Michigan, Minnesota, New York, North Carolina, Pennsylvania, and Virginia. Most of these states and a few others specifically prohibit carrying air guns into schools. Incredibly, almost half of the states have no laws regulating air guns.[7]

It is instructive to frame the general issue of air guns before exploring the intransigent mindset of Junior Reserve Officer Training Corps (JROTC) Marksmanship Program officials, some school administrators, and parents of many of the children enrolled in shooting programs in the high schools. For many of these enthusiasts the suggestion that the presence of firing ranges in high school classrooms may be inappropriate or dangerous amounts to a preposterous infringement of 2nd Amendment rights. There's no poll data regarding public opinion over the use of classroom space for firing ranges.

The concern that shooting guns in classrooms send the wrong message to high school children may not be enough to sway public opinion to the point where high school officials feel compelled to rein in the practice, although there have been some notable exceptions. In 2009, the San Diego Unified School District's School Board voted to eliminate the JROTC Marksmanship Program in the city's high schools after a community-led movement called for the shut-down. Rick Jahnkow, a coordinator for the Project on Youth and Non-Military Opportunities (YANO), said having air rifles on campus sent the wrong message to students. "Students and parents felt it was inconsistent with the philosophy of the district to try to encourage students to not think about using violence to solve problems," Jahnkow said. "So they felt that these ranges did not belong." [8]

These outcomes are extraordinarily rare as the public is either unaware of the practice or has come to accept the increasing number of firing ranges in the nation's high schools with a shrug of the shoulders. It is the potential for the exposure to lead that will ultimately require these JROTC programs to either shut down or switch to non-lead pellets.

The Civilian Marksmanship Program, through its *Guide to Lead Management for Air Gun Shooting* and other publications, seriously understates the health hazards associated with the use of air guns that shoot lead pellets in indoor firing ranges in the nation's high schools.

The guide is used by Junior Reserve Officer Training Corps (JROTC) instructors and high school officials to manage firing ranges that are typically located in high school classrooms and gyms.9

Hundreds of thousands of high school children and school staff across the nation come into contact with highly toxic lead particulate matter as a result of inadequate supervision and maintenance of indoor firing ranges. The CMP, along with the various JROTC programs run by the Army, Navy, and Marines, and high school officials in every state, together with private gun club owners, where target practices are also held, share the responsibility for safeguarding the health of the public regarding high school marksmanship programs. School districts typically don't monitor lead contamination caused by JROTC marksmanship programs. Instead, inspections are performed either by the Brigades/Area Commands, the CMP, or private firms.10

According to the CMP, there are over 2,400 Army, Navy, and Marine Corps JROTC units in the USA. Statistics kept by JROTC commands and the CMP indicate that at least two-thirds or approximately 1,600 JROTC units offer rifle marksmanship programs to their cadets.11 Interestingly, the CMP does not count the 800 Air Force JROTC programs across the country, so the total tops 3,200 units.12

Approximately half or 1,600 of these units offer rifle marksmanship programs to their high school cadets. Most of these JROTC units have rifle teams, and many provide basic safety and marksmanship training

High school students participate in Marine Corps JROTC Marksmanship practice. Programs like this are affiliated with the Civilian Marksmanship Program. WIKICOMMONS

to all of the cadets in their programs.13

The ARMY JROTC Marksmanship Program was first established

in 1916 using small-bore rifles. It was not until 1964 that the US Navy and the US Marine Corps established marksmanship programs using the .22 caliber small-bore rifles. The Air Force did not commence a shooting program until 2006. In 2009 Army JROTC units were issued the Daisy M887 CO2 air rifles.[14]

Today all JROTC units use air guns that shoot lead pellets, except for the Air Force, which has largely eliminated the use of lead ammunition in both its school-based JROTC Program and on its small arms training facilities. Rather than banning the use of lead pellets, the Air Force JROTC command "strongly recommends" using non-lead pellets due to health concerns.[15]

Incredibly, there are still many high school shooting programs affiliated with the CMP that continue to use small-bore .22 caliber rifles and hold practices at indoor firing ranges. The .22 small bore rifles fire standard bullets and deposit substantially more lead into the air and on the floor than the lead pellets fired from air guns. That is not to say that the lead exposure associated with air guns shooting lead pellets is not a problem—a view held by many shooters, thanks in large part to the misinformation spread by the CMP.

Too often, youth groups affiliated with high school JROTC programs are forced to use commercial firing ranges where .22 caliber rifles and larger guns are regularly fired. The nation has an estimated 6,000 commercial indoor and outdoor gun ranges, but only 201 have been inspected in the past decade, according to a Seattle Times analysis of Occupational Safety and Health Administration (OSHA) records. Of those inspected, 86% violated at least one lead-related standard, the analysis found. In 14 states, federal and state agencies did not inspect a single commercial gun range from 2004 to 2013, an analysis of OSHA records found.[16]

Although the Civilian Marksmanship Program claims inspections of JROTC firing ranges are performed either by the Brigades/Area Commands or by the CMP, someone dropped the ball at the Vancouver (Wash.) Rifle and Pistol Club, an organization affiliated with the CMP.[17]

In 2010, blood tests revealed that 20 youths had been overexposed to lead after shooting in the club's dirty, poorly ventilated range.

According to the *Seattle Times*, "The club allows the JROTC, the Young Marines and Boy Scouts of America to shoot there. While none of the shooters showed signs of being affected by the lead, the county's public health director said damage might not be noticed for many years. An examination of the range revealed lead nestled in the carpet, chairs and a couch. Surface tests showed dangerous amounts of lead stuck to counters, a soda machine, and the refrigerator. The floor was 993 times higher than a federal housing guideline for allowable lead on surfaces."[18]

The Center for Disease Control and Prevention says there is no safe blood lead level in children. Protecting children from exposure to lead is necessary to insure lifelong good health. Even minute levels of lead in blood have been shown to affect IQ, ability to pay attention and academic achievement. Effects of lead exposure cannot be corrected. The most important step parents, doctors, and others can take to prevent lead exposure before it occurs.[19]

In 2014 another CMP-affiliated firing range, Hopedale (MA) Pistol and Rifle Club, had three teenagers test for high lead blood levels.[20] An inspection conducted by the Massachusetts Workplace Safety and Health Program documented contaminated surface areas but also directed the shooting range owners to improve the pattern of air flow by improving the ventilation system. Air should flow from behind the shooter's back towards the target backstop, the report said.[21]

Hopedale's website says it is affiliated with the CMP and prominently displays the CMP logo along with a link to the CMP.

These dangerous indoor firing ranges for small bore .22 caliber rifles are still being formed in high schools. In 2014 Walla Walla High School officials announced the formation of the Blue Devil Smallbore Precision Rifle Club, which plans to practice at the Walla Walla High School Range.[22] Walla Walla is affiliated with the CMP.

The CMP holds regular youth competitions using standard firearms. Competitors for rim fire rifle matches are open to anyone 12 years of age or older, whereas competitors for "As-Issued Military Rifle and Pistol Matches" must be at least 14. The CMP may waive age requirements if they determine that the young shooters be competent.

All the while, the CMP's *Guide to Lead Management* asserts, "Target shooting with air rifles and small bore (rim fire) rifles does not create real health risks for shooting sports participants."[23]

There is substantial scientific evidence to refute the CMP's stance. Lead is a deadly toxin. Notice the use of the word "real" in the CMP statement. Throughout the world of shooting sports, there exists a kind of denial among gun enthusiasts of the truly harmful effects of lead ammunition. There is a sense, often expressed in online chat rooms, that the issue has no merit and is being employed as a ruse by anti-gun forces to mandate additional gun control measures.

The CMP advises against the use of non-lead pellets in its *Guide to Lead Management*, arguing they do not perform as well as their lead counterparts. "Non-lead or so-called "green" pellets have yet proven capable of producing ten-ring accuracy on air rifle targets. Most non-lead pellets are, in fact, so inherently inaccurate that they cannot even be satisfactorily used in the earliest stages of youth target shooting." It is a childish rant.

Notice again, this time - the depreciatory reference to "so-called green pellets." The technology of producing alternatives to lead pellets has come a long way in recent years. The Air Force's switch to non-lead pellets and the move by many high school districts across the country to do the same, along with laws like those in California that prohibit the use of lead pellets in hunting, (but not in the classroom) have conspired to create a hot market for non-lead substitutes.

In 2011, teams from the Battle Ground High School and Prairie High School AFJROTC marksmanship programs in Washington State became the first teams to use non-lead pellets in a national JROTC match. The shooting programs in those schools were shut down for nearly a year because of fears of possible contamination caused by the use of air guns that shot lead pellets in the indoor shooting ranges. The schools switched to a non-lead pellet from the Czech Republic made of tin and bismuth.[24]

According to the JROTC coach, "Once the other coaches started seeing our scores, they knew these pellets were for real." Battle Ground went on to win the precision class during the 2011 national championships, where Prairie High's riflemen also excelled.[25] The two schools shoot non-lead Predator brand international pellets.[26]

A second CMP publication rules out the use of non-lead pellets. In its Power Point Presentation, "Starting a JROTC Marksmanship Program", a required course for all JROTC Marksmanship instructors, the CMP *requires* JROTC programs in high schools to "use 4.5 mm (.177 cal.) lead flat nosed pellets only." There is no mention of the potentially harmful effects of lead or the existence of non-lead alternatives.[27]

While the CMP calls for the use of lead pellets, its other publications downplay the potential for lead exposure. JROTC Standard Operating Procedures for Air Rifle Safety and Air Rifle Range Management only mentions the possibility of lead contamination while discussing food. The procedures state, "No food items are permitted on an air rifle range. Eating food while handling lead pellets could cause lead ingestion."28

Likewise, the CMP's *Guide to Rifle Safety* downplays the health risks of lead exposure,

> The rules are simple: Do not bring food into the range or consume food on the range. Do not bring any drinks into the range unless they are bottled and can be closed. Wash your hands after handling air rifle pellets (preferably in cold water). Cleaning the target backstops of spent lead pellets must be done by the instructor or another adult.

Interestingly, the guide encourages participants to wear protective eye glasses "because it is possible for pellet fragments to bounce back to the firing line."

Lead particulate matter is flying all over the place, settling on skin and clothing.

Noordhoek, Niels. "4.5mm Pellet Exiting an Air Pistol, Photographed with a High-Speed Air-gap Flash." WIKIMEDIA COMMONS, 8 OCT. 2011. WEB. 10 AUG. 2014

Air gun rifles, like those used in high schools across the country, discharge lead at the muzzle end of the firing line. Many air gunners do not bother to clean their guns because every pellet being fired down the barrel scrapes out the deposits from the pellets that went before.29

The *Individual Junior Shooter Safety Pledge* that appears at the back of the CMP's Guide to Rifle Safety, and often hung in JROTC classrooms, contains 15 provisions that shooters must follow, but none address lead as a potential safety issue. The guide fails to mention the lead sprayed on the floor and in the air by the gun. These lax rules are contributing to lead exposure.[30]

The CMP's 2013 Guide to Lead Management relies on the findings of Health & Environmental Technology LLC (HET), an environmental testing firm in Colorado Springs, Colorado to dispel the notion that air guns shooting lead pellets create airborne particles. The sole employee of HET is Mr. Robert Rodosevich.

Rodosevich came under scrutiny in Colorado in 2012 for "gross technical incompetence in technical compliance." Meanwhile, HET's work performed for the CMP is cited by high school officials who are forced to defend the presence of indoor firing ranges in their schools by parents concerned about the potentially harmful effects of lead contamination.

HET came under official scrutiny when it was contracted by a listing realtor (selling agent) to prepare a "Preliminary Assessment" of the degree of contamination of a house used as a methamphetamine lab. HET came very close to giving the house a clean bill of health before properly licensed professionals were called in to conduct a thorough and legal evaluation of the highly contaminated residence.

"The Industrial Hygiene Review and Regulatory Audit Resulting in Findings of Noncompliance and Regulatory Misconduct at an Identified and Illegal Drug Laboratory," dated May 29, 2012, and performed by Forensics Applications Consulting Technologies found HET's work to be "fatally flawed."[31]

The state audit reported, "The HET document was not prepared by an individual documented as being capable or authorized under regulation to perform such work. The document prepared by HET exhibited gross technical incompetence in technical compliance." The state auditor continued, "Mr. Robert Rodosevich has violated state regulations by entirely failing to demonstrate that he has any kind of knowledge in performing the work at all." The auditor's report documented 35 violations of state regulations.

At one point, the auditor reported, "Mr. Rodosevich states that he sent the samples to Analytical Chemistry in Tukwila, Washington, but the laboratory reports are actually from ALS Laboratories in Salt Lake City, Utah."

From the state audit,

> Pursuant to state statute, if the seller of the property presents the work by Mr. Rodosevich as a genuine Preliminary Assessment, then this to would appear to meet the definition of "Offering a false statement for recording.
>
> Similarly, HET explicitly states they possess knowledge of the regulations, and therefore, establish the fact that they are aware of such recording. We recommend that the situation be forwarded to the District Attorney for proper evaluation, and to determine if the case rises to the level of criminal account. A legitimate preliminary assessment must be performed for the property.

The Civilian Marksmanship Program relies on the findings of HET to claim there is no airborne dust created by firing air guns that shoot lead pellets in America's high schools. Based on this finding, the CMP says normal ventilation systems are fine for shooting ranges in America's high schools and in private gun clubs where CMP affiliated clubs practice.

From *The Guide to Lead Management for Air Gun Shooting* (page 7):

> The issue of whether air gun firing creates airborne lead was re-examined in 2007 tests conducted by Health & Environmental Technology (HET), a professional environmental testing firm from Colorado Springs, Colorado. These tests were conducted on an air gun range at the U. S. Olympic Shooting Center. For these tests, air samplers were placed in the breathing space of the air gun shooters while they fired and next to the target backstops. No measurable airborne lead was detected by any of these monitors during air gun firing.
>
> Firing air rifles or air pistols at muzzle velocities prescribed for target shooting (<600 fps) does not generate any detectable air- borne lead. There is therefore no need for special ventilation systems on air gun ranges since there is no airborne lead to exhaust from the range. Normal ventilation achieved by modern HVAC systems provides more than adequate ventilation for air gun ranges.

HET found that "minute deposits of detectable lead fragments and residue are deposited on the range floor in front of the gun muzzles, lead residues are also deposited on the floor in the area around the backstops." HET reported that the lead fragments "are of sufficient density that they do not become suspended in the air, but rather fall to the floor."

A Swedish study in 1992 analyzed the air in an indoor firing range that was used exclusively for air guns and found the air had lead levels an average of 4.6 μg/m3 (range 1.8 - 7.2 μg/m3). The study documents the presence of airborne lead as a result of air rifle shooting and cast doubt on HET's findings, as well as the CMP's claim that there's no need for special ventilation systems.[32]

A 2009 German study examined the blood lead levels of 129 individuals from 11 different indoor shooting ranges who shot a variety of weapons.

- 20 individuals who shot only air guns showed a median BLL of 33 μg/l with a (range 18–127 μg/l). (Translated into standard American usage per deciliter – 3.3ug/dl or 3.3 micrograms per deciliter)
- 15 shooters who were users of air guns and .22 long rifles had a median of 87 μg/l with a range of14–172 μg/l.
- 51 shooters of the .22 caliber rifles and large caliber handguns (9 mm or larger) had a median of 107 μg/l (range 27–375 μg/l)
- 32 who only used large caliber handguns had a median of 100 μg/l with a range 28–326 μg/l.
- Finally, the study tracked an 11-member IPSC group (International Practical Shooting Confederation members employ all shooting disciplines - handgun, rifle, shotgun, and air gun.) The IPSC-group had the highest median of 192 μg/l with a range of 32–521 μg/l.

The survey size of the air gun-only shooters in the German study was small at 20, and it's possible the subjects developed elevated BLLs from a variety of sources, but it seems to be clear from both the Swedish and the German studies that air gun shooters using lead pellets may be exposed to harmful lead particulate matter. The authors of the German study call for the use of either lead-free ammunition or vastly improved ventilation systems.[33]

The Centers for Disease Control and Prevention is adamant that the smallest exposure to lead may be dangerous to children. In 2012, its Advisory Committee on Childhood Lead Poisoning Prevention released a report entitled *"Low-Level Lead Exposure Harms Children: A Renewed Call for Primary Prevention."* In this report, the committee recommended lowering the Blood Lead Levels (BLL's) considered to be poisoned from a minimum of 10 ug/dl to a minimum level of 5 ug/

dl. They cited that BLLs lower than 10 ug/dl still result in "IQ deficits," "behavioral problems, particularly attention-related behaviors and academic achievement," and "adverse health effects [such as] cardiovascular, immunological, and endocrine effects."[34]

Adverse developmental effects were also found by the National Research Council of the National Academies in infants and children at maternal blood lead levels under 10 μg/dL, and reduced fetal growth and low birth weight were observed at maternal blood lead levels under 5 μg/dL.[35]

The German study (Demmeler, Matthias, et.al.) showed blood lead levels of air gun shooters up to 12.7 μg/dL, more than twice the 5 ug/dL the Centers for Disease Control considers to be the threshold for poisoned blood in a child.

Only a few in this country have connected the dots. Regularly firing lead projectiles at 500 feet per second in programs involving 1,600 high schools is terrible public policy.

In 2013 parents (including the author) in Montgomery County, Maryland approached district officials regarding their concerns about the potential for lead exposure in regular classrooms used for both firing ranges and academic subjects. Montgomery County Public Schools Deputy Superintendent Dr. Erik J. Lang acknowledged that Gaithersburg, Kennedy, Paint Branch, and Seneca Valley high schools all had indoor firing ranges that operate in classrooms during the school day.

In a detailed response, parents received correspondence dated March 13, 2013, from Sean Yarup, Environmental Team Leader, Division of Maintenance, Indoor Air Quality Office of the Montgomery County, Maryland Public Schools. In the letter, Mr. Yarup cited the CMP's Guide to Lead Management and advised parents:

> There is no scientific evidence that firing lead projectiles in target air guns with velocities of less than 600 fps. generates any detectable airborne lead. All available medical testing shows that air rifle target shooting participants do not develop elevated lead levels as a result of this activity. Anyone who handles lead pellets during air rifle or air pistol shooting can effectively minimize their lead exposure by washing their hands after firing and by not consuming food or beverages on the range.

Apparently, Montgomery officials were satisfied that their students were only exposed to "minimal" amounts of lead.

In contrast, a neighboring jurisdiction, Fairfax County, Virginia was confronted by another group of parents with the same concerns back in 2007. They worried that JROTC air gun shooting ranges in classrooms and gyms at Mount Vernon, Hayfield, Herndon, Edison and South Lakes high schools posed a potential risk of lead exposure to the general school population. Unlike Montgomery County, Doug O'Neill, from the Fairfax County Office of Safety and Environmental Health, immediately took action - *once he became aware of the firing ranges!*

According to a story in the local Connection newspaper, O'Neill said, "Nobody really knew the ranges existed," but when he discovered them, his office began "asking hard questions."[36]

The spokesman from the Office of Safety and Environmental Health of the Fairfax County Public Schools, with 180,000 students and a $1.8 Billion budget, ranked as one of the nation's top school districts, didn't know the military used the school system's classrooms as rifle ranges? From the article:

> I don't think it ever crossed anybody's radar screen. I knew we had lots of programs; I've been in the schools 14 years," said O'Neill. "We went out to review what they were, and asked for wipe samples."

> The samples resulted in the discovery of lead dust, but there weren't any county standards in place to gauge whether the levels detected were dangerous, which O'Neill said concerned him. "I wrestled with that. We used the most conservative standard we could find."

> In the meantime, the county shut the ranges down until hired contractors could clean the lead out of the rooms.

> Letters were sent to parents of students whom school officials determined might have also been exposed to the dust. Art students at South Lakes also used the JROTC room for art class, and wrestlers at Mount Vernon used the JROTC room there for wrestling practice, said Doug O'Neill, school spokesperson from the office of safety and environmental health.

> Everyone who was in those rooms was sent a letter," said O'Neill. "Contamination was confined to the five rooms, one in each school, and did not affect other areas of the schools," O'Neill said. "We found lead that exceeded a very low standard, and we cleaned it up," said O'Neill.

Immediately after the incident Fairfax schools adopted a policy that mandated the use of non-lead projectiles in all of the firing ranges located in the county's schools. The policy states,

> Effective January 11, 2007, FCPS determined that the usage of lead-based air rifle pellets is inconsistent with the design of the JROTC classrooms. No lead projectiles are allowed on FCPS premises. Only non-lead projectiles will be used for air rifle activities within FCPS facilities. Lead projectiles may be used by participating air rifle programs at non-FCPS ranges that are properly ventilated and designed for air rifle activities. Air rifles must be thoroughly cleaned to remove all lead residues prior to being brought onto FCPS property! It is the responsibility of the JROTC instructor to effectively clean all air rifles prior to being transported onto FCPS property.[37]

Fairfax officials only allow their students to participate in air rifle programs at non-Fairfax facilities if the ranges are "properly ventilated and designed."

The unsettling notion that the Fairfax school administration did not realize that classrooms were being used for firing ranges may be understood in the way high schools across the country often grant the military autonomy in running the JROTC program, along with several dozen other military programs. School officials have little sense of the content of the curriculum and exercise no oversight regarding the professional credentials of "teachers". Instructors associated with the JROTC Marksmanship program are frequently the only non-degreed, non-certified individuals allowed to manage classrooms in the absence of professional supervision in most states.

Nine years later, in 2016, the Washington Post reported on firing ranges in Fairfax County High Schools, emphasizing the safety of the sport. The article stated that "air rifles can be shot anywhere, even in a garage, where ventilation systems and backstops aren't needed."[38] This may be the case with non-lead projectiles, but the Post did not make an important distinction between lead and non-lead pellets.

The CMP cautions that if shooters or coaches move forward of the firing line "they can potentially pick up lead fragments on their shoes and track them back to the firing points or areas behind the firing line. For this reason, personnel movements forward of the firing line should be reduced and restricted to marked lanes on either side of the firing points."[39]

It is difficult to see how these standards are rigorously and universally maintained, especially when the CMP calls for the meticulous use of shop or industrial vacuum cleaners and mops and disposable mop heads, along with a variety of other measures after each shooting session. (See the complete list of cleaning measures below). In Fairfax, VA, rooms used for shooting are also used for art classes and wrestling matches when students roll around on the floor. In Montgomery, Maryland, rooms are also used for other classes. Fairfax and Montgomery are among the nation's wealthiest jurisdictions, in a better financial position than most school districts across the country to provide separate housing for firing ranges.

To clean up the deposits of lead at the firing line and target area the CMP suggests using "relatively simple cleaning procedures" to remove lead from the classroom floor to the point where no detectable lead remains. To do so, the CMP advises, "a periodic wet mopping with a solution of water and tri-sodium phosphate" (TSP) should do the trick.[40]

In 2012, the US Department of Housing and Urban Development advised that tri-sodium phosphate should be avoided when cleaning up the lead because it is deadly to the environment and no better than many other less harmful cleaning agents. HUD does not recommend trisodium phosphate (TSP). Not only has TSP been banned in some areas because of destructive effects on the environment, but research indicates that phosphate content is not associated with effectiveness in removing lead-contaminated dust from residential surfaces.[41]

A 2006 study in the journal, Environmental Science & Technology found no evidence to support the use of TSP over all-purpose cleaning detergents for the removal of lead-contaminated dust. The authors concluded that childhood lead prevention programs should consider recommending all-purpose household detergents for removal of lead-contaminated dust after appropriate vacuuming.[42]

Back in 2002, (eleven years before the CMP lead guide) the Navy recognized that non-TSP phosphate cleaners may be more effective than TSP. The Navy's *Indoor Firing Ranges Industrial Hygiene Technical Guide* warned that diluted, TSP is a skin irritant and users should wear waterproof gloves. The Navy guide also warned that if TSP is used, eye protection should be worn, and portable eyewash facilities should be located in or very near the work area.[43]

Lead-based ammunition is likely the greatest unregulated source of lead knowingly discharged into the environment in the United States. In contrast, other significant sources of lead in the environment, such as leaded gasoline, lead-based paint, and lead-based solder, are recognized as harmful and have been significantly reduced or eliminated over the past 50 years.

More to the point, there is a large body of work to demonstrate the harmful effects of lead exposure associated with indoor firing ranges. No one disputes the fact that lead accumulates on the floor at the muzzle of an air gun, and the floor around the target area. Meanwhile, the CMP's lead guide says that high school children who fire lead pellet rifles in classrooms are safe from lead contamination if they wash their hands and keep open food and drink away from shooting activity.

In 1988, William L. Marcus, PhD., a researcher at the National Institute of Health, examined the issue of lead exposure for air gun shooters. He concluded that if young target shooters follow a few simple precautions, their use of lead pellets during target shooting does not constitute a health hazard. Dr. Marcus worked with shooting sports leaders to develop two simple rules that are still the basis for health guidelines that are taught to shooting coaches and shooting sports participants. Those rules are:

> 1) Anyone who handles air gun pellets during shooting must wash their hands, with soap and water, after they finish shooting.
>
> 2) No food or open beverage containers may be taken into the range and no food may be consumed on air gun ranges. It also should go without saying that pellets should never be placed in a shooter's mouth.[44]

The research by Dr. Marcus was conducted in 1988, a Neanderthal age in the world of monitoring the effects of lead on the public. According to a study by the National Institute for Occupational Safety and Health (NIOSH) in 2011, washing hands with soap and water is not completely effective in removing lead from the surface of the skin.

NIOSH researchers developed and patented a novel and highly effective skin decontamination/cleansing technology. NIOSH recommends use of this technology to reduce the risks of lead exposures after firing weapons.[45]

Lead enters the body when we breathe in tiny lead particulates or ingest them mostly by hand to mouth contact. It is also possible to enter our bodies through the skin. In Fairfax County, Virginia wrestling rooms and art studios were used as firing ranges. Unless the stringent procedures to protect the health of children outlined by the CMP (below) are meticulously followed by JROTC and school officials by each of the 1600 high schools with marksmanship programs, children and staff are at risk. Anecdotal evidence in Maryland and Virginia suggests that high school students in the JROTC marksmanship program sometimes cross the firing line on the floor with their hands, arms legs, and feet. When the class period is over, floors may remain untouched, and the firing line disappears, and furniture is rearranged while the next group of students file in for an unrelated academic subject. Meanwhile, the lead dust is stirred into the air and picked up by students on their shoes, hair, clothing, and backpacks to be transported throughout the school. Kids become like dust mops, spreading the deadly material throughout the building.

Meanwhile, the number of children considered at risk of lead poisoning jumped more than five-fold after the U.S. Centers for Disease Control and Prevention lowered its threshold for the diagnosis in 2012. Like the CDC, the American Academy of Pediatrics has stated there is no safe level of lead exposure.[46]

While the CMP says target shooting with lead pellet rifles does not create "real" health risks, the organization publishes a very stringent list of the necessary procedures to protect the health of children in high schools with shooting ranges. The CMP's guidelines are extraordinarily tedious and there is evidence these guidelines are not being meticulously followed by all 4,664 CMP-affiliated clubs across the country. We should also bear in mind that children are not the only potential victims of lead exposure. Custodial staff may suffer the highest levels of exposure.

According to the CMP's Guide to Lead Management, the following is a list of the necessary procedures to protect the health of children in high schools with shooting ranges:

- Pellet traps designed to effectively contain the pellets and pellet fragments must be used.
- Only authorized adult personnel who follow proper procedures should remove lead from pellet traps or target holders.

- With this type of pellet trap, you must still ensure all residues fall behind the target line by carefully inspecting the areas behind and in front of the target line before establishing the range map.
- Lead consisting of spent pellets or pellet fragments that is removed from the pellet traps is regarded as a recyclable material. After a quantity of this lead is accumulated, take it to a recycling center.
- If you are working with an older range that does not have a smooth floor, consider replacing or covering the floor to achieve a smooth surface that is easier to clean.
- In order to carry out recommended air gun range management procedures, range managers should have these supplies and materials available to them: (1) Shop or industrial vacuum cleaner; (2) mops and disposable mop heads; (3) Container (bucket) with secure closure for spent pellets; (4) Container (bucket) with secure closure for vacuum filters and mop heads.
- On ranges where the target system allows lead pellet residues to deposit on the floor forward of the targets, it is recommended that the range staff establish a lane (paint or tape a line) to provide a designated walking path for the coach or authorized athlete to follow while moving to the target line.
- At the target line, it is recommended that the designated target changer put on disposable shoe covers before walking over any residues that may be in front of the targets.
- Once targets are changed, the designated target changer should remove the disposable shoe covers before stepping onto the walking path and returning to the firing line. Shoe covers are disposable, elasticized paper.
- If the air gun range is in a multi-use facility where other activities will take place in the downrange area after air gun firing concludes, that area must be cleaned after every training or competition session.
- After firing activities have ended, have the athletes remove shooting equipment from the firing line, ensuring that they do not step over the firing line. Using a shop vacuum, start from behind the firing line and move parallel to the firing line, carefully vacuuming from the firing line downrange for ten feet. Start again from ten feet in front of the target line and move

parallel to the target line, vacuuming to the tar- get line (or beyond if there is lead pellet residue behind the target line.
- Ensure that the shop vacuum's cord, wheels and hoses do NOT drag through un-vacuumed area. Always keep the vacuum and the vacuum operator in the clean area of the range. The operator should not step on or stand in a potentially contaminated area.
- Range floors that are roughly textured or porous and may require mopping with tri-sodium phosphate, a buffering solution that suspends particulates long enough to be picked up by the mop.

Around the Nation

Flint, MI - Flint has come under the national spotlight because of its lead-contaminated drinking water, although this is not the only source of lead contamination. Northwestern High School in Flint boasts an indoor firing range that is run by the Navy and affiliated with the Civilian Marksmanship Program. As we've seen from the CMP's Guide to Lead Management, the CMP cautions that if shooters or coaches move forward of the firing line "they can potentially pick up lead fragments on their shoes and track them back to the firing points or areas behind the firing line. For this reason, personnel movements forward of the firing line should be reduced and restricted to marked lanes on either side of the firing points."

Published photos show ROTC students at Northwestern High School remove their targets after a session at the school's indoor shooting range on Monday, Feb. 3, 2014.[47] The photo suggests officials in Flint are failing to minimize these risks. Apparently, the city's drinking water is not the only source of potential lead contamination. Other photos of the shooting range at Northwestern suggest there are no marked lanes. The CMP also calls for the use of disposable plastic shoe covers when going downrange which also does not appear to be happening in Flint. Kids at Northwestern are likely to be tracking lead throughout the school.

Meanwhile, parents of children participating in Flint's Northwestern High School are required to sign a form that releases NJROTC "from any and all claims, demands, actions or causes of actions due to death, injury or illness, the government of the United States and all of its officers, representative and agents acting officially and also the local, regional, and national Navy officials of the United States."[48]

Waimea, Hawaii - The Menehune High School Junior ROTC Marksmanship Program in Waimea, Hawaii has operating procedures that direct custodial staff to "sweep up lead pellets."[49]

Peoria, Illinois - Will it play in Peoria? Apparently so. The Richwoods High School Marine Corps JROTC Rifle team's range supports six full-time firing points. For air rifle matches for up to 20 shooters, the team uses the local roller skating rink.[50]

Sanger, California - The Sanger High School NJROTC Marksmanship team did not have the kind of equipment or practice facility it needed so the school district manager of maintenance services found ways to convert an old, leaky stained shed into "a like-new, almost state of the art squad room and air rifle range." One of the parents applied for a grant to the NRA which came up with "almost $7,000 for precision marksmanship air rifles, pellets, safety shooting glasses, air cylinders, targets and lots more."

"The district didn't have money for the kind of new equipment we needed," said Naval Lt. Commander Bryan Kinyoun."[51]

Omaha, Nebraska – In 2006 Parents began complaining about potential lead exposure due to JROTC marksmanship programs at Benson, Bryan, Burke, Central, North, Northwest and South Bryan High's firing range located at Bryan Middle School. Reid Steinkraus, Supervisor of the Douglas County Child Lead Poisoning Program, who did not know the ranges existed, said the district had taken the necessary steps to assure that the schools were not contaminated. [52]

According to the "Omaha Public Schools Indoor Air Program", the JROTC programs use "small pellets instead of bullets at all OPS firing ranges." The manual states:

> No lead is discharged at the ignition point from this type of ammunition. The firing ranges use a system of baffles to slow the velocity of the projectile which were eventually deposited in sand filled troughs at the base. All of the sand in these firing ranges was removed, treated as hazardous waste and disposed of properly. In addition, the firing ranges are equipped with high efficiency particulate air (HEPA) filtered vacuum cleaners for cleaning purposes. Air monitoring was conducted during firing periods in the breathing zone of the cadets and at the exhaust port. No airborne lead was detected."[53]

Although lead is not discharged at the ignition point, it is deposited at the muzzle end of the gun at the firing line. Even if the delicate air testing was properly conducted and there was absolutely no airborne lead particulate matter, there's still the issue of contamination through exposure by students from lead deposited directly in front of them and the exposure by staff if they are not meticulously following lead management procedures outlined by the CMP.

Sheyboygan, Wisconsin - The Sheboygan Rifle & Pistol Club, an organization affiliated with the CMP, moved its shooting range out of a Wisconsin middle school after parents raised concerns about exposing students to lead. The club had an October 2011 deadline to either upgrade the range's ventilation system or move out. Parents raised concerns about how the children were being protected from the range's lead residue.[54]

Lathrop High School, Tanana Valley Alaska - In 2002, Youth shooting programs at the Tanana Valley (AK) Sportsmen's Association, an organization affiliated with the CMP, shooting range were halted after ten members of the Lathrop High School rifle team were found to have high concentrations of lead in their blood.[55]

As stated, the CMP is opposed to the use of non-lead pellets. Their position is reminiscent of reactionary stances by those who were opposed to federal steps to take the lead out of paint and gasoline. The CMP is joined by the NRA and other pro-gun groups in its adamant defense of lead in ammunition. The NRA, for instance, fought California's recent law to ban lead in ammunition used for hunting. Many nationally renowned scientists testified in California that ammunition used for hunting is the number one source of unregulated lead left in our environment.[56]

The NRA lobbied against the legislation by distorting the facts. NRA board member Don Saba claimed, "the lead that's in ammunition is fairly non-toxic." Like those who deny climate change, the NRA, through its proxies, "claims that the science showing lead ammunition harms wildlife is "riddled with false assumptions, faulty methodology, selective presentation of data and outright ignoring of plausible alternative explanations."[57]

It would be laughable if millions did not believe it.

The CMP is similarly fanatic. It argues in its *Guide for Lead Management* that lead is the only material that is "both practical and economically feasible for use in producing competition-quality air gun projectiles." Shouldn't the potential for lead exposure render lead pellets utterly impractical? Moreover, shouldn't the health of America's school children take precedence over the cost of .177 caliber pellets?

The Guide to Lead Management says there have been several attempts to produce air gun pellets from other materials such as tin, but that none is a satisfactory substitute for lead. However, we've seen the success of the Battle Creek Marksmanship team using pellets made of tin and bismuth and the Air Force strongly recommending the use of non-lead pellets for its ASJROTC marksmanship programs.

Congress is beginning to pay attention to the health risks associated with military firing ranges, although not the firing ranges run by the military in the schools. The National Academy of Science reported in December of 2012 that decades-old limits on lead exposure are inadequate to protect the health of workers on military firing ranges. The researchers reported that lead from ammunition fired on military ranges in the last five years has "frequently exceeded" those limits, "in some cases by several orders of magnitude."[58]

Sen. Ben Cardin expressed concern about the report's implications for workers at Maryland installations with firing ranges, such as Aberdeen Proving Ground. "They're at risk," he said.

Barbara Boxer, the chairwoman of the Senate Committee on Environment and Public Works, explained, "We want to protect our people from exposure to these dangerous toxins. And we will do everything in our power to ensure that our families are protected from toxins that harm the human body."[59]

Hopefully, Senators Boxer and Cardin will also take measures to protect schoolchildren from these dangerous toxins.

In the meantime, it'll be tough to dislodge cavalier attitudes about lead that pervade in high schools across the country. For instance, in 2013 when five students with the Somerset (PA) High School gun club were found to have elevated blood levels for lead, the school's athletic director was quoted in the local paper as saying, "Very few schools are getting their teams tested for this. Lead is prevalent in the sport and high levels are going to exist." The gun club members routinely practiced at a shooting range owned by Somerset Sportsmen Rifle & Pistol Association, Inc., affiliated with the CMP. The article explained that the rifle team "experienced high lead levels last year as well. This is a temporary side effect of shooting guns." The school superintendent assured the public that the school is working closely with the coach to implement proper hygiene guidelines for team safety and that the school purchased a new vacuum and had the shooting range at the Somerset Sportsmen's Club professionally cleaned.[60]

Notes – Chapter 9

1. Civilian Marksmanship Program Annual Report 2014. Retrieved July 27, 2015, from http://bit.ly/2f0017C.

2. "2013 Form 990 - Return of Organization Exempt from Income Tax." Corporation for the Promotion of Rifle Practice and Firearm Safety, Inc., 15 Feb. 2015. Web. 1 May, 2016. http://bit.ly/2fgTt0h.

3. Elliot, Jock. "The New World of Airguns." SHOT Business RSS. National Shooting Sports Foundation Shot Business, 1 June 2014. Web. 4 Aug. 2014. http://shotbusiness.org/the-new-world-of-airguns/.

4. "Operation Manual Avanti 887". Daisy Outdoor Products, 16 Oct. 2006. Web. 4 Aug. 2014. http://www.daisy.com/sites/default/files/manuals/887-888.pdf.

5. "Non-Powder Guns Policy Summary." Law Center to Prevent Gun Violence RSS. Law Center to Prevent Gun Violence, 28 Oct. 2013. Web. 4 Aug. 2014. http://smartgunlaws.org/non-powder-guns-policy-summary/.

6. "Federal Register / Vol. 66, No. 215 / Tuesday, November 6, 2001 / Notices". U.S. Government Printing Office, 6 Nov. 2001. Web. 4 Aug. 2014. http://www.gpo.gov/fdsys/pkg/FR-2001-11-06/pdf/01-27872.pdf.

7. "Non-Powder Guns Policy Summary."

8. Ruiz, Sebastian. "School board muzzles JROTC's rifle ranges". San Diego Community Newspaper Group, 12 Feb. 2009. Web. 4 Aug. 2014. http://bit.ly/2fFCe9B.

9. "Guide to Lead Management for Air Gun Shooting". Civilian Marksmanship Program and USA Shooting, 1 Jan. 2013. Web. 31 July 2014. http://bit.ly/2fXyiEk 10. "Starting a JROTC Marksmanship Program - JROTC Marksmanship Instructor Course, Section III." 3.22 Unit Marksmanship Inspections. Civilian Marksmanship Program, n.d. Web. 1 Aug. 2014.

11. CMP Develops New JROTC Marksmanship Instructor Course. (n.d.). Retrieved 1 Aug. 2014, from http://www.odcmp.org/0305/default_inc.asp.

12. "Air Force JROTC Units Across the Nation." AFJROTC - AJROTC Units. Jean M. Holm Center for Officer Accessions and Citizen Development, Web. 1 Aug. 2014. http://bit.ly/2gw87F6.

13. Miles, Dale. "CMP Develops new JROTC Marksmanship Instructor Course.". Civilian Marksmanship Program, n.d. Web. 31 July 2014. http://www.odcmp.org/0305/JMIC.asp.

14. "JROTC Marksmanship Instructor Training Course." . Civilian Marksmanship Program, n.d. Web. 1 Aug. 2014. http://bit.ly/2fXCy6v.

15. "Air Force Junior ROTC Reference Guide". Director, Air Force ROTC, 1 Jan. 2012. Web. 1 Aug. 2014. http://bit.ly/2ghnBgV.

16. Willmsen, C., & Kamb, L. (2014, October 20). Loaded with lead: How gun ranges poison workers and shooters. Retrieved July 28, 2015, from http://projects.seattletimes.com/2014/loaded-with-lead/3/.

17. CMP Club & Competition Tracker | Club Display. (n.d.). Vancouver Rifle & Pistol Club.

Retrieved July 29, 2015, from https://ct.thecmp.org/app/v1/index.php?do=clubDisplay&club=885.

18. Willmsen, C., & Kamb, L. (2014, October 20). Loaded with lead: How gun ranges poison workers and shooters. Retrieved July 28, 2015, from http://projects.seattletimes.com/2014/loaded-with-lead/3/.

19. "What Do Parents Need to Know to Protect Their Children?" CDC's Lead Program. Centers for Disease Control and Prevention, 19 June 2014. Web. 10 Aug. 2014. http://www.cdc.gov/nceh/lead/ACCLPP/blood_lead_levels.htm.

20. Hopedale Pistol Club 2014 Inspection Report. (2014, August 6). Retrieved July 29, 2015, from http://bit.ly/2eG1gZc.

21. Ibid.

22. "WA-HI Adds Small Bore Rifle Club." Week in Review. Walla Walla Public Schools. Web. 10 Aug. 2014. http://bit.ly/2fl4vEk.

23. "Guide to Lead Management for Air Gun Shooting." Civilian Marksmanship Program and USA Shooting, 1 Jan. 2013. Web. 31 July 2014. http://bit.ly/2fXyiEk.

24. "Off Beat: ROTC rifle squad gets the lead out for the win." The Columbian. Columbian Publishing Company, 21 June 2011. Web. 1 Aug. 2014. http://bit.ly/2fYPGWU.

25. Battle Ground Public Schools Director of Communications: Gregg Herrington.

26. Cooper, Steve, and Summer Wood. "CMP - First Shot Online!" CMP - First Shot Online. Civilian Marksmanship Program, 1 Mar. 2011. Web. 1 Aug. 2014. http://bit.ly/2fYQVW7.

27. "Starting a JROTC Marksmanship Program - JROTC Marksmanship Instructor Course, Section III." Google. Civilian Marksmanship Program, n.d. Web. 1 Aug. 2014. http://bit.ly/2fx9u5f.

28. "JROTC Standard Operating Procedures for Air Rifle Safety and Air Rifle Range Management". Civilian Marksmanship Program, 2 Feb. 2009. Web. 1 Aug. 2014. http://bit.ly/2fW9icR.

29. Pelletier, B.B. "How Should I Clean My Airgun Barrel?" Air Gun Blog Pyramyd Air Report. Pyramydair,com, 23 Apr. 2013. Web. 10 Aug. 2014. http://bit.ly/2fYWNPl.

30. "Guide to Air Rifle Safety - A guide for junior shooters on all aspects of air gun safety including safety rules, range procedures, air rifle range operations, proper storage and personal safety". Civilian Marksmanship Program, 1 Jan. 2012. Web. 1 Aug. 2014. http://bit.ly/2fgWYDV.

31. Connell, Caoimhin. "The Industrial Hygiene Review and Regulatory Audit Resulting in Findings of Noncompliance and Regulatory Misconduct at an Identified and Illegal Drug Laboratory." Forensic Applications Consulting Technologies, Inc., 7 Aug. 2012. Web. 1 Aug. 2014. http://bit.ly/2fFEUnM.

32. Svensson, BG;, Schütz, A; Nilsson, A; Skerfving, S. Lead exposure in indoor firing ranges. International Archives of Occupational and Environmental Health, 1992: 64(4) 219-221.

33. Demmeler, Matthias; Nowak, Dennis; Schierl, Rudolf. "High blood lead levels in recreational indoor-shooters." International Archives of Occupational & Environmental Health.

Feb 2009, Vol. 82 Issue 4, p539-542. 4p. 1 Graph. 1Institute for Occupational, Social and Environmental Medicine, University Munich, Germany.

34. "Low Lead Level Harms Children: A Renewed Call for Primary Prevention". Advisory Committee on Childhood Lead Poisoning Prevention of the Centers for Disease Control and Prevention, 4 Jan. 2012. Web. 1 Aug. 2014. http://www.cdc.gov/nceh/lead/acclpp/final_document_030712.pdf.

35. "Potential Health Risks to DOD Firing-Range Personnel from Recurrent Lead Exposure." . National Research Council of the National Academies, 3 Dec. 2012. Web. 1 Aug. 2014. http://www.eenews.net/assets/2012/12/04/document_daily_01.pdf.

36. "Lead Contamination at Five County High Schools." Lead Contamination at Five County High Schools. Connection Newspaper, 2 Apr. 2007. Web. 2 Aug. 2014. http://bit.ly/2fgU5TT.

37. "Fairfax County Public Schools - Regulation 8615.4P." P. 16. Fairfax County Public Schools, 27 Jan. 2014. Web. 2 Aug. 2014. http://bit.ly/2eG5kZB.

38. Goldwein, Eric. "High School Rifle Teams Stay the Course as National Gun Debate Rages on." Washington Post. The Washington Post, 14 Jan. 2016. Web. 02 May 2016. http://wapo.st/1RoMliy.

39. "Guide to Lead Management for Air Gun Shooting".

40. "Guide to Lead Management for Air Gun Shooting." Page 16.

41. "Guidelines for the Evaluation and Control of Lead-Based Paint Hazards in Housing (2012 Edition) Chapter 14 ". U.S. Department of Housing and Urban Development, 1 Jan. 2012. Web. 2 Aug. 2014. http://portal.hud.gov/hudportal/documents/huddoc?id=lbph-16.pdf.

42. Lewis, RD, et. al. "Removal of lead contaminated dusts from hard surfaces." Environmental Science & Technology 40(2):590-4. 15 Jan. 2006. Web. 3 Aug. 2014. http://www.ncbi.nlm.nih.gov/pubmed/16468407.

43. "Indoor Firing Ranges Industrial Hygiene Technical Guide (Technical Manual NEHC–TM6290.99-10 Rev.1)". Navy Environmental Health Center, 1 May 2002. Web. 3 Aug. 2014. http://bit.ly/2fxaI0j.

44. "Guide to Lead Management for Air Gun Shooting."

45. Volume 8, Issue 5 (May 2011) Handwipe Method for Removing Lead from Skin (Received 29 October 2010; accepted 21 March 2011) Published Online: 2011 http://bit.ly/2f4vV0V.

46. Peeples, Lynne. Healthy Living December 19, 2012 Wednesday Secondhand Bullets: The Not-So-Obvious Health Risks at the Gun Range.

47. Dadams5@mlive.com, Dominic Adams |. "Flint Northwestern Air Rifle Team Heads to National Championships in Ohio." Mlive.com. 5 Feb. 2014. Web. 24 Jan. 2016. http://bit.ly/2ghqMpb.

48. "NJROTC Standard Release Form." Northwestern High School, Flint MI. Web. 24 Jan. 2016. http://bit.ly/2f0uMVa.

49. "Menehune High School Junior ROTC Menehune Battalion Cadet Standard Operating Procedure, July, 2009." Waimeahighschool.org. Menehune High School Junior ROTC, 1 July 2009. Web. 11 Aug. 2014.

50. "Richwoods High School." Orion Results.com. Orion Scoring System. Web. 11 Aug. 2014. http://www.orionresults.com/mcjrtocrichwoods.

51. Sheppard, Dick. NJROTC relies on NRA and CMP to Help its Marksmanship Team. Sanger Herald July 3, 2014 http://thesangerherald.com/our_newspaper/contact_us/

52. Elfrink, Tim. "Lead Safety Examined at OPS Rifle Ranges." Omaha World Herald. 11 Jan. 2006. Web. http://bit.ly/2fW9mZY.

53. "Omaha Public Schools Indoor Air Quality Program." Omaha Public Schools, 1 Jan. 2006. Web. 11 Aug. 2014. http://bit.ly/2ghqPB9.

54. "Middle School Shooting Range." NBC 26. Associated Press, 26 Sept. 2011. Web. 11 Aug. 2014. http://www.jrn.com/nbc26/news/130574288.html.

55. Mowry, Tim. "High Amounts of Toxin Are Discovered in School Rifle Team." Shooters Forum RSS. Anchorage Daily News, 15 Nov. 2002. Web. 11 Aug. 2014. http://bit.ly/2fWfD88.

56. Hoffman, Lyz. "Lead Ammo Ban Passes Legislature." Lead Ammo Ban Passes Legislature. Santa Barbara Independent, 14 Sept. 2013. Web. 11 Aug. 2014. http://bit.ly/2fYUb45.

57. Greenberg, Maxx. et al., "NRA Pulled Its Science-Denying Website That Claimed Lead Ammunition Isn't Poisoning Endangered Wildlife." Media Matters for America. Media Matters for America, 8 Aug. 2013. Web. 7 Aug. 2014.

58. Brown, Matthew. "Lead limits on military firing ranges outdated, report says; Cardin wants new standards to protect range workers, public." The Baltimore Sun. December 4, 2012

59. The Baltimore Sun, December 4, 2012 Lead limits on military firing ranges outdated, report says; Cardin wants new standards to protect range workers, public By Matthew Hay Brown, The Baltimore Sun

60. Rosado, A. (2013, February 11). Somerset addresses elevated lead levels. Retrieved July 29, 2015, from http://bit.ly/2fWcAws.

Sixth Brigade recruiters selected to be digital recruiters, trained on how to use social media to find qualified prospects.
PHOTO – U.S. ARMY RECRUITING COMMAND PUBLIC AFFAIRS OFFICE

Chapter 10

THE PENTAGON IS TRACKING OUR KIDS
How the U.S. collects data on potential recruits

In 2015 Congress re-wrote section 9528 of the *No Child Left Behind Act* (NCLB), which provided for parents to opt out of lists of the names, addresses, and phone numbers of students being forwarded by high schools to military recruiters. The old law, passed in 2002, also allowed under-18 students to opt themselves out. When the law was passed it contradicted FERPA, the Family Educational Rights and Privacy Act, which only provided rights to students over the age of 18. Schools were often confused. Some allowed minors to opt out by themselves and some did not.

When Congress rewrote NCLB, it called the new law the *Every Student Succeeds Act*, (ESSA). Section 8025 of the new law removed the right of underage students to opt themselves out.[1]

There has always been confusion among parents, activists, and school officials across the country regarding how to remove a child's information from lists being forwarded to the Pentagon. Both NCLB and ESSA require schools to "notify the parents of the students served by the agency of the option to make a request." Nothing in either statute describes exactly *how* a school system is supposed to notify parents or identifies a particular form for accomplishing the task of opting out. Some systems were immediately proactive, produced an opt-out form, and made it available to parents. Others ignored the law.

Section 8025 of ESSA says a parent of a secondary school student may submit a written request to the school that the student's "name, address, and telephone listing" not be released to military recruiters. Upon receiving such a request, the school is prohibited from releasing the information to recruiters.

Colorado's Weld County School District uses an opt-out form that dates back to 2008. The form is very simple and also works for the new legislation. It has parents check a box and sign a statement that says,

"Do not disclose my child's name, address, telephone number or directory information to any United State military recruiter." The form also includes spaces for the child's name and date. That's it. A simple email to the principal or the child's guidance counselor stating a parent's desire to withhold student information from recruiters is sufficient.

The National Parent Teacher Association went on record in 2005 opposing the military opt-out provision of the No Child Left Behind Act. The PTA supported changing the law by providing for 'opt in' instead, so parents could choose to request contact from military recruiters. In 2005, the PTA's website also contained information on how to opt out pursuant to the No Child Left Behind Act and how to remove an individual's information from the JAMRS database. That information has since vanished from the PTA's website, like the widespread public indignation and activism that once defined this issue.

School systems were powerless to eliminate the requirement that parents submit a written request to stop the transfer of student information to recruiters. Community groups in every state organized opt-out campaigns in 2004 and 2005. Others, following the lead of the PTA, demanded that schools switch to an opt-in framework.

Many became convinced that opting out kept recruiters at bay, but this counter-recruitment cottage industry has been rendered largely inconsequential by a quantum leap in the Pentagon's information gathering capabilities since the passage of No Child Left Behind in 2002. From electronic trolling of social websites to purchasing information from yearbook and ring companies, military recruiting services know what's in Johnny's head, if Johnny has a girlfriend, and what *she* thinks of his decision regarding enlistment.

The military has enlisted the help of Nielsen Claritas, a cutting-edge marketing and research firm. Its "custom segmentation" program allows a recruiter armed with the address, age, race, and gender of a potential recruit to call up a wealth of information about youth in the area, including recreation and consumption patterns.

The laptops of local recruiters are loaded with personal information on youth. The information is merged with data from the DOD's Joint Advertising Market Research and Studies Recruiting Database (JAMRS) and social media sites like Facebook, and the result is staggering. Recruiters may also know Johnny reads wrestling magazines, weighs 150, can bench press 180, drives a ten-year-old Chevy truck, listens to "classic rock," and enjoys fly fishing.2

Name, address, and phone number? The Pentagon may know if a prospect has had gingivitis.3

The US military maintains an Orwellian database containing intimate details on 30 million youth between the ages of 16 and 25, providing local recruiters with personal information for a sophisticated psychological campaign to lure youth within their geographic zones. The DOD purchases information from private data brokers and it collects data that youth voluntarily contribute on recruitment brochures or questionnaires.4

According to the JAMRS website, the program explores the "perceptions, beliefs, and attitudes of American youth as they relate to joining the Military."5

Several federal agencies rely on the research conducted by JAMRS, while the agency's recruiting database serves as a foundation for the services' outreach efforts. According to the initial notice the DOD filed in the Federal Register on May 23, 2005, categories of individuals covered by the system include:

> [Names of] high school students, aged 16-18; current college students; and Selective Service System registrants. Individuals who have taken the Armed Services Vocational Aptitude Battery (ASVAB) test; Individuals who have responded to various paid/non-paid advertising campaigns seeking enlistment information since July 1992; Current military personnel who are on Active Duty or in the Reserves. Individuals who are in the process of enlisting. Individuals who have asked to be removed from any future recruitment lists.

Presumably, the database contains information from a variety of sources, from the host of military programs operating in the schools to various military websites and digital data-collecting schemes.

The categories of records in the system include:

> Full name, date of birth, gender, address, city, state, zip code, and where available Social Security Number (SSN), e-mail address, ethnicity, telephone number, high school name, graduation date, Grade Point Average (GPA) code, education level, college intent (if documented), military interest (if documented), field of study, current college attending, ASVAB Test date, ASVAB Armed Forces Qualifying Test Category Score.6

WIKIMEDIA COMMONS

The Army's Recruiting Handbook describes the importance of this data, "The science of recruiting requires a great deal of data gathering, interpretation, and analysis. Without accurate and timely operational data, recruiters would just be shooting in the dark. Recruiters who know how to access and use their market intelligence can effectively focus their prospecting efforts."[7]

By early 2007, the American Civil Liberties Union announced the settlement of a lawsuit it filed against the DOD alleging privacy violations regarding the way information in the JAMRS database was collected and used. The DOD agreed to collect Social Security numbers only from the Selective Service System, although it continues to collect hundreds of thousands of Social Security numbers through the administration of the Armed Services Vocational Aptitude Battery in 12,000 high schools across the country.

The military was required to allow the public to opt out of the JAMRS system, although there is no way to keep an individual's personal information out of the database. As a result of the settlement, someone may complete an opt-out form and send it to the JAMRS office. The information will be kept in a "suppression file," inaccessible to recruiters.[8]

Unlike the *Every Student Succeeds Act*, which prohibits youth under 18 from opting out of lists high schools forward to military recruiters, the JAMRS program allows under-age youth to remove their information from the database. From the Federal Registry:

> Individuals, who are 15 1/2 years old or older, or parents or legal guardians acting on behalf of individuals who are between the ages of 15 1/2 and 18 years old, seeking to have their name or the name of their child or ward, as well as other identifying data, removed from this system of records (or removed in the future when such information is obtained), should address written Opt-Out requests to Joint Advertising, Marketing Research & Studies (JAMRS), ATTN:

Survey Project Officer, 4040 N. Fairfax Drive, Suite 200, Arlington, Virginia 22203-1613. Such requests must contain the full name, date of birth, and current address of the individual.[9]

Because opt-out screening is based on the current address of the individual, any change in address requires the submission of a new opt-out request with the new address.

The New York Civil Liberties Union has posted a JAMRS opt-out form on its web site to facilitate opting out of the database.

To be clear, there are two separate opt-out protocols, one pertaining to the *Every Student Succeeds Act* and the other regarding the JAMRS database.

Opting out is important because the DOD can take the information in the JAMRS database and forward it to the following entities without an individual's consent:

- Law enforcement
- Other agencies when DOD requests information in order to engage in hiring and firing decisions
- Other agencies when requested for a variety of government decision making
- Congress in response to Member inquiries
- Foreign law enforcement
- State and local taxing authorities
- The Office of Personnel Management for pay, leave, and benefits administration
- The Department of Justice for litigation
- Military banking facilities
- The General Services Administration for records management inspections
- The National Archives and Records Administration
- The Merit Systems Protection Board
- Almost any entity for national security purposes [10]

The notion of an all-encompassing database like JAMRS has largely slipped from public consciousness, if it was ever there. Aside from an initial flurry of press when a mention of the organization first appeared in the Federal Registry in 2005 and publicity surrounding the ACLU's suit in 2007, JAMRS has pretty much disappeared from mainstream consciousness, although it is occasionally mentioned as a source of data in military-funded academic studies regarding recruitment numbers and strategies.

The **Selective Service System** maintains a database of 17 million names and contact information of men between the ages of 18 and 25 who have registered. There are 11,000 volunteers across the country who work part-time on local draft boards.[11]

JAMRS seized the opportunity to partner with the Selective Service System to make a pitch for recruitment during the draft registration process. Additionally, Selective Service provides the names of all registrants to JAMRS for inclusion in the JAMRS Consolidated Recruitment Database. These names are distributed to the Services for recruiting purposes on a quarterly basis.[12]

Since 1980, all male citizens between the ages of 18 and 26 are required to be registered with the Selective Service System. Although there has been no draft since 1973, the US wants to be ready for a massive mobilization in case there's a serious threat. Young men are required to register during a 60-day period that begins 30 days before their 18th birthday.

Failure to register is a felony carrying a penalty of up to 5 years in prison and a fine of up to $250,000.

It sounds terrifying, although there have been no prosecutions for failure to register since 1986. Just 73% of 18-year-olds registered on time during the 2015 fiscal year ending last Sept. 30. The registration rate for men aged 20-25 was 94 percent.[13]

Considering the punitive measures in place to discourage non-registration, they don't need prosecution.

Under the Solomon Amendment, a federal law, young men who fail to register are denied the following:
- Federal financial aid to college students,
- Federal job training,
- Employment with federal agencies,
- And for immigrants, U.S. citizenship.

In addition, the Solomon Amendment mandates that institutions receiving certain federal agency funding must fulfill military recruitment requests for access to campus and for lists containing student recruiting information. If colleges do not comply, they may lose federal funds essential to their campus.[14]

Most of the states have piled on. According to the Center on Conscience & War, the country's leading independent authority on the draft,

44 states, the District of Columbia, and several territories have

enacted legislation that encourages or coerces registration with Selective Service. These laws take myriad forms: some states refuse government financial aid to unregistered students, some refuse enrollment in state institutions, some of those who do not register pay out-of-state tuition, and some states have a combination of these laws. Bills that restrict employment with state governments have passed in 20 states and one territory. Laws linking registration to a driver's license, learner's permit, or photo ID vary by state. Some states simply provide the opportunity to register with Selective Service as one applies for a license, while more than 30 make it mandatory.[15]

In December 2015, the Department of Defense announced a new policy to open all combat roles to women. Competing forces in Congress saw the writing on the wall and went to work introducing bills that would either eliminate the Selective Service System altogether or greatly expand the agency by mandating the registration of women between the ages of 18 and 26. Although a bill calling for the registration of women passed the Senate, it failed a test in the House in July of 2016.

Job Corps is a free education and training program that helps low-income young people ages 16 through 24 who need technical training, education, or counseling to complete schoolwork or to find and keep a job.[16] The U.S. Department of Labor administers the program. Job Corps' services are delivered through a nationwide network of 125 Job Corps centers operated by private companies under contract to the Department of Labor or by other federal agencies under the terms of interagency agreements.[17] Job Corps serves approximately 60,000 youths annually.

And Job Corps provides a direct pipeline to the military. If the military requires Job Corps clients to supplement their high school diplomas with additional courses for acceptance into branches of the military, centers must provide courses to students at no cost to the student.[18]

With the drawdown in military activity overseas, Job Corps Centers have been focusing more on training returning veterans for civilian careers. Three Job Corps Centers provide dormitories exclusively for veterans who are transitioning from the military to civilian life. At the same time, recruiters target Job Corps Centers, convincing at-risk youth to enlist, promising valuable career training in the military.[19]

The ASVAB is wildly popular at Job Corps Centers. The military enlistment test was given to thousands of students during 1,334 separate testing sessions throughout the 2012-2013 school year.[20]

March 2 Success is a free website providing study materials to help users improve their scores on standardized tests like the SAT, the ACT, and the ASVAB. Content also covers math, English and science instruction appropriate for grades 8-12. The site is based on Peterson's online courses. March 2 Success also has information to help students with the entire college application process.

Like the Armed Services Vocational Aptitude Battery (ASVAB), and the Junior Reserve Officer's Training Corps (JROTC), two widely prevalent programs in the nation's high schools, March 2 Success is all about recruiting for the armed forces. Students are prompted to click on various links:
- Email a Question to a Recruiter,
- Army Career Explorer
- Army Videos
- SGT Star: The Army's Virtual Guide

According to the *U.S. Army Recruiter's Handbook*, March2Success is designed primarily to build an image with students, parents and educators that the Army is high tech and career oriented.

Before signing up to use the March 2 Success site, students must read and agree to the privacy and security policy. Students do not have to provide personal information to the Army but refusal to do so precludes the use of the instructional portion of the site. The Army will collect personally identifiable information from children as young as 13 without parental consent.

March 2 Success complements the ASVAB Career Exploration Program. The recruiting command emphasizes both of these programs while addressing students, particularly during career fairs. For instance, U.S. Army Lt. Col. Jason Kerr was the keynote speaker during the annual Putnam County, Ohio Student Career Fair, held in October, 2015. The Lt. Colonel stressed the importance of taking advantage of the free tools.[21]

Digital military recruiters are stationed in recruiting companies across the country to find prospects using Craigslist, Facebook, Twitter, Instagram and ZipRecruiter.com. Recruiters say it's a lot easier to convince youth to become soldiers if the initial contacts happen online.

Fresno Battalion digital recruiter Staff Sgt. Kevin Newell explained the process in an interview in the Army's *Recruiter Journal*. "When you run into students in schools, they know more about us," he said. "You don't get that initial shock and they say, 'Oh that's the Army.' They say, 'Hey we've seen your stuff you've been posting on Facebook and it's really interesting.'[22]

Marine Corps recruiters often use a chin-up bar in high schools to attract the attention of youth. Recruiters invite students to show off their physical prowess on the chin-up bar and offer prizes like water bottles, t-shirts, or a hat. Before they are allowed to participate, students must complete a liability waiver. It is ludicrous for the Marines to suggest the form has any legal bearing since the students filling out the form are minors. The form collects personal data for recruiting purposes.

High school guidance offices and career centers routinely encourage students to visit a number of popular DOD-sponsored websites, most of which collect personally identifiable information for marketing purposes. High school students who click on links on many of the sites below to request information about the military share their personal information for recruiting purposes. The DOD compiles, processes, and distributes this information to the services.

A few of these websites follow:

Todaysmilitary.com is an obvious DOD site that collects information on users. "When it comes to learning about the Military, knowing where to start your research may seem daunting. Don't worry — we're here to help."

For high achieving students, the Army sponsors Ecybermission.com, a web-based engineering and mathematics competition where teams of 10-14-year-olds compete for awards.

Armystrongstories.com is an Army recruiting website program ostensibly dedicated to telling the Army story. Although soldiers are invited to share their "unfiltered perspective" on life in the military, submissions that do not comply with content guidelines are not posted.

Military.com is operated by Military Advantage, Inc., which is a subsidiary of Monster Worldwide, Inc, a global leader in employment services. Military.com has a host of military resources, including pay charts, mobile apps, and job search engines for military occupations.

The Department of Defense has several recruiting websites that collect information. Often, the military hides its true recruiting intentions.

Researchers have to dig pretty deep on the **ASVAB Program.com** site to find out what the acronym stands for. The website never explains that the primary purpose of the ASVAB test is to produce leads for recruiters.

My Future.com is a sophisticated DoD site that provides rather biased career, education and military options for youth and never reveals its tie-in to recruiting. Its affiliation with the military is buried. Users are required to register to use the site.

Each of the branches, reserves, and Guard units has its own websites that collect data. Most have a presence on Facebook, You Tube, and Twitter. Recruiters spend countless hours trolling these sources. Recruiters collect a mountain of information during frequent, popular displays of military hardware at schools, malls, and public parks. They methodically gather leads during air shows and parades and they seldom miss career fairs, particularly those at high schools. All the while, recruiters are collecting data on index cards and PCs that are fed to the JAMRS database and ultimately to neighborhood recruiters.

From 2014 to 2016, more than half of the states enacted legislation aimed at protecting the privacy of high school students. A Student Privacy Pledge has attracted the support of 200 companies in the business of providing online services to students in America's classrooms.[23]

The White House, too, has proposed a Student Digital Privacy Act, modeled after California's stringent Student Online Personal Information Protection Act, (SOPIPA), which was passed in 2014 and went into effect in 2016.[24]

Meanwhile, the military, the nation's most egregious violator of student privacy rights, gets a pass.

Several elements are common to most of these laws, according to Jules Polonetsky and Brenda Leong of the Future of Privacy Forum. They summarize the new laws regulating school-based digital data collectors:

> [Data collectors] are barred from selling student information, delivering targeted advertising to students, or changing privacy policies without notice and choice. They must use data for authorized educational uses only, support requirements for parental access to data, and delete data when required.[25]

If a school promotes an online product and requires or encourages students to use it, then it has responsibility for making sure the tool complies with many of these new privacy laws.

Like yearbook and ring companies that sell student information to the highest bidder, DOD recruiters and civilian employees routinely pass sensitive information about underage students to JAMRS. In turn, JAMRS subcontracts the massive database of approximately 30 million youth, ages 16-25, to the data goliath Equifax.

On a scale that dwarfs corporate competitors, the DOD delivers targeted advertising to students. It changes privacy policies without notice or choice to consumers. The recent changes to USMEPCOM Regulation 601-4 concerning the Armed Services Vocational Aptitude Battery, ASVAB, provide an example.[26]

The military does not use the data it collects for educational purposes, and it works against providing for parental consent or access to data. Furthermore, the military retains data collected on students long after laws demand their destruction.

While proposing the Student Digital Privacy Act last year, President Obama forcefully declared, "data collected on students in the classroom should only be used for educational purposes — to teach our children, not to market to our children." However, the president's proposal leaves the DOD alone.

The framework of the President's proposal is taken from the California law:

> Operators may not collect information that is descriptive of a student or otherwise identifies a student, including, but not limited to, information in the student's educational record or email, first and last name, home address, telephone number, email address, or other information that allows physical or online contact, discipline records, test results, special education data, juvenile dependency records, grades, evaluations, criminal records, medical records, health records, social security number, biometric information, disabilities, socioeconomic information, food purchases, political affiliations, religious information, text messages, documents, student identifiers, search activity, photos, voice recordings, or geolocation information.

The DOD collects most of this through the ASVAB enlistment test alone.

Federal law says military recruiters may request the names, addresses, and numbers of students for direct marketing purposes, an act prohibited in all the new privacy laws. As we've seen, the law allows parents to request that their child's name not be forwarded to the Pentagon.

Maryland is the only state that has a law requiring an opt-out form to be placed on the mandatory emergency contact card, leading most parents to remove their child's information from lists being sent to recruiters. The new data privacy laws fail to address this obvious invasion of privacy in the 49 states that are reluctant to check this military overreach.

The military has multiple avenues of data flowing into its databases. High school guidance offices and career centers encourage students to visit the websites of each of the military branches, reserves, and Guard units. They all collect volumes of personally identifiable data. Schools also promote the websites listed above, and they often provide instruction in navigating a host of military or military-supported sites like todaysmilitary.com, ecybermission.com, march2success.com, armystrongstories.com, military.com, asvabprogram.com, and myfuture.com.

Unwary students are prompted to click on military links to Facebook, YouTube, and Twitter, resources where newly formed units of recruiters across the country spend countless hours assembling a virtual portrait of children before first contact.

Kentucky is the worst state in the union when it comes to protecting student information from recruiters. Its law says, "All student academic records are made available upon request to any agency of the federal or state government for the purpose of determining a student's eligibility for military service."[27]

When President Obama endorsed the Student Privacy Pledge, he called for companies to make a firm commitment to using student data only for educational purposes. The Student Privacy Pledge asks data collectors to abide voluntarily by the same standards in many new state laws.

"We pioneered the Internet," Obama said at the Federal Trade Commission. "But we also pioneered the Bill of Rights and a sense each of us as individuals have a sphere of privacy around us that should not be breached by our government but also [not] by commercial interests." [28]

The DoD has not signed the pledge and is not likely to do so anytime soon because so much of the Pentagon's strategy for recruiting the nation's youth depends on deception.

The Pledge applies to all personal student information whether or not it is part of an "educational record" as defined by federal law. The federal law known as the Buckley Amendment says schools may not release educational records to third parties without seeking parental consent, although the DOD does so with the administration of the ASVAB.

Meanwhile, other giants in the student testing industry, like the College Board and Houghton Mifflin Harcourt, have signed on.

When the ACLU settled their lawsuit with the DOD over the illegal JAMRS database in 2007, the DOD agreed to the following:

- limit to three years the length of time that DoD retains student information;
- stop collecting student Social Security numbers; and
- establish and clarify procedures by which students can block the military from entering information about them in the database and have their information removed. 29

The DOD has fallen short on all three accounts. Student information is retained indefinitely, although JAMRS data is placed in a "suppression file" after three years. The Recruiting Command routinely collects Social Security numbers through the ASVAB program and the DOD has failed to make anything clear to students or their parents regarding the JAMRS database or ways to have information removed.

This is not what democracy looks like. The DOD defends its actions, arguing, in effect, that this heavy-handed arrangement is preferable to the return of the draft.

Relatively few want to enlist and those who do increasingly come from a shrinking number of deep red states in the south. The realities of a vicious and unresponsive command structure after 15 years of unnecessary warfare have filtered down to potential recruits and their families. The Pentagon feels it must violate our 1st Amendment rights while operating a highly deceptive recruiting apparatus to achieve its yearly quotas. What's needed is a sincere national discussion on the size, cost, and mission of the Department of Defense, particularly as it relates to the inability of this nation to address the overwhelming needs of its citizenry. A serious downsizing of the military, accompanied by a substantial reduction of troop strength and recruiting quotas will engender a more relaxed, democratic and transparent recruiting command.

Notes – Chapter 10

1. "S.1177 - Every Student Succeeds Act." Congress.gov. 10 Dec. 2015. Web. 23 Jan. 2016. http://bit.ly/1Ldv8Wi .

2. U.S. Army Recruiter Journal. "Are you a mover and a shaker?" Nov. 2007 USAREC - The United States Army http//www.usarec.army.mil/hq/apa/download/.../nov07.pdf.

3. Ferner, Mike. "Pentagon Database Leaves No Child Alone." Www.counterpunch.org. 04 Feb. 2006. Web. 14 May 2016. http://bit.ly/2fXztTT.

4. "Joint Advertising Market Research Studies (JAMRS) | New York Civil Liberties Union (NYCLU) Web. 14 May 2016. http://www.nyclu.org/milrec/jamrs. 5. "JAMRS." Joint Advertising Market Research & Studies. Web. 14 May 2016. http://jamrs.defense.gov/.

6. "Dodd-Frank Wall Street Reform 280 in the Last Year." Federal Register. 18 May 2005. Web. 14 May 2016. http://bit.ly/2f4zgNz.

7. "Recruiter Handbook USAREC 3-01." U.S. Army Recruiting. 22 Nov. 2011. Web. 16 July 2015. http://www.usarec.army.mil/im/formpub/rec_pubs/man3_01.pdf.

8. Liptak, Adam. "Defense Dept. Settles Suit On Database for Recruiting." The New York Times January 10, 2007 http://www.nytimes.com/2007/01/10/washington/10recruit.html?_r=0.

9. "Federal Register." Federal Register Volume 73, Number 142. 23 July 2008. Web. 14 May 2016. http://bit.ly/2eG3JTC.

10. "EPIC - DOD Recruiting Database." EPIC - DOD Recruiting Database. Electronic Privacy Information Center. Web. 14 May 2016. https://epic.org/privacy/student/doddatabase.html.

11. Wood, David. "Uncle Sam Needs Coders. Here's How The Military Could Draft Them." Huff Post Politics. Huffington Post, 10 May 2016. Web. 14 May 2016. http://huff.to/1WmycW1.

12. "Affiliations." Joint Advertising Marketing Research Systems. Department of Defense. Web. 14 May 2016. https://web.archive.org/web/20061022001158/http://jamrs.org/aff.php.

13. Lardner, Richard. "House Committee Votes to Require Women to Register for Draft." The Big Story. Associated Press, 28 Apr. 2016. Web. 14 May 2016. http://apne.ws/1TgmKUX.

14. American Association of Collegiate Registrars and Admissions Officers. The Solomon Amendment - A Guide for Recruiters and Student Records Managers. 2001. Web 14 May 2016 http://bit.ly/2fxihE6.

15. "Center on Conscience & War - Selective Service Registration: Coercion of Conscience." Center on Conscience & War - Selective Service Registration: Coercion of Conscience. Web. 14 May 2016. http://bit.ly/2fVC5ze.

16. "Start Your Career. Join Job Corps." Welcome to Job Corps. U.S. Dept. of Labor. Web. 14 May 2016. http://www.jobcorps.gov/home.aspx.

17. "Job Corps Program Assessment Guide." Job Corps. U.S. Department of Labor, 6 Aug. 2013. Web. 14 May 2016. http://www.jobcorps.gov/Libraries/pdf/pag.sflb.

18. "Requirements - High School Diplomas." Job Corps - Program Assessment Guide. Department of Labor. Web. 14 May 2016. http://www.jobcorps.gov/Libraries/pdf/pag.sflb. p. 233.

19. Newman, Mark. "Job Corps Explores Military Opportunities." Ottumwa Courier. 15 Mar. 2016. Web. 14 May 2016. http://bit.ly/2fxit6i.

20. "State Data." National Coalition to Protect Student Privacy. Web. 14 May 2016. http://www.studentprivacy.org/state-data.html.

21. Bush, John. The Lima News. Career Fair Helps Putnam County Students 'Bridge the Gap. 7 Oct. 2015 Web. 16 May 2016.

22. Bock, Fonda. "Fishing Where the Fish Are; the Social Media Ocean." Recruiter Journal. U.S, Army, 13 Nov. 2014. Web. 14 May 2016.

23. "Pledge to Parents & Students." 200 Companies Serving Students and Schools Have Now Signed the Student Privacy Pledge –. Student Privacy Pledge, 12 Nov. 2015. Web. 14 May 2016.

24. Herold, Benjamin. "Obama Calls for Stronger Protections on Student-Data Privacy." Education Week. 20 Jan. 2015. Web. 14 May 2016. http://bit.ly/2fXIAE7.

25. Leong, Brenda. "Passing the Privacy Test as Student Data Laws Take Effect (EdSurge News)." EdSurge. 12 Jan. 2016. Web. 14 May 2016. http://bit.ly/1W3W2SP.

26. "USMEPCOM Regulation 601-4 Personnel Procurement Student Testing Program." United States Military Entrance Processing Command. 13 Nov. 2006. Web. 14 May 2016. < http://bit.ly/2fXIGvt.

27. "Kentucky Legislature." Kentucky Revised Statutes. Web. 15 May 2016. http://www.lrc.ky.gov/Statutes/statute.aspx?id=4231.

28. Carson, Angelique. "Obama Stops by FTC; Announces Privacy Bills on ID Theft, Student Data, Consumer Privacy." 12 Jan. 2015. Web. 15 May 2016. http://bit.ly/2f4DDbH.

29. "Defense Department Reforms Student Military Recruiting Database to Settle NYCLU Lawsuit." American Civil Liberties Union. Web. 15 May 2016. http://bit.ly/2fFMej1.

THE FUTURE IS BRIGHT

ASVAB program.com, U.S. Department of Defense, Defense Manpower Data Center

From the ASVAB website:

What do you see when you look at the future?
As Dr. Seuss puts it,

"You have brains in your head.
You have feet in your shoes.
You can steer yourself
any direction you choose.
You're on your own.
And you know what you know.
And YOU are the one who'll decide where to go..."

Chapter 11

"CAREER PROGRAM" IS ENLISTMENT TOOL IN CAMO

How the military collects valuable demographic and cognitive information about high school youth using a deceptive career exploration program

The Armed Services Vocational Aptitude Battery, (ASVAB) is the military's entrance exam that is given to fresh recruits to determine their aptitude for various military occupations. Taking the ASVAB is the first step in the military enlistment process. The test is also the cornerstone of the school-based ASVAB Career Exploration Program, (ASVAB-CEP), which is one of the military's most effective recruiting tools. The ASVAB-CEP was administered to 691,042 students in 11,893 high schools across the country during the 2013-2014 school year.[1] That's nearly half of all high schools.

The ASVAB-CEP collects an individual's name, Social Security Number, address, telephone number, date of birth, sex, ethnic group identification, educational grade and rank, individual's plans after graduation, and individual item responses to ASVAB subtests and associated accession tests, test dates and test scores.[2]

The Department of Defense promotes the ASVAB-CEP in schools, often without revealing its tie-in to the military and never revealing its primary function as a recruitment tool. School counselors and administrators encourage students to participate in the program that many claim assists students in matching their abilities with certain career paths.

The ASVAB-CEP has two components. One is comprised of the three-hour enlistment exam, and the other is made up of an "interest self-assessment" and several "career exploration tools." The interest inventory, known as the "Find Your Interests" or FYI Program, asks students questions about the kinds of activities they most like to do. The DOD claims this will allow students to explore civilian and military occupations in line with their skills demonstrated on the test and their interests reflected on the FYI Program.

At its core, the ASVAB is extraordinarily sexist. The high school version of the ASVAB is comprised of eight subtests. Five of these subtests: General Science, Arithmetic Reasoning, Word Knowledge, Paragraph Comprehension., and Math Knowledge are quite similar to other standardized tests. Three of the subtests, Electronics Information, Auto & Shop Information, and Mechanical Information measure a student's knowledge of how mechanical things work. For instance, the Auto & Shop subtest may ask,

Shock absorbers on a car connect the axle to the
  A. wheel.
  B. chassis.
  C. drive shaft.
  D. exhaust pipe. or

If a car is driven mostly in a city so that the spark plug tip never gets hot enough to burn off excess carbons in the cylinder, then
  A. lower voltage should be applied to the spark plug.
  B. the tip should be pulled farther out of the cylinder.
  C. the tip should be pushed further into the cylinder.
  D. a thicker conducter [sic] in the plug must be used.[3]

Most males probably know shocks operate between the axle and the chassis and it is obvious to many men that spark plugs are hotter further into the cylinder, causing excess carbon to be burned off. It is doubtful most women know these things.

Women have poorer scores on subtests that examine mechanical knowledge because many haven't shown an interest in mechanical things up to this point in their lives. Although they may possess the aptitude to excel in a particular field, women may be discouraged from seeking these occupations as a result of participating in the ASVAB-CEP.[4]

After the test is administered, military representatives typically meet with youth at school to discuss their scores and suggest career paths. Later, recruiters make calls to the students, using sophisticated, individualized profiles gathered from the test and a host of sources.

From electronically monitoring social websites to purchasing a wide variety of commercially available personally identifiable information, military recruiting services know a lot about Johnny, although they don't know exactly how smart he is. Enter the ASVAB. The test opens the door to a potential recruit's cognitive abilities; something recruiting services can't purchase or find online. Johnny's social, intellectual, and mechanical dimensions are combined to create a precise, virtual portrait. As one DoD official put it, "It's all about info before first contact."

Federal and state laws strictly monitor the release of student information, but the military manages to circumvent these laws with the administration of the ASVAB-CEP. Students are usually given the test at school without parental consent and often without parental knowledge. ASVAB test results are the only student information released from U.S. schools to a third party without the opportunity provided for parental consent.

The Family Educational Rights and Privacy Act (FERPA) requires a signed parental release statement before "education records" are released to third parties. The Pentagon's position, explained in the ASVAB Counselor Guide, is that the ASVAB is proctored by DOD personnel and that ASVAB results become education records only *after* the test is scored by the DOD and returned to the school. This way, the brass argues, ASVAB results are not education records. Instead, they're "military records".[5]

ASVAB testing in the schools is a particularly egregious violation of civil liberties that has been going on almost entirely unnoticed and largely unchallenged since the late 1960's.

Aside from managing to evade the constraints of federal law, the military may also be violating many state laws on student privacy when it administers the ASVAB. Students taking the ASVAB are required to furnish their social security numbers for the tests to be processed, even though many state laws specifically forbid such information being released without parental consent. In addition, the ASVAB requires under-aged students to sign a privacy release statement, a practice that may also be prohibited by many state laws. The issue provides a textbook case of a clash between federal and states' rights. As an exception to the general rule, conservatives tend to side with the federal government in this debate.

Since 1925 the U.S. Supreme Court has recognized the "fundamental right" of parents or guardians to make decisions regarding "the care, custody, and control of their children." Parents and guardians have a legal interest in deciding whether or not they would like their children to participate in the ASVAB-CEP program. For an examination of the respective rights of schools and parents, see "A Guide to Best Practices for ASVAB-CEP Administration", a publication of The Center for Law and Justice, Rutgers, The State University of New Jersey.[6]

Regardless of the legality of the ASVAB-CEP, the program is terribly deceptive. A typical school announcement reads:

> All Juniors will report to the cafeteria on Monday at 8:10 a.m. to take the ASVAB. Whether you're planning on college, a technical school, or you're just not sure yet, the ASVAB Career Exploration Program can provide you with important information about your skills, abilities and interests – and help put you on the right course for a satisfying career!

Announcements like this are copied from the ASVAB Career Exploration Program's "Snippets" webpage. There's no mention of the military or the primary purpose of the test, which is to find leads for recruiters.[7]

Although military regulations allow the test to be administered while precluding test results from reaching recruiters, the collective experience of parents and activists across the country has revealed that many school administrators are unaware of the option.

U.S. Military Entrance Processing Command (USMEPCOM) Regulation 601-4 identifies eight options schools have regarding the administration and release of ASVAB information. These options range from Option 1, which permits test results and other student information to be released to military recruiters without prior consent, to Option 8, the only one that prevents test results from being used for recruiting purposes.

Until recent changes to the program were announced, inaction on the part of a school caused USMEPCOM to select Option 1. (see below). Students and parents may not determine which release option is used. They cannot individually opt out of releasing the information

Table 3-1 – USMEPCOM 601-4

Recruiter Release Options - Instructions for providing access to student test information to recruiting services:

> **1** Provide student test information to recruiting services no sooner than 7 days after mailed to School

> **2** Provide student test information to recruiting services no sooner than 60 days after mailed to School

3 Provide student test information to recruiting services no sooner than 90 days after mailed to School

4 Provide student test information to recruiting services no sooner than 120 days after mailed to School

5 Provide student test information to recruiting services no sooner than the end of the SY for that specific school

6 Provide student test information to recruiting services no sooner than 7 days after mailed to school with instruction that no telephone solicitation by recruiters will be conducted as a result of test information provided

7 Invalid test results. Student test information is not provided to recruiting services

8 Access to student test information is not provided to recruiting services[8]

Options 1-6 basically say the same thing. Recruiters get the data. Option 7 is frequently used for 10th graders, or when there's some sort of goof up. ASVAB results may be used for enlistment purposes for up to 2 years, making most sophomores too young to use their results to join. Option 8 says the military cannot use test results for recruiting purposes.

In 2005, approximately 1-2% of all students taking the test had Option 8 selected. According to data provided by a series of FOIA requests, that figure rose to 4.4% in 2007; to 8.6% in 2009; to 12.2% in 2010; to 14.2% in 2011; to 15.0% in 2012 and to 16.5% during the 2012-2013 school year.

A February, 2016 story in Education Week quoted Shannon Salyer, the national program manager for the ASVAB Career Exploration Program, "Of the 650,000 tests last year, results from about 400,000 were provided to recruiters as leads."[9] Salyer was apparently referring to those tested under Option 7 and Option 8.

The National Coalition to Protect Student Privacy and its state affiliates have been partly responsible for the surge in schools moving to select Option 8. Most schools, school boards, and state legislatures across the country were unaware that release options existed until activists informed them. To reiterate, military regulations made Option 1 the default selection if a guidance counselor failed to contact the Military Entrance

Processing Station (MEPS) to express the school's desire to select a particular option. Option 1 sends results to recruiters in seven days.

The changes made by the US Military Entrance Processing Command to Regulation 601-4 on November 16, 2015 may adversely impact the privacy of hundreds of thousands of American high school students. The change to the regulation appears in bold:

> Only a school official will select the recruiter release option for their students. **If an option isn't selected, the MEPS must contact the school to determine the release option. If no option is received from the school, the test will be scored using Option 8 (no release).** Release options are provided in Table 3-1 (Recruiter release options). The release option chosen by the school will be honored without discrimination and without adverse effect of quality or priority of service to the school. **All MEPS scheduling communications with schools will include a listing of all release options.**[10]

At first glance it appeared that sustained activism advocating for the selection of ASVAB Release Option 8 to protect student privacy was leading to the ultimate demise of this deceptive ruse, but upon closer examination, it's apparent the military is adjusting its strategy to a changing landscape for greater advantage.

Until the change, school officials were expected to be proactive in communicating to the Recruiting Command whether they wanted to make the test results available to be used for recruiting purposes. Guidance counselors were to select one of the eight release options for their students taking the test.

"If no option is provided by the school the test will be scored using Option 8" sounds like the military took a progressive step forward, but the second part about scheduling communications with all schools, including a listing of release options suggests the command is going after all those Option 8 schools to get them to switch to an option that will ultimately allow the release of student information to recruiters. Previously, schools that selected Option 8 did so one time and that selection typically stayed in place. Now, it appears, the slate is cleared annually.

If Military Entrance Processing Command representatives cannot talk a school into moving from Option 8, they may suggest the school allow for a split option. That means some students will be allowed to take the ASVAB under Option 8 and some under Options 1-6.

An example of this strategy may be found in the recent change to

Chancellor's Regulation A-825 in New York City.[11] For years, the city's schools were required to select Option 8 for all students taking the test. If a student wanted to use her scores for enlistment purposes, she was required to visit with a recruiter to sign a form that released the results. (or her parents had to sign if she was under 18)

Now, schools in New York where the military gives the ASVAB are required to send home written notification in advance of the test to the parents of each student scheduled to take the ASVAB. The form asks parents if it is OK to release results to recruiters.

Counselors across the country are already overwhelmed with their workload, and this new military regulation will add to it. Counseling staff will be required to keep track of the notifications and sort students accordingly. Counselors will be subject to blame and potential litigation if results are forwarded to recruiting services from a child whose parents did not authorize consent.

The military could no longer use test results from tens of thousands of students annually tested, so it changed the rules.

The data received by the National Coalition to Protect Student Privacy includes the name of every high school in the country where the ASVAB is administered, the numbers of students who take the test, along with their release options. The data also includes information regarding whether testing sessions are mandatory. Military regulations prohibit recruiters from suggesting the test be made mandatory while guidance counselors have reported that recruiters routinely push mandatory testing. This data is crucial in allowing analysts to track the progress of the Option 8 outreach efforts and to document improper procedures regarding the administration of the test. When presented with the data, school officials often report different numbers for mandatory testing, the overall numbers of students tested, and their release options. After examining erroneous data, state legislators and school administrators are more likely to call for the universal selection of Option 8.

The 2013-2014 school data shows that 908 high schools required students to take the test, even though military regulations prohibit DOD personnel from suggesting to school officials that the test is made mandatory. In Arkansas alone 141 high schools required the administration of the test.[12]

The Army recruiter's handbook calls for military recruiters to take ownership of schools and this is one way they're doing it. The U.S. Army Recruiting Command ranks each high school based on how receptive it is to military recruiters. Schools are awarded extra points when they make the ASVAB mandatory.[13]

Meanwhile, USMEPCOM Regulation 601-4 specifically prohibits the test from being made mandatory:

> Voluntary aspect of the student ASVAB: School and student participation in the Student Testing Program is voluntary. DOD personnel are prohibited from suggesting to school officials or any other influential individual or group that the test be made mandatory. Schools will be encouraged to recommend most students participate in the ASVAB Career Exploration Program. If the school requires all students of a particular group or grade to test, the MEPS will support it.[14]

It's unlikely that hundreds of schools will continue to require students to take the test without sustained pressure from the recruiting command. Apparently, the Department of Defense has regulations in place solely for public consumption that it has no intention of following.

In response to an email survey by the National Coalition to Protect Student Privacy, several guidance counselors in Nebraska and Maryland indicated they did not know they were given the ability to select release options. Some explained they thought the No Child Left Behind Act required all students to take the ASVAB. Some thought the opt-out component of the No Child Left Behind Act covered ASVAB testing. If parents failed to opt-out, they were told by recruiters it's OK to allow the release of student information gathered through the administration of the ASVAB.

Still, others reported that they had selected Option 8 only to find the database showing that Option 1 had instead been selected and all results had been forwarded to recruiters. One school official in Prince George's County Maryland reported using an ASVAB Release Option form provided by the recruiting command that omitted Option 8.[15]

The Pentagon is under-reporting the number of schools with mandatory testing. There are hundreds of schools with required testing that are not reported by the DoD. For instance, the data shows there is no mandatory testing in Ohio. However, it is possible, using a simple Google search, in this case, ["k12.oh.us" asvab "all juniors"] to uncover several dozen schools that require students to take the ASVAB that are not reported by the Pentagon.

Several press accounts have documented public resentment against mandatory military testing in the high schools. A few examples follow.

Several students at **Durango High School in Durango, Colorado** reported hearing an Army recruiter refer to students as "f*ing faggots" while administering the ASVAB to 500 students during a mandatory testing session. The resulting uproar, captured in the Durango Herald, focused on the anti-gay slur, not the forced testing of 500. One of the students who heard the comment told the author that several students who were not happy about being forced to take the test were singled out by the recruiter. "My mom doesn't want you to use my name. The soldier picked on us because of the way we looked."[16]

These egregious violations of decency and privacy were reported by the media after outraged mothers of students contacted reporters.

In 2008, three public high school students at **Cedar Ridge High School in Hillsborough, North Carolina**, refused to take the required ASVAB test on privacy grounds and were sent to the detention room for the day. Principal Gary Thornburg explained, "I don't have a lot of patience with people who are refusing to take the assessment--or refusing anything that their entire grade level is participating in."[17]

In 2006, juniors at **Pepperell High School in Lindale, Georgia** were told by their principal that the ASVAB was mandated by federal law. Posting on social media and distributing fliers on the day of the test, a small group of student activists convinced half of the junior class to refuse to take the test. With social media postings and a handful of flyers, 17-year-old high school seniors Robert Day and Samuel Parker decided to act after Day overheard some teachers at Pepperell High School saying that first thing Monday morning the school's juniors would be made to take the ASVAB military aptitude test. One of the military recruiters present attempted to snub their efforts, claiming the No Child Left Behind Act allows access to all of their information, so they might as well take the test. Some of the students deliberately filled in faulty information.[18]

In 2009 several Juniors at **Suwannee High School in Suwannee, Florida** stayed home rather than take the ASVAB, an annual requirement for all Juniors. "If they come to school on that day, they take it," said Jim Simpson, assistant principal at SHS. Donna Odom, a parent of an 11th-grade student, complained that student privacy was not protected. She protested to school officials and the local press that the school had the option to withhold personal information, including social security numbers, from recruiters but that the school decided to share the results with recruiters. [19]

In 2012, Mark Rutherford and a fellow classmate at **North Salem High School in Salem, Oregon** were required to sit for the ASVAB after their request to pass on the test was denied. In protest, Rutherford and his buddy randomly chose answers, causing the two boys to be removed by the 1st Sergeant in command. Rutherford said, "When we explained we chose to opt out by voiding the test due to its military connection the 1st Sergeant informed us as did Vice Principle Rolland Hayden, that the ASVAB is in no way related to the military." Rutherford describes the encounter with the recruiter:

> He removed us from the testing area (gym full of other students) and as we were walking out through a hallway I asked him "Are we in trouble?" and he responded in a very rude and intimidating tone "Why? Are you scared?" Since he didn't give me a direct answer to my question and due to his rude and intimidating manner I stated my belief that I felt "it was against my constitutional rights to be forced to take a military test which I felt was not appropriate for a public school environment." The 1st Sergeant laughed, mocking us and making remarks about our knowledge of our constitutional rights. He then said to us in the presence of a member of the school administration and loud enough for other staff members to hear "What do you know about constitutional rights when you haven't fought for this country?"

The young radical wrote a complaint to the local superintendent of schools, quoting the author. He sent it to several news sources.[20]

When seniors at **North Hardin High School in Radcliffe, Kentucky** were told they would be required to take the ASVAB they organized a senior skip day instead. More than half of the seniors stayed away from school the day the test was administered. "I am not focused on a military career, I am only focused on college and my academics so I didn't want to take the test and skipped," Jason Ingram ('12) said.[21]

The Pentagon often hires non-military personnel known as Civilian Test Administrators (TA's) to proctor the ASVAB. TA's frequently get together to exchange war stories. One TA who asked not to be identified, shared this story about a fellow DOD employee giving the test to a group of Texas high school seniors:

"He was giving a mandatory ASVAB and was having a lot of trouble keeping order. The students were rebellious and refusing to cooperate. Several teachers were in the room trying to control the chaos. When this

TA collected the test, he found that many students had blackened in the bubbles on the answer sheets in the shape of offensive symbols and words. I'm sure you can imagine what they were. So the TA took the answer sheets into the principal's office and she raised hell with the students."

The same TA relates that it was not unusual for students to refuse to take the test.

In some instances, a student would simply refuse to provide any information other than his/her name and would sit quietly with their hands folded. Others would randomly fill in the answers without reading the questions. The TA explained:

> In one mandatory session where the student refused to accept the test booklet, the assistant principal approached and threatened the student stating: "There will be consequences," but the student remained defiant. There was no yelling or shouting. Just a flat, monotone refusal, like they were coached.

Another TA described a testing session during which a teacher entered the testing room and began browsing through the answer sheets to see that no Social Security Numbers had been included. When he found one, he proceeded to erase it. That action caused a confrontation between the TA and the intruding teacher. "I don't know what happened in the end," said the TA.

TA's receive no instruction on legal issues regarding the test. They are simply instructed to read the testing instructions verbatim. TA's are routinely asked probing questions by students, and they hear concerns from school counselors. They witness relevant questions from fellow TA's posed during DoD training sessions being side-stepped and shut down, and they begin to question the ethicality of the entire program.

The collection of Social Security numbers (SSN's) is particularly problematic. The TA explained:

> I can tell you from my experience that students will include their SSN's simply because they want to be cooperative. Even after telling students that providing their SSN is optional, I have had students ask for permission to call their parents to get their SSN. I was dismayed to see that students had brought their social security cards to the test site and were pulling them from their purses and wallets. Some even had their SSNs on their cell phones.

Test Administrators ask for a student's SSN's three times, and students are prompted three times to fill it in on the answer sheet. TA's threaten to negate the test unless the information is provided. If a student is taking the ASVAB for its alleged value as an aid in identifying suitable careers, the SSN is inconsequential.

Meanwhile, in early 2016, President Obama ordered a systematic review of where the Federal Government can reduce reliance on Social Security Numbers as an identifier of citizens. [22] Furthermore, the Social Security Administration's Office of Inspector General has warned against the unnecessary collection and use of Social Security Numbers, citing "a significant vulnerability for this young (K-12 school) population."[23]

In 2008, the DoD ordered a substantial reduction of the collection of SSN's within the department. However, the 122-page, "DoD Social Security Number (SSN) Reduction Plan" fails to incorporate ASVAB testing.[24]

The TA explained that he had heard of several complaints from counselors regarding the legality of the Privacy Act Statement students are required to sign when they take the ASVAB. Guidance counselors complained that students did not understand what they were signing. The counselors claimed students did not have the authority to release their information.

The statement appears on the answer sheet, DD Form 1304-5AS:[25]

Student Testing Program

Privacy Act Statement

Armed Services Vocational Aptitude Battery

Principal Purpose(s): To compute and furnish test score products for career/vocational guidance and group assessment of aptitude test performance; for up to two years, to establish eligibility for enlistment (only for students of the eleventh grade or higher and only with the expressed permission of the school); for marketing evaluation, assessment of manpower trends and characteristics; and for related statistical studies and reports.

Disclosure: Voluntary. However, if you do not provide the requested information, your test will not be scored or otherwise processed.

Signature: _____

Date: _____

Requiring youth to sign this form is reprehensible, especially when they are forced to take the test. Children under 18 are not legally empowered to make legal decisions regarding the release of their own academic records to a third party. The military claims it does not need parents to sign off on the release of ASVAB results because they say these records are military records, not school records. Including this charade as a part of this deceptive program is unconscionable.

The Texan test administrator advised students not to sign the form, although, he estimates, thousands of these unsigned tests were still scored and processed.

Kevin Haake of the Nebraska Coalition to Protect Student Privacy sums up public resentment toward forced military testing:

> We'd rather not have the military actively recruiting in our schools but I don't see an egregious violation of civil rights when a couple of kids voluntarily sign up to take this military test. It's another matter when entire classes of children are told they've got to take this thing and all their information is shipped to the Pentagon without mom and dad knowing about it.[26]

Many principals and counselors are sold on the utility of the ASVAB as a useful career exploration program that assists students in determining career paths. Interestingly, not all elements of the Pentagon's vast recruiting apparatus are in accord on this point.

The U.S. Marine Corps Military Personnel Procurement Manual contains the following, "The ASVAB is used by the Armed Forces for recruiting purposes and by school counselors for vocational guidance counseling. The ASVAB's ability for determining civilian job skills has not yet been proven."[27]

The Marine Corps questions the validity of the ASVAB in helping student's measure civilian job skills, while the official ASVAB website says the test does a poor job as a predictor of success for students who desire to go to college.

From the website:

> Why can't I use my ACT or SAT score to enter the military? "The ASVAB is designed for a different purpose than the ACT and SAT. The ASVAB is designed to predict success in the military, while the ACT and SAT are designed to predict success in college.[28]

In contrast to the examples from the Marines and from the official ASVAB website, this "snippet" fed to schools to promote the ASVAB to students tells a different story:

> Whether you're planning on college, a technical school, or you're just not sure yet, the ASVAB Career Exploration Program can provide you with important information about your skills, abilities, and interests – and help put you on the right course for a satisfying career. See your counselor for more information.

Many school officials feel it is a good program. Once the test is administered and scored, the recruiting command sends recruiters to the schools after the tests are scored to discuss "career paths" with students.

The DOD database of testing purports to reflect the number of schools and students that participate in mandatory testing, although there are several problems with its accuracy.

The ASVAB provides the first, massive, national litmus test for enlistment. Consider five schools in the Miami area. North Miami Beach HS tested 855. It has a minority population of 96%. Coral Gables HS tested 695 with a minority population of 90%. Coral Park HS had 429 take the test. It has a minority population of 96% Miami Central High School tested 645 and Miami Northwestern HS sat down 642. Both have minority populations of 99%. None of these five schools are listed in the DoD database as having "mandatory" testing and there's no evidence online that students were required to take the test.

Voluntary?

Just two of the top 20 Dade County, Florida high schools ranked by reading performance scores allowed the ASVAB to be administered during the 2012-2013 school year. Conversely, all of the system's bottom 20 schools, aside from two, allowed military testing.[29]

A web search of seven Michigan high schools listed in the Pentagon's data as "Not Mandatory" clearly shows that students are required to take the ASVAB. Pickford, Watersmeet, Goodrich, Manistique Lake Linden, Rapid River, and Ironwood High Schools all forced students to take the test. Munford High School in Munford Tennessee tested 855 but is listed in the database as not mandatory. Perhaps patriotism is rampant in Munford, but how, exactly, do they manage to get 855 teenagers to sit voluntarily for three hours to take a military exam?

We can identify hundreds of schools that require testing in states across the country that are not identified as being mandatory in the official ASVAB data we've received from USMEPCOM. For instance, the information released by the DoD shows there is no mandatory testing in Ohio, however, it is possible, using a simple Google search tool, in this case: ("k12.oh.us" asvab "all juniors") to uncover many schools that require students to take the ASVAB that are not reported by the Pentagon.

The Pentagon has figured out another way to require students to take the ASVAB.

Nearly 50,000 New Jersey high school seniors were required to take an alternative end-of-year assessment at the completion of the 2015-2016 academic year because they opted out of taking the Partnership for Assessment of Readiness for College and Careers, (PARCC) test the year before. School officials said "a significant number" of these students would have to take either the College Board's ACCUPLACER test or the Armed Services Vocational Aptitude Battery, (ASVAB) as approved pathways to graduation.[30]

School systems pay a hefty price when they use the ACCUPLACER, a product of the College Board, especially when the test is given to tens of thousands of students. Meanwhile, the military's enlistment test is free of charge.

In 2014, New Jersey began allowing students to take the ASVAB as a substitute for the PARCC test. To graduate, students are expected to score a 31 on the Armed Forces Qualifications Test, (AFQT). A 31 is the minimum score for enlistment in the Army. The AFQT uses sections of the ASVAB to calculate the score.

AFQT scores are computed using the standard scores from four ASVAB subtests: Arithmetic Reasoning (AR), Mathematics Knowledge (MK), Paragraph Comprehension (PC), and Word Knowledge (WK). AFQT scores are reported as percentiles between 1-99. An AFQT percentile score indicates the percentage of examinees in a reference group that scored at or below that particular score.[31]

SAT-AFQT Concordance Table (For SAT administered in 1995 of later)

SAT Composite Score	AFQT Category (and AFQT score range)
500-530	IV-C (10-15)
540-590	IV-B (16-20)
600-680	IV-A (21-30)
690-800	III-B (31-49)
810-900	III-A (50-64)
910-1180	II (65-92)
1190-1600	I (93-99)

Source: Defense Data Manpower Center Personnel Testing Center, Monterey, CA

An AFQT score in Category I opens the door to almost any Military Occupational Specialty (MOS) in any of the branches. Scores in Category II or III-A usually ensure enlistment. If a score falls into Category IIIB, a potential recruit may or may not be able to enlist, depending on what the exact score is and how the particular branch is performing regarding its recruiting quotas. Congress says the military cannot accept more the 4% of its recruits from Category IV and none from Category V.

The Army requires a minimum AFQT score of 31 for those with a high-school diploma. The Navy wants recruits with a minimum of a 35 on the AFQT. For the Marines, it's a 32, while the Air Force requires a 36.

According to the table, a 31 on the AFQT equates to a 690 SAT composite score, based on the critical reading and math sections on the SAT test. The 690 score excludes the optional writing section. This score would land a student in the bottom 6% nationally, likely to be too low to gain admittance to a New Jersey state college.[32]

According to Dr. Fred Zhang of Prep Scholar, a 700 is the median 8th grade combined score on the SAT, meaning the Army's minimum ASVAB score of 31 is equivalent to the performance of a below-average 8th grader.[33] In the case of New Jersey, students can satisfy their assessment graduation requirement if they can demonstrate the academic ability of a below-average 8th grader by scoring a 31 on the ASVAB.[34]

The staggering numbers of New Jersey 11th graders who opted out of taking the PARCC test during the 2014-2015 school-year may have done so as a result of a coordinated campaign. A passing score on the PARCC Test is a graduation requirement. South Brunswick New Jersey's Board of Education Vice President Dan Boyle explained during a board meeting in January 2016, "Throughout the state, there are an inordinate amount of students that are not qualified to graduate," Boyle said at the time. "That is almost directly a result of the (PARCC) opt-out movement."[35]

A robust testing opt-out movement in New Jersey and in several states throughout the country has targeted the corporatization and standardization of American education. United Opt Out National serves as a focal point of resistance to corporatized education reform. The group demands "an equitably funded, democratically based, anti-racist, desegregated public school system for all Americans that prepares students to exercise compassionate and critical decision making with civic virtue."[36]

The Army, with a keen eye on educational currents, witnessed tens of thousands of New Jersey students refusing to take the PARCC tests and was eager to cash in on the PARCC opt-out movement by offering its free ASVAB Career Exploration Program in place of the PARCC. After all, the Army reasoned, the kids have to have a pathway toward graduation, and the Army was honored to provide the "public service."

An article in the April, 2015 Army Recruiter Journal described the Army's lobbying campaign in New Jersey and gloated that the ASVAB "would be accepted as a substitute competency test for students who fail to pass the PARCC."

In the meantime, the military claims the ASVAB is being shut out of schools. In one of his last public comments in the fall of 2014, departing US Army Recruiting Commander Maj. Gen. Allen Batschelet said, "We're seeing an increasing trend with schools shutting us out from access or making access pretty restricted," "Schools are either choosing to not administer the ASVAB or withholding results from recruiters," he explained.[37]

The Military Entrance Processing Command has managed to convince school officials in a half-dozen states to make the ASVAB an alternative option for end-of-year senior year assessments to provide a path for students who cannot pass the front-line tests.

In **Minnesota**, a new law radically changes graduation testing requirements, allowing high school students who fail mandated exit exams to take the Armed Services Vocational Aptitude Battery (ASVAB) as an alternative assessment. According to the Minnesota Department of Education, students simply have to take the ASVAB or one of two other exams to earn a diploma once minimal course requirements are met. There is no specific score required. Of the three tests, the ASVAB is the only one that is free.[38]

At Blaine High School, just north of Minneapolis, students are greeted with this message about the ASVAB:

> The ASVAB is a multiple-aptitude battery that measures developed abilities and helps predict future academic and occupational success. The ASVAB is offered to high school and post-secondary students as part of the ASVAB Career Exploration Program. The program provides tools to help students learn more about career exploration and planning, in both the civilian and military worlds of work. The ASVAB Career Exploration Program is free of charge. For seniors who have not yet met the high school graduation testing requirement, the ASVAB will meet the grad requirement.[39]

There are no privacy protections built into Minnesota's new the law, meaning that many of the lowest achievers throughout the state who take the military entrance exam will have their information forwarded to military recruiters - without Mom and Dad's OK.

New Mexico allows a score of a 31 on the ASVAB to provide a path to graduation. The New Mexico Public Education Department publishes an Alternative Demonstration of Competency Guide that includes the following erroneous account of the ASVAB:

> The Armed Service Vocational Aptitude Battery (ASVAB) has 10 tests. The score of ten tests are combined to compute the Armed Forces Qualification Test (AFQT) scores. Candidates need to receive a score of 31 to be accepted into the ARMY and 51 to be accepted into any other branch of the military.[40]

The Student Testing Program has eight sections, not ten. AFQT scores are computed using the standard scores from four ASVAB subtests, and the other branches accept recruits with scores a just little higher than the Army, but nowhere near the 51 stated herein. Notice how "ARMY" is capitalized. It appears as if the Army is operating at an advantage in New Mexico.

Mississippi wants seniors to score a 36 on the AFQT before they can graduate. The Mississippi Board of Education Chairman, Dr. Wayne Gann said he, "felt strongly that we should provide options for students who lacked passing scores on one or more subject area tests if the student is able to demonstrate readiness to transition to college or the workforce through other assessment measures." A 36 on the AFQT is high enough to enlist in all four services. [41]

Kentucky calls for a 50 on the AFQT for a student to earn a diploma. A 50 on the AFQT is the same as a composite SAT score of 810, according to the ASVAB Concordance Table. An 810 won't open many college doors.[42]

The **Missouri** School Improvement Program establishes five standards of accountability used to rate school performance. The third standard calls on high schools to administer the ASVAB to determine whether students are "College and Career Ready." Like the other states above, there are no privacy protections built into the Missouri School Improvement Program.

Missouri's Nevada High School, about 50 miles south of Kansas City, advises children not to be concerned with the privacy implications of the ASVAB-CEP. The school apparently mirrors the attitudes of state school officials.

From the school's website:

> There is a fear that you will be recruited. And you will be. But that is completely unrelated to taking the ASVAB at school, or even having heard of the ASVAB. Being recruited is a function of being the age you are. There are lots of recruiters out there. They have access to lots of databases (census, school directories, DMV, credit and bank records, etc.), including ours. Their job is to find you and ask if you want to join the military and they are very good at their job. If you do not want to, simply say no. Throughout your life, you will have endless similar opportunities to turn down the chance to change your long distance carrier, have your carpets cleaned, or siding put on your house. Think of it as a case of "welcome to adulthood, here is your junk mail." Such a false hope of not being recruited is a poor and ultimately pointless reason to avoid the value of using the ASVAB to learn of and use your aptitude scores.[43]

Like the officials with the Missouri Department of Elementary and Secondary Education, Nevada High School fails to explain to the school community that the ASVAB may be administered without results being forwarded to recruiters. While many states are taking steps to strengthen privacy protections for children, Missouri is moving in the wrong direction. Just 4.3% of students taking the ASVAB in Missouri's schools during the 2012-2013 school year had Option 8 selected by school officials.

Robin Marty, a Missouri resident, was so outraged when the Missouri Department of Education included the ASVAB as a regular assessment for students, she started a "Care2" Petition. The petition called for an end to the use of the test as a graduation requirement. 29,000 signatures were delivered to Missouri state education officials.[44]

In **Colorado**, beginning with the graduation class of 2021, local school boards and districts will select from a menu of graduation requirements, including the ASVAB, to create a list of options their students must use to graduate from high school. School districts may offer some or all of the state menu options.[45] The minimum allowable score for the ASVAB in Colorado is a 31.

Published reports from New Jersey and the states mentioned herein fail to address the raison d'etre of the ASVAB testing regime, which is to provide leads for recruiters. Furthermore, state departments of education and local school boards routinely state that school officials will be giving the ASVAB, when in fact, military officials give the test. If schools administered the ASVAB, results would be regarded as educational records and therefore subject to the Family Educational Rights and Privacy Act, (FERPA). This federal law precludes the release of sensitive student information to third parties without parental consent. When the military gives the test, ASVAB records are considered to be military documents.

The ASVAB is often the only "free" assessment on "test days" in high schools across the country. These are the days set aside on each school calendar to heed the call for increased student testing. About a third of all high school students are not college bound. If these students are offered a choice between taking the PSAT, which is an entrance exam for the college-bound crowd and involves paying a fee, or taking the ASVAB, which is free, they may be more likely to pick the ASVAB. The military lists these students as voluntarily taking the ASVAB, although, in a sense, they're forced to do so.

The website of Crown Point HS, about ten miles south of Gary, Indiana carried this announcement for students:

> 11th grade students that wish to take the PSAT, and potentially qualify fornational merit scholarships, will be required to pay $14.00. Juniors may register to take the PSAT in room c-203 from September 7-14th. 11th grade students that do not wish to take the PSAT will be administered the ASVA exam. The ASVAB exam is free of charge.[46]

Crown Point tested 469 students during the 2012-2013 school-year and they're listed as not mandatory. All students had their results shipped to recruiting services without parental consent.

Activism
In 2008, groups affiliated with ASVAB campaigns in Hawaii, California, and Maryland set their sights on statewide initiatives to mandate the universal selection of Option 8.

After a rash of disturbing news pieces that exposed the deceptive and predatory nature of military recruiting in Hawaii's high schools, including numerous reports of sexual advances by recruiters toward high school girls, Hawaii's Department of Education implemented the nation's first statewide mandatory Option 8 policy.

Next, a brilliant campaign by California activists led the California legislature to pass an Option 8 measure in 2008, but it was vetoed by Gov. Arnold Schwarzenegger. Schwarzenegger was not persuaded by arguments that California parents, rather than representatives from the US Military Entrance Processing Command, should make decisions regarding the release of student information.

In 2010, a campaign directed by the Maryland Coalition to Protect Student Privacy resulted in Maryland becoming the first state to enact a law that prohibits the automatic release of student information to military recruiters gathered as a result of the administration of the ASVAB.[47]

The NAACP of Maryland, the ACLU of Maryland, and the Maryland PTA testified in support of the measure.

Elbridge James from the NAACP-MD glanced at the database of the schools that administered the ASVAB and immediately saw a pattern of discrimination. The test simply wasn't administered in the wealthiest and whitest schools. James of the NAACP testified:

> This legislation is about the simple idea that parents need to have the final say over the release of information regarding their children. This especially applies to black families and low-income households whose children seem to be the target of military recruiters. We believe military recruiters currently administer the test in schools with students whose families have few financial resources and limited education more than they do in schools where families have greater economic and education opportunities. Military recruiters rarely, if ever show up at some high schools in the state like Bethesda-Chevy Chase High School, while they appear to be permanent fixtures in Baltimore City and Prince George's schools. From a Pentagon data sheet, we know that last year, 148 took the ASVAB test at Largo Sr. High School in Prince George's County while nobody took it at Churchill High School in Montgomery County.[48]

Cynthia Boersma, Legislative Director of the ACLU-MD, also testified:

> Parents and students should be afforded the opportunity to decide whether they want to contact military recruiters and share this information, not the schools or the military recruiters. This bill gives the parents the right to decide whether they want to be contacted by military recruiters and safeguards the privacy rights of students who take the ASVAB.[49]

Merry Eisner, Vice President for Legislation of the Maryland PTA told Maryland legislators,

> The National PTA seeks to increase awareness and community sensitivity about the collection and dissemination of information regarding students and believes that such records should respect the rights to privacy and be relevant to a child's education [50]

Lt. Col. Christopher Beveridge, Commander, 12th Battalion, U.S. Military Entrance Processing Command, the state's top military recruiter, opposed the universal selection of Option 8, arguing that the military, not parents, should ultimately decide on the release of student information gathered through the administration of the ASVAB. When the Pentagon's man tried to convince legislators that privacy activists behind the legislation were against the military, it failed miserably.

Beveridge wrote in his testimony:

> Much of the rhetoric behind this bill is bent on disrupting any efforts to build, support, or sustain the military. There has been a disinformation campaign targeted at school officials throughout Maryland, Northern Virginia, and D.C. that preys upon school officials' fears of potential litigation associated with safeguarding students' personal information. Ultimately, the goal is to dissuade high schools from ASVAB testing altogether. HB 778 would be the first step along this path.[51]

Lawmakers didn't buy it. Several expressed their appreciation for the military's free career service and enthusiastically praised the military. The bill passed the legislature and was signed into law by Governor Martin O'Malley. Stories in several national media outlets, including USA Today, NPR Radio and the Washington Post brought national attention. Interestingly, the Washington Post repeated a frequent Pentagon claim that children can "opt-out" from having their test results sent to recruiters. A robust letter-writing campaign forced the paper to print a correction.[52]

New Hampshire also passed a law mandating the universal selection of Option 8 in 2014. New Hampshire Peace Action Executive Director Will Hopkins was most instrumental in passing ASVAB legislation in the Granite State. The measure quietly sailed through the state house and was signed into law without attracting media attention or the opposition of the military.

New Hampshire's school board was lobbied by the NEA New Hampshire, the state's NEA affiliate. The (National) NEA Annual Meeting and Representative Assembly, however, has been unwilling to get behind a resolution calling for the universal selection of ASVAB Option 8.

It was another story in Connecticut, where an Option 8 bill was defeated by the Democratically-controlled General Assembly in 2014.[53]

The proposed legislation was overwhelmingly approved by the General Assembly's Education Committee along party lines and was set for a floor vote that was expected to pass. In an unprecedented maneuver, the Veterans' Committee objected to the bill, citing opposition by the recruiting command and several inaccurate claims.

Connecticut was victimized by a military whitewash campaign. The testimony submitted to the legislature by U.S. Army Recruiting Battalion Commander Lt. Col. Michael D. Coleman was incorrect on a fundamental and crucial point. He was not accurate when he wrote, "Moreover if enacted, students will lose a proven occupational, vocational and technical counseling tool and the opportunity afforded by the Career Exploration Program"[54]

Military regulations say that a school can prohibit the release of student data to recruiters but still take advantage of the Career Exploration Program.[55]

Three states and 2,000 additional schools enjoy the benefits of the Career Exploration Program without allowing recruiters to use student data for recruiting purposes.

Defending the decision to kill the Connecticut legislation, Veterans' Affairs Committee Chair Rep. Jack Hennessy said, "To my knowledge, parents already have this ability to limit the dispersal of information, and we thought it unnecessary."[56] Hennessy was wrong. Military regulations state that only school or military officials may decide if ASVAB results are released to recruiters.[57] This is why the Education Committee thought the legislation was necessary! Perhaps Senator Hennessey didn't understand the measure. Perhaps he was fed inaccurate information by the recruiting command. Lt. Col. Coleman and Senator Hennessey misrepresented the truth to the people of Connecticut.

After the measure had been defeated, the *New Haven Register* published a story on the defeat of the ASVAB bill.[58]

Connecticut school officials contacted by the paper didn't have a problem with the wholesale transfer of student information to recruiters without parental consent. They had been relying on the recruiting command for information. They're victims of the same whitewash campaign occurring across the country.

The paper reported, "In New Haven schools, parents are given an opt-out letter at orientation "that allows parents to declare that they do not wish for their child's student information to be shared with military recruiters," said school's spokeswoman Abbe Smith in an email." Smith apparently didn't realize that ASVAB results aren't subject to the opt-out clause of the No Child Left Behind Act. If this were the case, the legislation would not be necessary. This is the same claim Rep. Hennessy made.

Officials at Hillhouse High School told the *Register*, "The school only shares information with recruiters if the student indicates that he or she is interested in pursuing a future with the military."

This is wrong on three counts, although it is a common falsehood spread by the recruiting command in schools across the country. First, most students taking the ASVAB are minors, and they're legally prohibited from making decisions regarding the release of personal information from the schools. Second, students must sign the ASVAB privacy statement that asks for their signature to release information. The statement says the tests will not be processed if students don't sign. Third, the decisions regarding the release of ASVAB results are either made by school officials or the recruiting command, not kids or parents!

To finish the whitewash, Rep. David Alexander, a member of the Veterans' Committee, published an op-ed in the *Connecticut News Junkie* "In Support of Connecticut Military Service," in which he advocated circumventing parental decision- making regarding the release of their children's information.[59]

In arguing against giving parents the right to consent to information leaving the state's schools and heading to the Pentagon, Alexander wrote, "I can envision that many well-intended parents may discourage their children from joining the military as they enter adulthood post-high school." Alexander referred to the privacy issue as a 'red herring" and argued that "Vietnam-era distrust is imbued within SB 423." He wrote that SB 423 "only furthers the cultural divide between the all-volunteer force and the civilian population."

If there is a cultural divide, as Alexander suggests, it might be lessened if the military began operating in a truthful and transparent fashion according to the dictates of a democratic society.

Diane Wood with the Texas Coalition to Protect Student Privacy reflects common sense Lone Star State attitudes:

> I got fired up when I discovered this egregious violation of civil liberties that's been going on entirely unnoticed. I don't care if it's the Department of Defense or whoever. The thing that's surprised me is that this privacy campaign has resonated with both progressives and Tea Party activists down here. We all see ASVAB testing as an unwarranted and illegal federal incursion into our lives.60

Wood's tireless organizing and her testimony to the nationally maligned Texas State School Board probably contributed to Texas testing 6,600 fewer students in 2012-2013 than the year before. In one year, Option 8 rates increased from 14.7% to 15.5% while the number of students forced to take the test shrunk from 15,805 to 4,825 and the number of schools requiring students to take the ASVAB decreased from 181 to 70.

This is a remarkable accomplishment, especially in a state like Texas where Governor George W. Bush proclaimed an "ASVAB Day" in 1995 to encourage Texan youth to take the test in school.61 A dozen state governors have issued proclamations calling on all students to take the ASVAB, although none encouraged protecting student privacy.

In many states, smart, targeted community activism has been shown to translate into quantifiable results. Barbara Harris, with the New York Coalition to Protect Student Privacy, has been at it for years and has helped to eliminate mandatory testing in the Empire State. "We've witnessed several trends here in New York. The number of test-takers continues to drop, the percentage of schools that have selected Release Option 8 continues to rise, and mandatory testing has disappeared. I'm hopeful we'll soon get the Board of Regents to mandate Option 8 across the state."

It's the same in Connecticut and Massachusetts. Seth Kershner with the Connecticut Coalition to Protect Students Privacy has led the effort in those states. Testing numbers in Connecticut and Massachusetts have plummeted in recent years to about 4,000 in each state. There's no mandatory testing. Nearly half of the students being tested do so under Option 8.

Notes – Chapter 11

1. "Military Releases High School Testing Data." National Coalition to Protect Student Privacy. Web 18 Sept. 2016 http://www.studentprivacy.org.

2. DoD Armed Services Military Accession Testing February 12, 2015 Privacy Act; Systems of Records Ms. Cindy Allard, Chief, OSD/JS Privacy Office, Freedom of Information Directorate, Washington Headquarters Service, 1155 Defense Pentagon, Washington, DC

3. "ASVAB | Sample Questions." ASVAB | Sample Questions. Web. 27 May 2016. http://official-asvab.com/questions/app/question_ai3_app.htm.

4. "Technical Aptitude: Do Women Score Lower Because They Just Aren't Interested?" Association for Psychological Science. 31 Oct. 2011. Web. 27 May 2016. http://bit.ly/2fXNWiV.

5. "ASVAB Counselor Guide." ASVAB Career Exploration Program. Web. 27 May 2016. Page 14 http://bit.ly/2fxtc0R.

6. "ASVAB-CEP Best Practices." Rutgers School of Law. Constitutional Rights and International Human Rights Clinics, 4 Oct. 2013. Web. 27 May 2016. http://bit.ly/2fWu4sy.

7. "ASVAB Career Exploration Program Snippets." ASVAB-CEP. Web. 27 May 2016. http://bit.ly/2fFWS9t.

8. "Personnel Procurement Student Testing Program Regulation 601-4." U.S. Military Entrance Processing Command, 16 Nov. 2015. Web. 27 May 2016. http://bit.ly/2fZa5vl.

9. Adams, Caralee. "Military Career Testing Could Get ESSA Boost." Education Week. Education Week, 23 Feb. 2016. Web. 27 May 2016. http://bit.ly/2ghkBjS. 10. "Personnel Procurement Student Testing Program Regulation 601-4."

11. "Regulation of the Chancellor – A-825." New York City Department of Education. 21 Jan. 2016. Web. 27 May 2016. http://on.nyc.gov/2fZ7QYD.

12. July 29, 2016, from Corynne N. Gerow OSD/JS FOIA Specialist; Freedom of Information Office of the Secretary of Defense and Joint Staff FOIA Request Service Center http://www.dod.mil/pubs/foi/ 1155 Defense Pentagon Washington, DC 20301-1155.

13. "USAREC Regulation 601-107." U.S. Army Recruiting Command, 15 Dec. 2006. Web. 27 May 2016. http://www.usarec.army.mil/im/formpub/rec_pubs/r601_107.pdf. p. 25

14. "Personnel Procurement Student Testing Program Regulation 601-4." p. 8

15. "ASVAB School Information Form." Provided by Prince George's County Public Schools Student Privacy.org. National Coalition to Protect Student Privacy. Web. 27 May 2016. http://bit.ly/2ghbDmH.

16. "Military Recruiter Uses Homophobic Slur during ASVAB Test." Colorado Indymedia. 5 Nov. 2009. Web. 27 May 2016.

17. Tiemann, Amy. "High School Students Stand up for Privacy, Refuse to Take Military Test." CNET. Raleigh News & Observer, 14 Feb. 2008. Web. 27 May 2016. http://cnet.co/2fZ8K7v.

18. Horton, Scott. "Teens Frustrate Military Recruiter's ASVAB Scam." Anti War.com. 24 Nov. 2006. Web. 27 May 2016. http://antiwar.com/horton/?articleid=10055.

19. Suwannee Democrat (Live Oak, Florida) McClatchy-Tribune Business NewsDecember

1, 2009 Military test provokes ire of some parents BY Carnell Hawthorne Jr., Suwannee Democrat, Live Oak, Fla.

20. Rutherford, Mark. "Students Complain to School Mandating Military Recruiters' Test." War Is A Crime .org. Web. 27 May 2016.

21. KY seniors skip rather than take required ASVAB.   March 30, 2012 North Hardin High School, Radcliff, Kentucky http://bit.ly/2fhdZ0W.

22. "FACT SHEET: Cybersecurity National Action Plan." The White House. Office of the Press Secretary, 09 Feb. 2016. Web. 30 May 2016. http://bit.ly/1QpaZdq.

23. "A-08-10-11057 - Alternate Format." OFFICE OF THE INSPECTOR GENERAL SOCIAL SECURITY ADMINISTRATION, July 2010. Web. 30 May 2016. http://bit.ly/2f0Jnjk.

24. "Directive-Type Memorandum (DTM) 2007-015-USD(P&R) – "DoD Social Security Number (SSN) Reduction Plan"." DOD - Personnel and Readiness. Department of Defense, 28 Mar. 2008. Web. 30 May 2016. http://bit.ly/2ghPIwG. 25. "Student Testing Program ASVAB Answer Sheet." DD Form 1304-5AS. Department of Defense, July 2014. Web. 28 May 2016. http://bit.ly/2fxroF9.

26. Haake, Kevin. Phone interview. 11 Feb. 2013.

27. "MILITARY PERSONNEL PROCUREMENT MANUAL, VOLUME 2 ENLISTED PROCUREMENT." MCO P1100.72C. Headquarters U.S. Marine Corps, 18 June 2004. Web. 28 May 2016. http://bit.ly/2eGmJBw.

28. "ASVAB | Frequently Asked Questions." ASVAB | Frequently Asked Questions. Web. 28 May 2016. http://www.official-asvab.com/faq_app.htm.

29. "Assessment, Research, and Data Analysis." Miami-Dade County Public Schools. Web. 29 May 2016. http://bit.ly/2fZbC4p.

30. Baldwin, Carly. "How Many South Brunswick Students Opted Out of PARCC?" South Brunswick, NJ Patch. 12 Feb. 2016. Web. 29 May 2016. http://bit.ly/2ghKFMN.

31. "ASVAB | Understanding ASVAB Scores." ASVAB | Understanding ASVAB Scores. Department of Defense. Web. 29 May 2016. http://official-asvab.com/understand_coun.htm.

32. "Is 1030 a Good SAT Score?" 1030 SAT Score: Is This Good? Prep Scholar. Web. 29 May 2016. http://bit.ly/2fWz2pi.

33. Zhang, Dr. Fred. "What's a Good 8th Grade ACT / SAT Score?" What's a Good 8th Grade ACT / SAT Score? Prep Scholar, 5 Feb. 2015. Web. 29 May 2016. http://bit.ly/2fLLk70.

34. "Graduation Requirements for the Classes of 2016, 2017, 2018 and 2019." State of New Jersey Department of Education. 7 Jan. 2016. Web. 30 May 2016. http://bit.ly/2fl2cB6.

35. Kim, Charles W. "South Brunswick: District Providing Alternate Testing For PARCC 'Opt Outs' " TAP Into South Brunswick-Cranbury. 8 Feb. 2016. Web. 29 May 2016. http://bit.ly/2fhahV0.

36. "UNITED OPT OUT: The Movement to End Corporate Education Reform" The Web. 30 May 2016. http://unitedoptout.com/.

37. Davis, Clifford. "As Number of Youth Eligible to Serve Shrinks to 3 in 10, U.S. Army Adapts Recruiting Strategy." Jacksonville.com. 23 Oct. 2014. Web. 30 May 2016. http://bit.ly/2ghiw7I.

38. "Graduation Requirements (GRR)." Minnesota Department of Education, 2015. Web. 30 May 2016. http://education.state.mn.us/MDE/SchSup/DataSubLogin/GRR/.

39. "ASVAB Test." Blaine High School Career Center. 2015. Web. 30 May 2016. http://www.anoka.k12.mn.us/Page/27522.

40. "College and Career Readiness (CCR) Benchmarks." New Mexico Public Education Department. July 2013. Web. 30 May 2016. http://bit.ly/2eGnqe6. p.7

41. "Graduation Requirements." Mississippi Department of Education. Apr. 2015. Web. http://bit.ly/2fFQG1q.

42. "Kentucky Department of Education College and Career Readiness Measures 2011-12." Kentucky Department of Education. 26 Sept. 2012. Web. 30 May 2016. http://bit.ly/2fxuDMN.

43. "ASVAB Test - NHS Counseling." ASVAB Test - NHS Counseling. Nevada High School. Web. 30 May 2016. http://bit.ly/2ghPWDN.

44. Marty, Robin. "Are Missouri Schools Helping the Military Recruit Kids?" Care 2 Petitions. 1 Mar. 2014. Web. 30 May 2016. http://bit.ly/2fVPWFV.

45. "Menu of College and Career-Ready Demonstrations." Graduation Guidelines. Colorado Department of Education. Web. 01 June 2016. http://www.cde.state.co.us/postsecondary/gradmenu.

46. "Testing." Crown Point Community School Corporation. Web. 31 May 2016. http://www.cps.k12.in.us/site/Default.aspx?PageType=6.

47. "Chapter 105 Laws of Maryland." Maryland.gov. Web. 30 May 2016. <http://bit.ly/2fxvn4l.

48. "NAACP-MD Testimony." Student Privacy.org. National Coalition to Protect Student Privacy. Web. 30 May 2016. http://bit.ly/2f4NtKv.

49. "ACLU-MD Testimony for the Senate Education, Health & Environmental Affairs Committee March 17, 2010." Student Privacy.org. National Coalition to Protect Student Privacy, 17 Mar. 2010. Web. 30 May 2016. http://bit.ly/2fZbimh. 50. "PTA-MD Testimony." Student Privacy.org. National Coalition to Protect Student Privacy. Web. 30 May 2016. http://bit.ly/2fxnlbS.

51. "Lt. Col. Beveridge Testimony." Student Privacy.org. National Coalition to Protect Student Privacy. Web. 30 May 2016. http://bit.ly/2fFY1xL.

52. Birnbaum, Michael. "Md. Law Limits Military Recruitment of High School Students." Washington Post. 15 Apr. 2010. Web. 30 May 2016. http://wapo.st/2fWpRFu.

53. "File No. 390." AN ACT CONCERNING STUDENT PRIVACY AND THE ADMINISTRATION OF THE ARMED SERVICES VOCATIONAL APTITUDE BATTERY. Connecticut General Assembly. Web. 30 May 2016. http://bit.ly/2eGov5A.

54. "Letter from Lt. Col. Coleman to Members of Connecticut's Education Committee." Connecticut General Assembly. Web. 30 May 2016. http://bit.ly/2fhghNH.

55. "The access option chosen by the school will be honored without discrimination and without adverse effect of quality or priority of service to the school." See USMEPCOM Regulation 601-4; Recruiter Release Option 3-2 a.

56. Connecticut Veterans' Committee Chair quoted in Vice Magazine. How the US Military Collects Data on Millions of High School Students. By Charles Davis; 4/24/14 http://www.vice.com/read/how-the-military-collects-data-on-millions-of-high-school-students

57. See Sec. 3-2 a. Recruiter Release Options USMEPCOM Regulation 601-4 "Only a school official will select the recruiter release option for their students. If no option is requested, the MEPS ESS will assign" http://bit.ly/2fXIGvt.

58. Group wants military recruiting info on students kept private by Ed Stannard 5/3/14 http://bit.ly/1ibOhEi.

59. In Support of Connecticut Military Service; by Rep. David Alexander; CT News Junkie, 4/28/14. http://bit.ly/2fFUFLt.

60. Telephone conversation with Diane Wood, December 28, 2013. Privacy campaigns tend to attract allies on opposite ends of the political spectrum.

61. "An Inventory of Governor George W. Bush Correspondence." Texas State Library and Archives Commission. Web. 31 May 2016. http://www.lib.utexas.edu/taro/tslac/60005/tsl-60005.html

More than 500 Navy Junior Reserve Officers Training Corps (NJROTC) cadets stand ready at Naval Station Great Lakes, Il.   WIKIMEDIA COMMONS

Chapter 12

JROTC MILITARIZES AMERICAN YOUTH

Reactionary curriculum, unqualified instructors, weapons program foster militarism

The Junior Reserve Officer Training Corps (JROTC) is a military program offered at over 3,402 high schools nationwide – 65% of them in the South – with a total enrollment of 557,129 students.[1]

Over half of these JROTC units are run by the Army, while the Navy, Air Force, and Marines each run several hundred programs. In 2009, Congress required the Secretary of Defense to implement a plan to increase the number of JROTC units to not less than 3,700 by 2020.[2]

Despite assurances by the Cadet Command regarding the voluntary nature of the JROTC program, 9th grade students are sometimes required to enroll in the military program. Quite often, schools allow JROTC to substitute for legitimate academic courses, providing a lifeline to JROTC programs that would otherwise have trouble maintaining minimum enrollment numbers.

Like other military programs operating in the nation's high schools, JROTC is marketed as a public service to American communities without revealing its tie-in to recruiting or other controversial aspects of the program. The Army says JROTC "teaches students character education, student achievement, wellness, leadership, and diversity" while fostering in each school a "more constructive and disciplined learning environment." From the perspective of the military mind, this may all be true, but in the civilian world, where there is greater emphasis on developing critical thinking skills, military notions of a more disciplined learning environment stifle creativity and smother individuality. Take, for instance, the unit on the U.S. Constitution in the Army's sophomore-year textbook. It is called "You the People" rather than "We the People." Obedience to the chain of command is valued above all. Questioning authority is not part of the curriculum.

The JROTC curriculum includes coursework on leadership, civics, geography and global awareness, health, and wellness, language arts, life skills, and U.S. history. History is described as a series of necessary military encounters and victories. The U.S. is viewed as the epicenter of the world, while multilateral solutions to complex problems are discouraged. There are numerous historical inaccuracies throughout the textbooks. Meanwhile, local school authorities exercise no control over instruction.

The curriculum is taught by retired Army personnel who rarely have teaching credentials and often have only possess a high school diploma. Their lack of formal teacher training, combined with the reactionary curriculum, produces a dangerous academic cocktail that serves to undermine the foundations of an enlightened, democratic society. In 2013, the Army alone was recycling 4,000 retired officers to run its programs in the high schools.[3]

According to the Civilian Marksmanship Program, approximately 1,600 Army, Navy, and Marine units offer rifle marksmanship programs to their cadets.[4] There are an additional 123 high school Air Force JROTC units with marksmanship programs operating in high schools across the country, according to the Civilian Marksmanship Program's Club Tracker.[5]

JROTC programs often operate in schools that aggressively enforce "no gun" zones. Many of these schools have federal and state-supported programs that teach children ways to solve conflicts nonviolently. Providing rifle practice as an integral part of state-supported education is awful public policy.

The JROTC program is controversial for several other reasons. JROTC is a non-academic elective that may put students at a disadvantage in applying for colleges and universities. Although the military claims the JROTC program is valuable to communities because it cuts down on drop-out rates, there is no statistical evidence to support the claim. Despite federal dollars to support the program, JROTC units may entail a financial loss to schools.[6] JROTC is used as a substitute for physical education programs as well as academic subjects in many schools.

The DOD spent $365 million on the program in 2013, providing uniforms, textbooks, and salaries. The funding also covers the cost of providing rifles for the JROTC Marksmanship Program.[7]

History of JROTC
JROTC programs were established by Congress in 1916 when the US public was being prepared for war against Germany. While the news-

papers relayed the drumbeat of war, the Army militarized many high schools as a means of providing ready-made soldiers should the call come for an all-out mobilization. The year before, Germany sunk the Lusitania, killing 1,197, including 128 Americans. (We know now that the ship was carrying hundreds of tons of war munitions, and the German government had published repeated warnings to passengers.) It's important to understand the mindset of the nation when Congress moved to establish junior-military squads in the nation's high schools. Just a year and a half after JROTC was established, the same Congress passed The Sedition Act of 1918, which made it a crime to "willfully utter, print, write, or publish any disloyal, profane, scurrilous, or abusive language about the form of the Government of the United States" or to "willfully urge, incite, or advocate any curtailment of the production" of the things "necessary or essential to the prosecution of the war."[8]

That would include questioning JROTC Programs that flourished in the decades to come.

Fast forward to 1964, when the US was mobilizing for the Vietnam War, and many of the same dynamics were at play. In that year, the ROTC Vitalization Act expanded JROTC programs to the Navy, Marines, and Air Force. Also, active duty Army instructors were replaced with military retirees.

Eight years later, in 1972, when the draft was coming to an end, females were first invited to participate in JROTC programs. Nationally, girls account for 42% of all Army JROTC cadets.[9]

In the aftermath of the Vietnam War, military planners, wondering how youth might be persuaded to volunteer, set their sights on the JROTC program.[10] JROTC provides a pipeline to college ROTC programs, but more importantly, the program primes the pump for a trusted supply of enlisted soldiers.

Despite repeated assurances by the Cadet Command and high school officials that the JROTC program is voluntary, there are programs across the country that require participation. For instance, all freshmen at Vincent High School in Vincent, Alabama are automatically enrolled in the school's JROTC program. Major Stanley Murrell, Commander of the public school's JROTC program, explained in 2015, "We view mandatory first semester enrollment as a huge positive and so do our administrators." Taking JROTC fulfills Alabama's mandated Character Education Instruction. Perhaps the biggest advantage is that kids who would have never considered JROTC find out it's fun and stick around."[11]

In 2010, the entire freshman class at Carvers Bay High School in South Carolina was enrolled in JROTC classes. The principal, retired from the Navy, explained the Marine Corps JROTC also fulfills the physical education requirement at the Freshman Academy.[12] In 2005, JROTC spokesperson Paul Kotakis told *The Nation* magazine that requiring students to take JROTC, "is a decision made by the individual school, not the Army."[13]

The same charade is being played out in a thousand schools that require students to take the military's enlistment test, even though the military says it's not mandatory.

The Pentagon knows how to sell JROTC in the nation's high schools. Recruiters and civilian DOD employees convince like-minded school officials to change graduation requirements to allow JROTC to substitute for academic subjects.

In 2012, Cadet Command Regulation 145-2 signaled a marked acceleration in the militarization of the nation's high schools. In it, the Army called for the creation of additional academic incentives for students to register for JROTC classes. The Army's appeal to the command structure and high school officials jeopardizes millions of instructional hours that were more likely to develop heightened creativity and critical thinking skills among millions of American youth.

From the Regulation:

> The school must, at a minimum, grant elective credit, and support credit for embedded subjects, such as physical education, performing arts, practical arts, civics, health, government, freshman focus or orientation, etc., that are taught in the JROTC curriculum (note: the JROTC curriculum will be used to meet the requirements of these courses.) Elective hours may be used for requirements outside the core, but only if four phase lesson plans are not available. Third and fourth-year Cadets should be able to earn honors credit based on their leadership and teaching responsibilities. Schools with low Cadet enrollment need to seek as much substitute credit as possible.[14]

The Army is specifically asking schools to allow its untrained instructors to meet the curricular requirements of physical education, performing arts, practical arts, civics, health, and government within the confines of its JROTC program. Where is the public indignation? Where are the unions? The policy is causing an academic train wreck.

Florida allows JROTC to substitute for physical science, biology, practical arts, and life management skills.[15] For instance, students at Boca Ciega High School in Gulfport, Florida who take JROTC for two years satisfy both the physical education and fine arts requirements for graduation.[16]

It's deeply troubling that state schools throw the arts under the bus in favor of classes that foster strait-jacketed military indoctrination.

At Spaulding High School in Barre, Vermont, students may satisfy a .5 credit requirement for U.S. government by taking JROTC for a semester.[17] The kids in Vermont may never come to understand the phrase, "We the People."

It's the same at Eagleville High School in Eagleville, Tennessee.[18] The Volunteer State provides a glimpse into how the process of accepting JROTC as a legitimate academic course works. In Tennessee students may substitute:

- Two credits of JROTC for one credit of wellness required for graduation.
- Three credits of JROTC for one-half unit of United States Government required for graduation.
- Three credits of JROTC for one-half unit of Personal Finance.

Tennessee education officials deliberated on the changes in 2014 pertaining to substituting JROTC for the required and rather complex Personal Finance course standards along with the efficacy of allowing military retirees without an appropriate subject credential to teach the contents of the course, rather than state-certified teachers. The record from the Tennessee State Board of Education provides insight into their decision to grant the waiver:

> In order to determine the best policy option to address this discrepancy, the Department of Education reviewed the Personal Finance course standards, researched the JROTC programs in Tennessee, and met with supervisors and teachers of multiple JROTC programs across the state. The Department found that JROTC instructors could meet all of the Personal Finance course requirements within the third year of JROTC, if they have received training on the Personal Finance course requirements.[19]

The measure was adopted. Aside from JROTC instructors, all other teachers must be licensed to teach Personal Finance. Only teachers who are certified in Economics, Business, Marketing, and Family and Consumer Sciences meet the employment standards.[20]

Personal finance is extraordinarily important in the lives of American school children. We examined the complexity of the Military Enlistment/ Re-enlistment Contract in the 1st chapter and the genesis of a culture that produces high school graduates who cannot understand or negotiate the complex contracts and agreements that increasingly run their lives.

Tennessee's Personal Finance Course Standards are quite impressive and cover, in detail, subjects including: the Free Application for Federal Student Aid (FAFSA) credit card agreements, consumer protection standards, writing argumentative essays, consumer credit, investment strategies, and identity theft, to mention a small sampling. Army Instructors without the necessary professional training and credentials are unqualified to teach Personal Finance.

In 2014, California became the first state to allow JROTC instructors to apply for official authorization to teach physical education in their JROTC classes. The measure was strongly opposed by PE teachers, who saw the act as an affront to their profession.

All California students must take a minimum number of PE classes; whereas JROTC is an elective. Students often register for PE to satisfy graduation requirements, rather than registering for the military course. Allowing JROTC instructors to teach PE provides a new lease on life for JROTC. Instructors must pass two tests, one in basic academic skills and another in knowledge of physical education.[21]

An examination of high school PE and JROTC classes, by Kathryn Anne Holt and others of the University of Nevada, Las Vegas, compared four JROTC classes with four PE classes, and found that students were engaged in moderate to vigorous physical activity 60% of the time in physical education and 24% of the time in JROTC.[22]

SHAPE America, The Society of Health and Physical Educators, is the nation's largest membership organization of health and physical education professionals. The group is committed to insuring that all children have the opportunity to lead healthy, physically active lives. SHAPE calls on school districts to prohibit students from substituting JROTC for PE class time or credit requirements.[23]

Meanwhile, the President's Council on Fitness, Sports, and Nutrition prominently cites several disturbing statistics on its website:
- Only one in three children are physically active every day.
- More than 80% of adolescents do not do enough aerobic physical activity to meet the guidelines for youth.
- Children now spend more than seven and a half hours a day in front of a screen (e.g., TV, video games, computer).

- Only about one in five homes have parks within a half-mile, and about the same number have a fitness or recreation center within that distance.[24]

Nonetheless, 23 states allow JROTC to take the place of physical education classes: AL, AZ, AR, CA, FL, GA, IL, IA, KY, LA, MA, MI, MS, MO, NE, NV, NM, OH, SC, TN, TX, WV, and WI.[25]

Eleven of the states are from the old south, a region of the country steeped in military traditions. The region also boasts the most overweight population in the country. Mississippi, for instance, is "the fattest state again," according to the *Washington Examiner*.[26]

Eight of the ten "fattest states" in the nation allow students to skip PE classes in favor of JROTC.[27]

Responsible school systems do not grant physical education credit for JROTC. This practice serves the narrow interests of the military but fails to address many of the standards, indicators, and objectives of physical education curricula. PE standards encompass exercise physiology, biomechanics, social psychology, and motor learning. There are numerous cross-curricular connections among PE and other disciplines.

Like the ASVAB Career Exploration Program and other recruiting operations in the schools, JROTC is extraordinarily deceptive. Military programs would be less welcome in the schools if the Pentagon fessed up about its true intentions. The Army describes the JROTC program this way:

> JROTC is a program offered to high schools that teaches students character education, student achievement, wellness, leadership, and diversity. It is a cooperative effort between the Army and the high schools to produce successful students and citizens, while fostering in each school a more constructive and disciplined learning environment. The outcomes of the JROTC program are:
>
> - Act with integrity and personal accountability as they lead others to succeed in a diverse and global workforce
>
> - Engage civic and social concerns in the community, government, and society
>
> - Graduate prepared to excel in post-secondary options and career pathways
>
> - Make decisions that promote positive social, emotional, and physical health

- Value the role of the military and other service organizations[28]

JROTC is marketed as some sort of value-driven social work program for segments of society that need remedial courses in things like character, emotional development, and personal integrity. High school websites that describe the program routinely say JROTC is not a recruiting program.

Elda Pema and Stephen Mehay, researchers from the Graduate School of Business and Public Policy at the Naval Postgraduate School in Monterey, California, recognize JROTC as a program that trains youth for military service. They wrote:

> Although it is similar to vocational education and School to Work programs, JROTC has been overlooked by education researchers. This oversight may stem from the perception that military science classes represent extracurricular activities that do not affect employment, a perception fostered by the U.S. Department of Education's classification of high school military science classes as 'enrichment/other' rather than vocational education (Levesque et al., 2000).
>
> This designation contradicts the Department of Education's own definition of career technical education as classes that teach skills required in specific occupations or occupational clusters. More important, this classification misrepresents the scope and content of JROTC. The curriculum, the use of military instructors, and the close link with the employer are clear indicators of the program's vocational orientation.
>
> Military science 'concentrators' (students with at least 3.0 Carnegie credits) receive an advanced pay grade if they enlist. About 40% of such concentrators enter the military (Taylor, 1999), which is similar to the 43% of vocational students who find jobs in training-related civilian occupations (Bishop, 1989).[29]

Policy Memorandum 50 (PM 50) from the U.S. Army Cadet Command, dated March 30, 1999, ordered JROTC teachers to help the military recruit students into the Army. The policy outlined several ways JROTC instructors were to collaborate with military recruiters.[30]

PM 50 was rescinded in 2008 after the military was forced to reconcile its public position that JROTC was founded on altruistic principles rather than serving primarily to recruit unwary youth into the armed forces. The rescission notice for Policy Memorandum simply says PM

50 is rescinded. It does not prohibit JROTC instructors from engaging in recruiting activities.

Students who spend three years in a JROTC program are eligible to enlist at the E-3 level (instead of E-1), and if they enter college ROTC, they may be given a full year of ROTC credit.[31]

As Project YANO's Rick Jahnkow puts it, "If it looks like a duck and quacks like a duck…"

Is JROTC a Recruiting Program?
- From the Navy JROTC Web site: "Approximately 40% of all NJROTC program graduates enter military service."[32]
- Defense Secretary William Cohen, testifying before the House Armed Services Committee in 2000, named JROTC "one of the best recruiting devices that we could have."[33]
- Chief of staff of U.S. Army Training and Doctrine Command, Lt. Gen. David P. Valcourt, in his address to the 2008 Joint Warfighting Conference in Virginia, said JROTC was helping "young people to consider joining the military or to make it a career."[34]
- Brig. Gen. Malcolm Frost, chief of public affairs for the U.S. Army: "It's the human aspect of touching, influencing, leading, mentoring, coaching, and counseling youth, whether they are in JROTC in high school, or whether they are in college, because if you don't get them there, then you're not going to have them five, 10, 20, or in my case, 27 years down the line."[35]
- Senate Armed Services Committee Report on the National Defense Authorization Act for Fiscal Year 2000 (S. 1059), May 17, 1999:

"The committee recognizes that there is a direct relationship between the JROTC program and recruitment. Strong testimony from the Joint Chiefs of Staff this year confirmed this relationship. More than half of the young men and women who voluntarily participate in this high school program affiliate with the military in some fashion after graduation."[36]

Aside from the work of Rick Jahnkow and The Project on Youth & Non-Military Opportunities which he heads, there is little work being done exposing the deceptive nature of the JROTC program, especially the hidden costs associated with operating a high school unit. The following segment is taken from an article entitled, "How Jr. ROTC

Contributes to the School Funding Crisis," that appears on the Project YANO website.37

> Although JROTC is a non-academic elective that does not count toward meeting admission requirements at state colleges and universities — and schools are scrambling to provide electives that do help students meet those requirements — JROTC is usually given privileged treatment by school trustees who are politically intimidated by the pro-JROTC lobby and often deceived about the money that could be saved by cutting the program.
>
> In comparison to alternative classes, JROTC is much more expensive to maintain than school administrators and trustees have been led to believe. The reason their initial assumptions are often wrong is that promoters of JROTC encourage the false belief that federal money will cover any extra costs. After approving the program, most school administrators never realize that the partial subsidy offered by the Pentagon (which comes from its recruiting budget, by the way) does not match the additional expenses generated by the high staffing requirements of the JROTC contract.
>
> Under the standard JROTC contract, the Department of Defense provides students with books, uniforms and special equipment such as air rifles. The school district must provide insurance, building facilities and maintenance, and must assume responsibility for paying instructors' salaries and all the normal employment taxes and benefits that cover regular teachers.
>
> The school district receives only a partial contribution from the DoD toward instructors' salaries and nothing toward the substantial cost of employment taxes and benefits. The subsidy amount for each instructor is calculated based on the military pay and housing allowance the officer would receive on active duty, minus his or her military retirement pay. This difference is then cut in half, and the result is the maximum amount the DoD will pay the school district.
>
> The JROTC contract requires the hiring of a minimum of two retired officers (one a non-commissioned officer) for the first 150 students enrolled as cadets at a school. After 150, another instructor must be hired for each additional increment of 100 cadets (e.g., three instructors for 151-250).

> It's important to note that only one non-JROTC classroom teacher would normally be hired to teach 150+ students. Furthermore, JROTC cadets are generally allowed by schools to take the class in place of physical education, and a single PE teacher would normally support 250+ students. So if JROTC were eliminated in a school district, less than half as many teachers would need to be hired to replace them.
>
> In other words, to have JROTC, a school district must more than double the staff normally required for the number of students involved. Because the federal subsidy amount will likely cover less than half the total salaries and none of the employment taxes or benefits for two (or more) JROTC instructors at each school, schools wind up using extra money from their budgets to, in effect, subsidize a high school military training/recruiting program for the Pentagon.

The military mandates that JROTC class enrollment must not drop below 100 students or 10% of the total student body, whichever is smaller. School officials sometimes involuntarily place students into JROTC classes to insure minimum numbers are met. A JROTC unit must be disbanded if it does not meet the enrollment threshold by the beginning of the following academic year.

The Army's JROTC curriculum includes course work in leadership training, civics, geography and global awareness, health, and wellness, language arts, life skills, and U.S. history. There is a separate Leadership, Education, and Training (LET) textbook for each of the four high school years.[38]

Instructors are rarely certified as in the subjects that they will be covering, and some of them have only high school diplomas.

The textbook, published by Prentice Hall, teaches a reactionary and dangerous version of US history and government. American high school officials offer no curricular oversight.

Consider the treatment of the dropping of atomic bombs over Hiroshima and Nagasaki at the start of the cold war. The authors of the JROTC course book, "Leadership, Education and Training (LET 3) Custom Edition for Army JROTC," grapple with the decision to drop the atomic bomb on Japan within the context of an ethical case study where students discuss the choices and consequences inherent in a series of historical events. Rather than presenting an unbiased version of events, the discussion is tainted by a strong preference toward bombing Japan, complete with falsehoods and inexcusable omissions.

From the LET 3 Army JROTC Textbook:

ETHICAL CHOICE	CONSEQUENCES	IMPACT
Should the U.S. have invaded the home islands of Japan?	Estimated 1,000,000 Americans and many More Japanese killed.	Does the President have an obligation to reduce American casualties at the expense of the enemy?

Ultra-conservative orthodoxy courses throughout the JROTC textbook. Examine this one-sided discussion of American foreign policy taken from the LET 3 book:

> What do Americans hope for in relations with other countries? To think about that question, you might ask yourself what we, as individual Americans, want in our relations with the people around us. First of all, we want to be respected. We want others to treat us as equals. We would like to live in a safe place, free from the fear of harm. As adults, we would like to be able to earn a living. These goals are like the goals we have as a nation. In general, the foreign policy goals of the United States are to protect citizens' safety, to promote prosperity, and to work for peace and democracy in other countries. **(LET 3 p. 305)**

The JROTC textbook says a goal of foreign policy is to spread human rights and democracy:

> Human Rights and Democracy: To encourage all countries to respect the human rights of freedom, justice, and equality. Americans believe that democracy, in which citizens have the final say in their government, is the best way to protect human rights. Thus, they want to help people in other countries who are trying to form or keep democratic governments. **(LET 3 p. 306)**

These statements may seem reasonable to many, but the track record of the United States during the post-war period has earned it the scorn of much of the world. In fact, the US has been voted as the most significant threat to world peace according to a global survey conducted by the Worldwide Independent Network and Gallup at the end of 2013. People in 68 nations were asked: "Which country do you think is the greatest threat to peace in the world today?" The US topped the list, with 24% of people believing America to be the biggest danger to peace.[39]

(The survey also asked respondents which country they would most like to live in and the U.S. topped the charts.)

Although the JROTC program professes to foster critical thinking skills, it fails to allow for an examination of political currents that stray from accepted military-political orthodoxy. The cumulative effect of subjecting more than a half million American school children to this reactionary ideology has a long-term detrimental effect on the political discourse of the nation.

The following segment on "intelligence" from the textbook is unconscionable because it brazenly legitimizes violence as a tool of foreign policy.

> Much of intelligence is secret. Information is sometimes gathered by spying. Sometimes intelligence agencies have helped overturn the government of a country. In Chile in 1973, for example, the CIA took part in overthrowing the government of Salvador Allende. The United States government thought Allende was not favorable to our national interest. Like defense, diplomacy, foreign aid, and trade measures, intelligence is an important tool of foreign policy. **(LET 3 p. 308)**

This statement shamelessly appears on the same page as the discussion of the CIA overthrow of Allende's government:

> Can you remember settling a disagreement with someone by talking it out? In a similar way, the American government tries to settle disagreements with other countries peacefully. **(LET 3 p. 308)**

The Marine Corps JROTC textbooks are no better as far as historical accuracy is concerned. The Marines' treatment of post-war US history is amazingly misleading. Periods of history are purposely mischaracterized to paint the US as defenders of truth and justice. For instance, the freshman year Marine Corps text contains a completely inaccurate account of the beginnings of the Mexican-American War:

> The massing of Mexican troops on the southern bank of the Rio Grande led President Polk to order General Zachary Taylor to move to the borders. Taylor marched to the Rio Grande and fortified a position on the northern bank. The Mexican and the American troops were thus facing each other across the river. When Taylor refused to retreat to the Nueces River, the Mexican commander crossed the Rio Grande, ambushed a scouting force of 63 Americans, and killed or wounded 16 of them.[42]

The problem with this account is that the Rio Grande wasn't the border. U.S. soldiers were in Mexican territory. The Nueces River, further to the north, was the border between the two nations. The U.S. had simply made an offer the Mexicans could not refuse and that offer entailed expansion to the Rio Grande.

The Marines' brief treatment of the US invasion of the Dominican Republic in 1965 further illustrates the point that this "history" shouldn't be taught to the nation's children:

> When Donald Reid Cabral, President of the Dominican Republic was assassinated in 1965 as part of a coup, the Marines were called in to protect U.S. citizens who wished to leave the area. On April 28, 1965, Col Pedro Bartolome Benoit asked for the help of the Marines to help restore order. On April 29, 1,500 Marines were ashore at Santo Domingo until peace was restored.

President Cabral wasn't assassinated in 1965. He died in 2006 at the age of 83. President Johnson's decision to invade the Dominican Republic was based on faulty intelligence. The U.S. military was invading the Dominican Republic to protect U.S. business interests for the fourth time in 58 years, although the authors of the JROTC text fail to mention it.[43]

Not to be outdone, The *Navy's Naval Science 2* JROTC text also misrepresents history. The textbook carries this account of the 1983 Grenada invasion:

> In late October 1983, in response to a takeover of the Caribbean island nation of Grenada by Cuban-backed Communist forces, a joint U.S. task force with elements of all services conducted a major amphibious operation and took control of the island in three days.[44]

Grenada never experienced a takeover by Cuban-backed forces. The Reagan Administration cited an airstrip that Cuban nationals were helping to build as a premise for the attack. The British government was helping to fund the project which was designed to enable large commercial jets to land on the island, helping to expand tourism. The U.N. General Assembly condemned the invasion as "a flagrant violation of international law" by a vote of 108 to 9. These crucial details are omitted from the text.

The services claim JROTC programs help students academically. In 2013, however, researchers at Northwestern University compared two groups of Chicago high school students of "low socio-economic status" who were enrolled in either a music training program or JROTC. After two years, the students who'd had music training showed measurable neurological development while kids in the JROTC program showed no significant change. The Army says the JROTC program promotes the "capacity for life-long learning." Evidence shows, however, that music training may be more beneficial.[46]

The Navy JROTC command claims its cadets "are better behaved, have higher attendance, are role models for the avoidance of substance abuse, have higher self-esteem, develop positive life skills, on average have higher grade point averages and graduate at a higher rate."[47] Perhaps, but JROTC cherry-picks its students by excluding those who don't meet academic and behavioral standards.

The Western New York Maritime Charter School in Buffalo provides a telling case study. Maritime is affiliated with the Navy Junior ROTC program, and Maritime's student cadets are all JROTC participants. The school has the highest attrition rate by far of any of Buffalo's 15 charter schools, almost three times the other schools, according to a 2015 report by the Buffalo News. 24.2% of Maritime's students were expelled, suspended or withdrew during the 2013-2014 school year. The average of those who departed from the other 14 charter schools was just 8.4%. 27 of the Maritime students who returned to the regular district schools were expelled by Maritime. No local charter school expelled so many children. The senior class was only half the size of its freshman class.[48]

According to Army regulations, a student must maintain an acceptable standard of academic achievement and standing as required by JROTC and the school. Essentially, this and other JROTC regulations mandate removing those cadets who are not making normal progress toward graduation, which makes it impossible to establish whether the program is responsible for improving student's academic success.[49]

Each Army JROTC unit is staffed with a minimum of one retired Army Officer known as a Senior Army Instructor (SAI) and one retired Non-commissioned Officer, known as an Army Instructor. (AI) Both must be recently retired from the Army. SAI's must possess a Baccalaureate degree or higher from an accredited educational institution while AI's must possess a minimum of an associate's degree within five years of the initial hire date.[50]

According to the Cadet Command Regulation 145-2, "Cadet command encourages all JROTC Instructors to be recognized as certified teachers and future training and educational experiences should be tailored to reflect that commitment." The JROTC regulations make it clear that Army certification of instructors is not meant to "supersede or usurp the state/district licensing or school requirements for local continuing certification." It's a good thing. Otherwise, educational standards would suffer.

The Army JROTC website for prospective employees directs candidates to click on the links to each state's teacher licensing website to determine additional licensing requirements, although most states defer to the Army to certify woefully under-qualified instructors. Although the Army encourages its instructors to be recognized by state authorities as fully-certified instructors, this is wishful thinking. States typically require Baccalaureate degrees for high school teachers, along with several classes of teacher education courses, in addition to a semester of student teaching. Many states now require teachers to earn a Master's degree in their discipline after a few years of teaching.

Meanwhile, many states offer a special subjects teaching credential for JROTC instructors that allows them to significantly circumvent the standards for regular teaching credentials. In California, for example, the academic requirement for a JROTC special subjects credential is a high school diploma or GED. For additional criteria, the state mostly relies upon the certification given by the military.[51]

The JROTC School of Cadet Command administers certification and recertification training. Certification includes completion of two courses, a distance learning course, and a resident course. To be certified, new instructors must complete the distance learning course within six months of hire and the resident course within twelve months of hire. That means new AI's may move from active duty to the classroom with a high school diploma and no training, while SAI's may teach without a single course on how to teach. It is an affront to the teaching profession.

In 2015, the Army relaxed its qualifications for classroom instructors. In 2006 the Army had strengthened its qualifications for noncommissioned officers seeking to fill an AI position in the high school JROTC program. The Army said all instructors had to be high school graduates and that all should hold the minimum of an associate's degree by January 1, 2009. Apparently, the regulation was too onerous for many. Now they allow AI's to teach for five years before earning an associate's degree.[52]

As we've seen, approximately 1,723 JROTC units, a little over half of the total, carry marksmanship programs. People always seem to be shocked to learn that the local high school has a shooting range in the basement or converts its gym or classrooms for rifle practice. For the most part, the shooting ranges continue to operate with little public knowledge or opposition. As we discovered in our discussion of the Civilian Marksmanship Program, Fairfax County Virginia school officials who monitor environmental health, didn't realize hundreds of students in their system were engaged in firearm practice.

In 2007, however, a grassroots group in San Diego launched a successful campaign to ban all shooting ranges in the district's schools.

The San Diego Unified School District Board of Education approved this resolution:

> "WHEREAS, the San Diego Unified School District has a zero-tolerance policy on weapons in schools and seeks, as one of its primary goals, to teach students to resolve conflicts without resorting to violence; and
>
> "WHEREAS, the District cannot risk sending a mixed message to students when some of their lives have been recently taken by gun violence;
>
> "NOW, THEREFORE, BE IT RESOLVED, that any existing school district property used for shooting ranges shall be immediately closed for that purpose and converted for other educational uses by the beginning of the next regular school year.
>
> "BE IT FURTHER RESOLVED, that marksmanship training, whether it is conducted on-campus or off-campus, and through textbooks or physical instruction, shall not be taught in connection with the San Diego Unified School District and shall be discontinued immediately."

This was an amazing victory. Rick Jahnkow of Project YANO was involved in organizing opposition. He said there was a prevailing feeling in disadvantaged communities struggling to reduce violence rooted in poverty and political neglect, and that programs involving weapons training in the schools were insensitive and inappropriate.[53]

At San Diego's Mission Bay High School, a coalition of students, parents, and activists focused on eliminating the existence of rifle shooting ranges, the practice of falsely claiming that JROTC would help students qualify for college, and the automatic placement of students in the course. Organizers felt that concentrating on these factors would drive down enrollment numbers, causing units to fall below the 100-student minimum necessary to keep the program afloat. Within two years, enrollment in the Mission Bay High School JROTC program had fallen to just 58 students, ultimately causing the complete removal of the program at that school.[54]

Americans are taking steps to halt the militarization of their public schools. In the next chapter, we'll examine international pressure to support them.

Notes – Chapter 12

1. Jones, Ann. "TomDispatch.com." Tomgram: Ann Jones, Suffer the Children. Tommdispatch, 15 Dec. 2013. Web. 22 June 2016. http://bit.ly/2fZfyC8.

2. NATIONAL DEFENSE AUTHORIZATION ACT FOR FISCAL YEAR 2013; R E PO R T OF THE COMMITTEE ON ARMED SERVICES HOUSE OF REPRESENTATIVES ON H.R. 4310 Junior Reserve Officers' Training Corps

3. Jones, Suffer the Children.

4. Miles, Dale. "CMP Develops new JROTC Marksmanship Instructor Course.". Civilian Marksmanship Program, n.d. Web. 31 July 2014. http://www.odcmp.org/0305/JMIC.asp.

5. "CMP Club & Competition Tracker | Club Search." CMP Club & Competition Tracker | Club Search. Civilian Marksmanship Program, n.d. Web. 22 June 2016. https://ct.thecmp.org/app/v1/index.php?do=clubSearch.

6. "Some Objections to JROTC." Project on Youth and Non-Military Opportunities. N.p., n.d. Web. 22 June 2016. http://www.projectyano.org/pdf/Jrotcobj_11-02.pdf.

7. Jones, Suffer the Children.

8. "The Sedition Act of 1918." PBS.org. PBS, n.d. Web. 23 June 2016. http://to.pbs.org/2f4M1b5.

9. Parker, Chris. "More Women Joining JROTC Programs." Tribunedigital-mcall. N.p., 27 May 2002. Web. 23 June 2016. http://bit.ly/2fVQUSw.

10. Jones, Suffer the Children.

11. Robinson, Phoebe Donald. "Vincent JROTC Cadet Interviews WW II Vet." Shelby County Reporter. N.p., 21 Oct. 2015. Web. 12 July 2016. http://bit.ly/2eGrVW9.

12. Martin, Anthony. "Is the Government Pushing High School Students into Junior ROTC Programs?" Examiner.com. N.p., 26 Aug. 2010. Web. 12 July 2016.http://bit.ly/2fXSllL.

13. Houppert, Karen. "Who's Next?" The Nation. N.p., 2005. Web. 12 July 2016. https://www.thenation.com/article/whos-next/.

14. Cadet Command Regulation 145-2 Junior Reserve Officers' Training Corps Program (A Citizenship and Leadership Development Program) Organization, Administration, Operations, Training and Support Headquarters U.S Army Cadet Command Fort Knox, Kentucky 1 February 2012 http://tinyurl.com/jomdhnt.

15. "FLORIDA DEPARTMENT OF EDUCATION DOE INFORMATION DATABASE REQUIREMENTS." Florida Department of Education. N.p., 1 July 2013. Web. 26 June 2016. http://bit.ly/2fWAZlC.

16) "Curriculum Guide 2015-2016." Boca Ciega High School. Michael Vague, Principal, n.d. Web. 12 July 2016. http://bit.ly/2ghgh4a.

17. Ibid.

18. "Welcome to Eagleville High School!" Eagleville High School. N.p., n.d. Web. 12 July 2016. P. 3 http://bit.ly/2fFXNqD.

19. "JROTC Course Substitution for Personal Finance." Tennessee State Board of Education. N.p., 25 July 2014. Web. 13 July 2016. http://bit.ly/2f4VbEx.

20. "JROTC Course Substitution for Personal Finance." Tennessee State Board of Education. N.p., 25 July 2014. Web. 13 July 2016. http://bit.ly/2fFWMyO.

21. EdSource Military instructors granted PE authorization. By Jane Meredith Adams | July 10, 2014 Ed Source http://bit.ly/2fVUMD6.

22. Holt, et al., Kathryn Anne. "Digital Scholarship@UNLV." Digital Scholarship @ UNLV. University of Las Vegas, 1 May 2012. Web. 24 June 2016 http://digitalscholarship.unlv.edu/thesesdissertations/1577/.

23. "Shape of the Nation - Status of Physical Education in the USA." SHAPE.org. Society of Health and Physical Educators, 2016. Web. 26 June 2016. P. 13 http://bit.ly/2fhetEb.

24. "President's Council on Fitness, Sports & Nutrition." Facts & Statistics -. N.p., n.d. Web. 24 June 2016. http://www.fitness.gov/resource-center/facts-and-statistics/.

25. AL, AZ, AR, FL, GA, IL, IA, KY, LA, MA, MI, MS, MO, NE, NV, SC, TN, TX "President's Council on Fitness, Sports & Nutrition." Facts & Statistics N.p., n.d. Web. 24 June 2016. http://bit.ly/2ghlTM0.

CA - "Physical Education FAQs." - Physical Education (CA Dept of Education). N.p., n.d. Web. 24 June 2016. http://www.cde.ca.gov/pd/ca/pe/physeducfaqs.asp NM, WV, WI - "Shape of the Nation - Status of Physical Education in the U.S." Voices for Healthy Kids.org. N.p., n.d. Web. 24 June 2016. http://bit.ly/2fhha8G.

OH - "Frequently Asked Questions about the Physical Education Graduation and Waiver Requirements." Home. Ohio Department of Education, n.d. Web. 24 June 2016.

26. Mississippi the fattest state again By ROBERT KING • 5/27/15 Washington Examiner http://washex.am/1FP94gQ

27. "Mississippi Is the Fattest State for 10th Straight Year, Colorado Still Leanest, Arkansas Getting Fatter, D.C. Slimmer." Calorie Lab. N.p., n.d. Web. 26 June 2016. http://calorielab.com/news/2015/10/31/fattest-states-2015/.

28. "JROTC Program Information - U.S. Army JROTC." JROTC Program Information - U.S. Army JROTC. U.S. Army, n.d. Web. 23 June 2016.

http://bit.ly/2cxLaLk.

29. Economics of Education Review 31 (2012) 680–693 Economics of Education Review journal homepage. April 2012. www.elsevier.com/locate/econedurev.

30. "Memorandum for Region Commanders." United States Army Cadet Command. U.S. Army, 30 Mar. 1999. Web. 23 June 2016. http://bit.ly/2ghoSnl.

31. "Department of Defense Instruction Number 1205.13." Department of Defense. N.p., 6 Feb. 2006. Web. 23 June 2016. http://bit.ly/2fxumJO.

32. "Navy Junior Reserve Officers Training Corps - Basic Facts." Navy Junior Reserve Officers Training Corps - Basic Facts. U.S. Navy, n.d. Web. 23 June 2016. http://www.njrotc.navy.mil/facts.html.

33. Jones, Ann. "TomDispatch.com." Tomgram: Ann Jones, Suffer the Children. Tomdispatch, 15 Dec. 2013. Web. 22 June 2016. http://bit.ly/2fZfyC8.

34. Gilmore, Gerry J. "General Cites Challenging Recruiting Environment." U.S. Army.mil. N.p., 19 June 2008. Web. 24 June 2016. http://bit.ly/2fXRn9n.

35. Ferreira, Gabby. "General Spreads Word about the Army." Indianapolis Star. N.p., 2015. Web. 24 June 2016. http://indy.st/1KUcPV4.

36. "NATIONAL DEFENSE AUTHORIZATION ACT FOR FISCAL YEAR 2000."
106TH CONGRESS 1ST SESSION SENATE, 17 May 1999. Web. 24 June 2016. http://bit.ly/2f4QBWS.

37. Jahnkow, Rick. "How Jr. ROTC Contributes to the School Funding Crisis." Project on Youth and Non-Military Opportunities. N.p., n.d. Web. 24 June 2016. http://bit.ly/2fXSuWx.

38. "Leadership, Education & Training 3."FLHS PATRIOT BATTALION JROTC. Army Junior Reserve Officer Training Corps, Prentice Hall, 2005. Web. 24 June 2016. http://www.flhspatriotbattalion.com/let-3.html

39. "US the Biggest Threat to World Peace in 2013 – Poll." RT International. Russia Today, 2 Feb. 2014. Web. 24 June 2016. https://www.rt.com/news/us-biggest-threat-peace-079./.

40. "Strong Protest by the Chinese Government Against The Bombing by the US-led NATO of the Chinese Embassy in the Federal Yugoslavia". Ministry of Foreign Affairs of the People's Republic of China. November 17, 2001. Retrieved October 22, 2009.

41. "Truth Behind America's Raid on Belgrade." The Guardian. Guardian News and Media, 27 Nov. 1999. Web. 24 June 2016. http://bit.ly/2ghVs9D.

42. U.S. Marine Corps Junior Reserve Officers' Training Corps Textbook LE 1. p. 339 http://bit.ly/2fWz2FR.

43. MCJROTC Textbook LE 1. P. 357.

44. "Naval Science 2 Maritime History, Leadership, and Nautical Sciences for the NJROTC Student." Naval Institute Press, 2006. Web. 25 June 2016. P. 138 http://bit.ly/2f4Wao6.

45. Spence, Rebecca. "Church-State Crusader Takes Aim at ROTC." The Forward. N.p., 25 May 2007. Web. 25 June 2016. http://bit.ly/2f4UkUa.

46. Sukel, Kayt. "Music Offers a Boost to Education in Low-SES Environments." Music Offers a Boost to Education in Low-SES Environments. The Dana Foundation, 2 Dec. 2013. Web. 25 June 2016. http://bit.ly/2fZa62a.

47. "Navy Junior Reserve Officers Training Corps - What Is NJROTC?" Navy Junior Reserve Officers Training Corps - What Is NJROTC? N.p., n.d. Web. 25 June 2016. http://www.njrotc.navy.mil/what_is_njrotc.html.

48. Tan, Sandra. "High Number of Expulsions at Western New York Maritime Charter School Draw Questions - The Buffalo News." Www.buffaloNews.com. N.p., 10 May 2015. Web. 25 June 2016. http://bit.ly/1Rtapiq.

49. "Cadet Command Regulation 145-2." Organization, Administration, Operations, Training and Support. U.S Army Cadet Command, 1 Feb. 2012. Web. 25 June 2016. Section 3-14(c) http://bit.ly/2eGv5sV.

50. "Cadet Command Regulation 145-2." Organization, Administration, Operations, Training and Support. U.S Army Cadet Command, 1 Feb. 2012. Web. 25 June 2016. Section 4-9(4) http://bit.ly/2eGv5sV.

51. State of California Commission on Teacher Credentialing. Designated Subjects, Special Subjects,, Teaching Credentials. Credential Leaflet 699. http://www.ctc.ca.gov/credentials/leaflets/cl699.pdf.

52. "Instructor Qualification Packet." US Army JROTC. U.S. Army Cadet Command, 18 June 2015. Web. 25 June 2016. P. 6 http://bit.ly/2f4Sanr.

53. Jahnkow, Rick. "The Gun Problem No One Talks About: Shooting Ranges in Schools." Vietnam Veterans Against the War: THE VETERAN:. N.p., Spring 2013. Web. 25 June 2016. http://www.vvaw.org/veteran/article/?id=2241.

54. "Recruiting Policy Victory." Education Not Arms Coalition. Project YANO, n.d. Web. 25 June 2016. http://www.projectyano.org/educationnotarms.

United Nations

CRC/C/OPAC/USA/CO/2

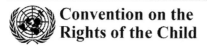
Convention on the Rights of the Child

Distr.: General

28 January 2013

ADVANCE UNEDITED VERSION

Original: English

Committee on the Rights of the Child

Optional Protocol on the involvement of children in armed conflict

Voluntary recruitment

1. The Committee expresses concern that approximately 10% of recruits enrolled in the armed forces are under 18 years and regrets that the State party does not intend to raise the age of voluntary recruitment to 18 years. The Committee is also concerned that:

(a) Recruitment policies and practices, including the quota system, undermine the safeguards contained in article 3.3 of the Optional Protocol and question the voluntary nature of the recruitment of children below the age of 18 years;

(b) Under the *No Child Left Behind Act*, schools are required to provide military recruiters access to secondary school students' names, addresses and telephone listings, and that parents are not always informed of their right to request not to release such information and parental or legal guardian's consent has not always been obtained, as observed in its previous concluding observations (CRC/C/OPAC/USA/CO/1 para. 15); and

(c) Parents and children are often unaware of the voluntary nature of the Armed Services Vocational Aptitude Battery (ASVAB) test organized in schools or its links to the military and that in some instances, students were reportedly informed that the test was mandatory.

Chapter 13

U.S. FLOUTS U.N. PROTOCOL ON CHILD SOLDIERS

Forced military testing, recruitment of 17-year-olds, lack of parental consent, violate treaty

In 2013, the UN's Committee on the Rights of the Child called on the Obama Administration to "Ensure that schools, parents, and pupils are made aware of the voluntary nature of the Armed Services Vocational Aptitude Battery (ASVAB) before consenting to the participation [sic] into it." The remarks were adopted by the Committee on the Rights of the Child at its sixty-second session (14 January–5 2013) regarding the Optional Protocol on the Involvement of Children in Armed Conflict (OPAC).[1] This was the first time the U.N. had indicated its concern with widespread military testing in American public high schools.

Mandatory ASVAB testing is a violation of OPAC Article 3.3, which states:

> States Parties that permit voluntary recruitment into their national armed forces under the age of 18 years shall maintain safeguards to ensure, as a minimum, that:
>
> (a) Such recruitment is genuinely voluntary;
>
> (b) Such recruitment is carried out with the informed consent of the person's parents or legal guardians;
>
> (c) Such persons are fully informed of the duties involved in such military service;
>
> (d) Such persons provide reliable proof of age prior to acceptance into national military service.[2]

American high school students who take the ASVAB, a military enlistment test, often do so involuntarily without parental consent. The primary purpose of the testing regime is to procure leads for recruiters.

The U.N. targeted the U.S. military's practices partly based on the 2012 report by London-based Child Soldiers International to the Committee on the Rights of the Child. Child Soldiers International cited the concerns of the National Coalition to Protect Student Privacy regarding the ASVAB's circumvention of privacy laws and the military's ability to extract sensitive student information without parental consent.

CHILD SOLDIERS INTERNATIONAL

From the Child Soldiers International Report:

> The military also uses the ASVAB to obtain students' personal contact information, including their name, address, phone number and social security details. Crucially, unlike the No Child Left Behind (NCLB) act, parents do not have the ability to opt out and prevent their child's personal information from being released to third parties. Therefore, student information that has been withheld by opting out of NCLB can be released to the military via the ASVAB. Whilst schools have the ability to prevent data from being passed on to the military, information from the National Coalition to Protect Student Privacy indicates that few school administrators are aware of this. Various sources have indicated that children are often unaware of the voluntary nature of the test or its links to the military, and there have been instances of students being actively informed that the test was mandatory. Child Soldiers International contends that the ASVAB infringes children's privacy, and is an enabler for military recruiters to target under-18's.[3]

In response to the Committee's desire that the U.S. ensure that the public is aware of the voluntary nature of the testing regime, the Obama Administration denied the mandatory nature of the administration of the ASVAB. In the same year, the US replied to the Committee,

"Participation in the ASVAB CEP is entirely voluntary. The DOD does not require schools to participate, nor does it require schools to test all students within a participating school."[4]

Yet, statistics furnished to the National Coalition to Protect Student Privacy by the U.S. Military Entrance Processing Command clearly list nearly a thousand high schools that require testing. Meanwhile, many schools that allow the military to test entire classes of students are identified by USMEPCOM as voluntarily administering the ASVAB.

USMEPCOM regulation 601-4 is vague regarding the role of DOD personnel and the forced testing of children in American high schools:

> Voluntary aspect of the ASVAB CEP - School and student participation in the ASVAB CEP is voluntary. DoD personnel are prohibited from suggesting to school officials or any other influential individual or group that the test be made mandatory. Schools will be encouraged to recommend most students participate in the ASVAB CEP. If the school requires all students of a particular group or grade to test, the MEPS will support it.[5]

As we've read, the test is marketed as a "career exploration program" in the schools while its primary purpose is to "produce leads for recruiters," according to recruiting manuals.

The U.S. response to the committee is also off the mark regarding the release of student information to military recruiters gained through the administration of the ASVAB. The U.S. falsely states, "The school can choose an option that prohibits any information on any student from being made available to recruiters. If a school does not choose that option, each student can choose whether his or her information will be made available to recruiters."[6]

It is correct that school officials may allow the military to proctor the test without results being released to children, but military regulations are clear that "only school officials will select the recruiter release option for their students."[7] Students may not make this determination. After all, they're minors, and state laws generally prohibit the release of student information without parental consent.

The U.S defense of ASVAB testing is prefaced by the following:

> 20 USC § 7908 specifically provides access to name, address, and telephone listings of high school students by military recruiters and

institutions of higher education; § 7908 also provides that a parent or student may request that such information not be provided without prior written parental consent.[8]

20 USC § 7908 is the federal law that requires high schools to turn over a student's name, address, and phone number to recruiters provided that parents are given an opportunity to "opt out" of the lists being sent to recruiters.[9] However, students and parents do not play a role in the release of information to recruiters made possible through the administration of the ASVAB. The U.S. response is misleading.

To be clear, a parent may request that her child's name, address, and phone number not be forwarded to recruiters pursuant to 20 USC § 7908, but this information and much more is sent to recruiters through the administration of the ASVAB, even if a parent has exercised her right under the opt-out measure.

The Committee also asked, "Could the U.S. provide information on the measures taken to restrict the presence of military recruiters on school grounds?" Predictably, the US response was that it does not see a *requirement or need* to restrict the presence of military recruiters on high school grounds. The exchange points to the cultural sea of difference between the two entities. The internationalists in Geneva are abhorred at the notion of military recruiters mixing in with vulnerable youth within the safe confines of a high school campus. It's unheard of throughout Europe and unthinkable throughout most of the world, (aside from the practice of militarizing and recruiting children through the madrasas of a handful of Islamic states.)

The Americans don't see anything wrong with the practice. The parties hold deep resentments toward one another, and there's a kind of passive-aggressive element behind these questions and answers. The treaty requires the recruitment of minors to be carried out with the informed consent of a child's parents. From the U.N.'s perspective, this agreement is compromised if recruiters are allowed regular access to children at school. The Americans feel they must recruit 200,000 yearly to maintain force strength and access to the high schools is necessary.

U.S. exceptionalism factors into the philosophical rift between the world's greatest power and the world's leading international organization. When the U.S. ratified OPAC in 2002, it filed a declaration of reservations to the optional protocol, assuming no obligations under the Convention on the Rights of the Child.[10]

The U.S. signed the protocol with the "understanding" that nothing in the Protocol establishes a basis for jurisdiction by any international tribunal, including the International Criminal Court. It is an extraordinary act of unilateralism. The US took exception to Article 1 of the treaty which says in its entirety, "States parties shall take all feasible measures to ensure that members of their armed forces who have not attained the age of 18 years do not take a direct part in hostilities."

This is how the US responded:

> The term "feasible measures" means those measures that are practical or practically possible, taking into account all the circumstances ruling at the time, including humanitarian and military considerations; the phrase "direct part in hostilities"- means immediate and actual action on the battlefield likely to cause harm to the enemy because there is a direct causal relationship between the activity engaged in and the harm done to the enemy; and does not mean indirect participation in hostilities, such as gathering and transmitting military information, transporting weapons, munitions, or other supplies, or forward deployment." It concludes, "Any decision by any military commander, military personnel, or other person responsible for planning, authorizing, or executing military action, including the assignment of military personnel, shall only be judged on the basis of all the relevant circumstances and on the basis of that person's assessment of the information reasonably available to the person at the time the person planned, authorized, or executed the action under review, and shall not be judged on the basis of information that comes to light after the action under review was taken.

These 'understandings' amount to a blanket reservation to Article 1, the substance of which runs contrary to the purpose of OPAC, and should be withdrawn, as the Committee on the Rights of the Child continues to demand. This is a slap in the face to the international community, although not surprising, considering the unilateralist stance of the U.S. regarding treaties designed to regulate weaponry and war making.

The U.S. provided the following statistics showing the number and percentage of 17-year-olds serving in the armed forces: [11]

	2009	2010	2011	3 Yr. Avg.	3 Yr. Total
Total Accessions	295,505	282,638	270,066	283,070	849,209
Total # 17 YO Access.	17.809	13,300	13,963	15,024	45,072
% Accessions that were 17	6.01	4.71	5.17	5,29	5.31

The committee asked what steps the U.S. is taking to disseminate the information related to the protocol to the general public and the training of professionals working with children. In response, the U.S. stated the US government is sharing the text of the Optional Protocol and related materials widely at all levels of government and to the public. However, school administrators across the country, who are on the front lines between recruiters and school children, are largely unaware of OPAC.

The U.S. was asked by the committee to respond to the conclusions of the 2010 US Government Accountability Office (GAO) report, "Clarified Reporting Requirements and Increased Transparency Could Strengthen Oversight over Recruiter Irregularities" which indicated that despite progress, the military's system of tracking and sharing recruiter irregularities was inadequate.[12]

The US responded to the committee, "The GAO stated in its conclusions that all components of the military services had made "substantial progress since 2006 in increasing their oversight over recruiter irregularities. The U.S. response continues, "Collectively, steps have been taken to improve the service components' sharing of recruiter irregularity data, the clarity of reporting guidance from the Office of the Secretary of Defense, and the transparency of the data reported to DOD."[13]

The US did not respond to the main findings of the GAO report pertaining to the year 2008:

- The most common type of recruiter irregularity reported by all service components except the Air Force Reserve involved the concealment or falsification of documents or information.

- Recruiters failing to obtain parental signatures on an applicant's application form constituted the second most commonly reported type of recruiter irregularity in the Army.

- The types of actions taken against recruiters who committed irregularities in fiscal year 2008 varied by service component. For example, the type of action most commonly applied in the Marine Corps was removal from recruiting. In contrast, the type of action most commonly applied in the Army was adverse administrative action, such as placing a letter of reprimand in the recruiter's permanent personnel file.[14]

As a result of the GAO findings, the DOD requested the RAND Corporation to produce its 2010 report, "An Analysis of the Incidence of Recruiter Irregularities."

The RAND report does not address systemic irregularities like those related to the administration of the ASVAB Career Exploration Program in the schools or the continued problems associated with the opt-out procedures outlined in Section 9528 of the No Child Left Behind Act. (Now Section 8025 Every Child Succeeds Act). Instead, RAND cites poor DOD record keeping regarding recruiter irregularities. It reports:

> Currently, it is unclear what information is concealed or falsified. Without understanding whether most cases involve medical conditions, ASVAB testing, dependency status, or other eligibility criteria, it is difficult to identify what aspects of the enlistment process require greater oversight or possible reengineering.[15]

The RAND report also points to recruiting irregularities that are more likely to occur at the very end of the month when recruiters are "on the hook" to meet their quotas.

The U.N. committee also asked the U.S. a series of questions pertaining to the administration of the JROTC program in high schools across the country. In its reply U.S. makes three assertions that are misleading.
- JROTC is voluntary
- JROTC instructors are employees of the schools
- Students in JROTC are not affiliated with any U.S. military service.

As we've seen, students in some public high schools are required to take JROTC when they register for 9th-grade classes. The military is playing the same game with the international community that it plays with the American public. JROTC isn't required by the military, but it may be required by school officials. It's the same with ASVAB testing. The military doesn't require high school students to take the ASVAB but it may be required by school officials who are willing to cede their authority to the military. There's a pattern to the obfuscation.

It is deceptive for the US to claim that JROTC instructors are employees of the schools. Being an employee of a school would suggest that school authorities exercise control over educational levels, training, and licensure of instructors. Schools exercise no such control over JROTC instructors. Being an employee of a school would also suggest that schools exercise curricular and instructional oversight over course materials. Schools cede this authority to the military regarding the JROTC program.

And, it is absurd to suggest that JROTC students are not affiliated with any U.S. military service. More than a half million students wear military uniforms. JROTC cadets receive special treatment if they directly enlist. They are given an advanced pay grade (E-2 or E-3 instead of the usual E-1). Graduating cadets are enticed to join college ROTC programs by offering them a year of ROTC credit.

After considering the U.S. response, the Committee adopted the following suggestions and observations:

- Amend the 2008 Child Soldiers Accountability Act in order to criminalize the recruitment and use of children in armed conflict up to the age of 18 years.

- Reconsider recruitment policies and practices, by inter alia amending the No Child Left Behind Act and to ensure that recruitment practices do not actively target persons under the age of 18.

- The Committee expresses concern that approximately 10% of recruits enrolled in the armed forces are under 18 years and regrets that the State party does not intend to raise the age of voluntary recruitment to 18 years.

- The military recruitment quota system undermines the safeguards contained in article 3.3 of the Optional Protocol and question the voluntary nature of the recruitment of children below the age of 18 years.

- Under the No Child Left Behind Act, schools are required to provide military recruiters access to secondary school students' names, addresses and telephone listings, and parents are not always informed of their right to request not to release such information.

- Ensure that schools, parents, and pupils are made aware of the voluntary nature of the ASVAB before consenting to the participation into it.

- Children are not always properly informed that enrolment into the JROTC program is of a voluntary nature; in some schools, this program is used as a substitute for students enrolled in oversubscribed classes from which children cannot withdraw without losing their school credit; children enrolled into the JROTC might be trained to use weapons.

- Ensure that JROTC is not used as a substitute for regular school activity.

- Prohibit disclosure of information on students without prior parental consent and ensure that recruitment policies and practices are brought in line with the respect for privacy and integrity of children.

- Continue and strengthen monitoring and oversight of recruiter irregularities and misconduct by effective investigation, imposition of sanctions and when necessary, prosecution of recruiter misconduct.[16]

Notes – Chapter 13

1. Concluding observations on the second report of the United States of America, adopted by the Committee at its sixty-second session (14 January–5 February 2013) Section IV Prevention; Paragraphs 20 & 21. 28 January 2013 Convention on the Rights of the Child - Committee on the Rights of the Child, OPAC. http://bit.ly/2fG3Uey.

2. Ibid.

3. See pages 13 & 14 of the April, 2012 Child Soldiers International Report to the Committee on the Rights of the Child in advance of the United States of America's second periodic report on the Optional Protocol to the Convention on the Rights of the Child on the involvement of children in armed conflict. http://bit.ly/2fl6tpL

4. OPAC - Written replies of the United States of America 3 December 2012 Committee on the Rights of the Child.

5. Sec. 3-2 a. Recruiter Release Options USMEPCOM Regulation 601- 4   http://bit.ly/2fG2HDQ Sec. 3-1.e

6. OPAC - Written replies of the United States of America 3 December 2012 Committee on

the Rights of the Child.

7. USMEPCOM 601-4 sec. 3-1

8. OPAC - Written replies of the U.S.

9. 20 U.S. Code § 7908 - Armed Forces recruiter access to students and student recruiting information https://www.law.cornell.edu/uscode/text/20/7908

10. OPAC - Written replies of the United States of America 3 December 2012 Committee on the Rights of the Child.

11. OPAC - Written replies of U.S.

12. Asch, Beth and Heaton, Paul An Analysis of the Incidence of Recruiter Irregularities Rand National Defense Research Institute, 2010. www.rand.org/pubs/technical_reports/2010/RAND_TR827.pdf

13) OPAC - Written replies of the United States of America, 3 December 2012 Committee on the Rights of the Child.

14) United States Government Accountability Office Report to the Subcommittee on Military Personnel, Committee on Armed Services, House of Representatives, Military Recruiting, January, 2010.   http://www.gao.gov/new.items/d10254.pdf

15. Asch, 39

16. Concluding observations on the second report of the United States of America, adopted by the Committee at its sixty-second session (14 January–5 February 2013) Section IV Prevention; Paragraphs 20 & 21. 28 January 2013 Convention on the Rights of the Child - Committee on the Rights of the Child. Optional Protocol on the involvement of children in armed conflict http://bit.ly/2fG3Uey.

Chapter 14

CONCLUSION

The recruiting command says it must have access to students in the nation's high schools because a return to the draft is unthinkable. The military argues that opening high school doors is preferable to a return of the draft, and they admit the School Recruiting Program is the cornerstone of all military recruiting. Although there has recently been some movement to require women to register, that measure was defeated by the House in July of 2016. Regardless, the return to conscription in the near future is unlikely.

Since the early days of the George W. Bush Administration, the military has embarked on an extraordinarily deceptive campaign in the high schools to enlist youth into the armed services. During debate in the House in 2001, Rep. David Vitter (R-LA) repeated the unsubstantiated claim of the Pentagon that 2,000 high schools nationally banned recruiters from school grounds. The falsehood led to the federal law that awarded the Pentagon with the names, addresses, and phone numbers of high school children.

Americans are conditioned to "support the troops" and every aspect of entrenched militarism, although a growing number recognize militarism as a cancer on the body politic. What's wrong with the military? Why should we be concerned with military recruiters "chillin" with kids in the cafeteria?

Nearly 40% of all Army enlistees never complete their first term. Imagine the emotional suffering and excruciating pain endured by those who really didn't "volunteer" in the first place. Americans are persuaded to believe we have a volunteer force, but it is actually a "recruited" force. The perpetual demand for new recruits, coupled with a military recruiter quota system, conspires to bring vast numbers of pathetic souls into an unforgiving, hostile environment that discards pitiful, failing youth like scrap materials filling military landfills.

Nearly half of the 770,000 soldiers polled in 2014 "have little satisfaction in or commitment to their jobs." Musculoskeletal injuries in the military result in 2.2 million medical encounters yearly. Nearly half of the 1.6 million veterans of the U.S. wars in Iraq and Afghanistan have filed injury claims with the Department of Veterans Affairs. Sexual assaults are at or near record levels in the military. Only 1 in 7 victims reported their attacks, and just 1 in 10 of those cases went to trial.

Meanwhile, military recruiters scour high school campuses and social media sites to find unwitting youth to agree to the terms of the fraudulent DD Form 4, the military's Enlistment/Reenlistment Document. School, municipal, and state officials have a fiduciary duty to protect students from this predatory arrangement.

This isn't an agreement. An agreement would imply the existence of two capable parties. 18-year-olds typically don't have a clue what they're signing and that's because the schools aren't teaching them the skills necessary to survive in our corporatized society. Vulnerable youths are incapable of negotiating the contracts (credit, student loans, insurance, leasing, etc.) that rule their lives. They're red meat.

This reality is in stark contrast to the relationship between the governments of our allies and their potential recruits. Germany, for instance, encourages members of its armed forces to join associations representing their interests. Throughout much of the world, militaries are subservient to the will of democratic parliaments. In the U.S. Congress exercises financial and regulatory authority over the military, but the military also exerts tremendous influence over Congress. That's because the military is sacred in the eyes of the public.

American military recruiting is a despicable, psychological pursuit that pits carefully selected and highly trained soldiers against vulnerable children. The American Public Health Association points to the greater likelihood that the youngest soldiers will experience increased mental health risks, including stress, substance abuse, anxiety syndromes, depression, post-traumatic stress disorder, and suicide. The APHA says recruiters engage in aggressive behaviors in an attempt to gain a child's confidence and trust. Recruiters are exceptionally charming while failing to honor clear boundaries. It is despicable public policy and it's time to end it.

Despite state-sponsored propaganda suggesting otherwise, the vast majority of youth aren't interested in joining the military, while a disproportionate number of enlistments come from the reddest of red states in the old South. The U.S. unemployment rate is under 5%, so youths generally have better prospects; prospects that don't jeopardize their lives, subject them to demeaning treatment, and rob their freedom. It is entertaining to witness the litany of reasons proffered by the Pentagon explaining why Johnny isn't signing up.

Meanwhile, American youths deflect an onslaught of attempts by recruiters from all four branches who are keen on getting them on the bus to boot camp. Recruiters call landlines, cell phones, and they send emails. They mail high-quality brochures that leave out crucial facts. They lurk in chat rooms and collect data from dozens of online venues. Recruiters chill in the parking lot with kids at the local high school, and they eat lunch in the cafeteria. They're on a first-name basis with students, most who nonetheless manage to remain aloof. Recruiters are child predators, and our kids know it, often better than their parents.

The Pentagon appears to be intent on developing a permanent military caste of southern boys and others they can develop and control from the cradle to the grave. Military planners are confident it is possible to create a force of completely obedient warriors who'll always

At Last a Perfect Soldier! By Robert Minor. First published on the back cover of The Masses, July 1916.

place the mission first and never accept defeat.

The military is run by hard-core zealots, many who attempt to merge a distinctively American arch-conservative Christian orthodoxy with military training and discipline. "For God and Country" is their mantra. Paradoxically, the Army Field Manual says religious beliefs aren't allowed to contradict the values of the Army, while the mainstream churches don't object. Meanwhile, the state encourages mass killing outside of the constraints of any sort of "Just War" paradigm. Several million have been systematically slaughtered in wars promoted by the United States since World War II, usually with the tacit support of the churches. The Catholic Church leads the pro-military religious bandwagon.

Aside from three historical peace churches, the Quakers, Mennonites, and the Church of the Brethren, most mainstream churches embrace American militarism. The peace churches recognize that loving one's enemies is the heart of Christian doctrine. They remind us that Jesus said no one could serve two masters.

Mainstream clergy rival Hollywood producers in their willingness to align their sermons with military minders. Their conservative congregations might empty if they spoke the unfiltered message of the Prince of Peace - and there'd be less in the collection baskets. After all, American flags are permanent fixtures on thousands of American altars. By contrast, filmmakers are required to submit their scripts to the censors to gain access to military land, men, and machines. Real planes, ships, and exploding things sell more tickets at the box office.

Military tractor-trailers with theatre-in-the-round and gun-toting, saber rattling soldiers on killing machine motorcycles crisscross the country, searching for teenage recruits in high school parking lots. They find them in desperado towns of rusted padlocks and jobs gone elsewhere.

Babies wear "camo" diapers, and children's television programming is laced with military messaging. 8-year-olds join the Young Marines, and the high school football team is known as the Warriors. Navy fighter jets fly over the football field during homecoming's halftime. America is witnessing the "grave implications" of the "economic, political and even spiritual" influence of the military-industrial complex President Eisenhower warned us about.

The Pentagon embraces the seductive power of the trigger as a recruiting device. Mass murderers practice their craft and become numb to their premeditated killing while playing first-person shooter video games like *America's Army 3*, rated Teen, Blood, Violence. Realizing the potential, the military exploits the technology to recruit and cultivate adolescent killers.

2,400 high schools have marksmanship programs affiliated with the Junior Reserve Officer Training Corps Program and the congressionally-chartered Civilian Marksmanship Program. Children are taught to fire air rifles that are classified as lethal weapons by the military. Many schools allow shooting to occur during school hours in classrooms and gyms that are contaminated by lead fragments that become airborne and are deposited on the floor at the muzzle-end and at the target backstop. Loose enforcement of regulations creates a health hazard for students and custodial staff. School and public health officials say the practice is safe and point to the Civilian Marksmanship Program's "Guide to Lead Management for Air Gun Shooting," a publication that relies on outdated and faulty science.

The US military maintains an Orwellian database known as Joint Advertising, Marketing Research & Studies (JAMRS) containing intimate details on 30 million youth between the ages of 16 and 25, providing local recruiters with sensitive, personal information to lure youth within their geographic zones. Since 2002, the Department of Defense has had access to the names, addresses, and phone numbers of nearly all high school students. The information is fed into the JAMRS database. The virtual presence of recruiters in the lives of American youth has become very real. Military recruiters infiltrate a myriad of social platforms where youth spend their lives. The data gained is meticulously stored, both locally and nationally.

The most sought-after data pertains to a child's cognitive abilities. It is data the Pentagon cannot purchase outright or find online, and it is gained through the deceptive administration of the Armed Services Vocational Aptitude Battery, (ASVAB) in 12,000 high schools. The ASVAB is a 3-hour exam masquerading as a career exploration program that tests a child's verbal and math abilities along with knowledge of general science, electronics, auto, and shop. ASVAB results are the only student information leaving America's classrooms without parental consent, a violation of FERPA, the Family Educational Rights and Privacy Act.

The Pentagon's greatest asset in the schools, however, is the Junior Reserve Officers' Training Corps, (JROTC). Over a half million children are indoctrinated into military culture while 40% who complete the program enlist in the armed forces. JROTC operates as a beachhead of sorts in the schools. It is often the center of military intelligence gathering. JROTC textbooks teach a rabid and reactionary brand of U.S. history and government, while classes are often taught by military retirees with no college education. The program puts guns into the hands of tens of thousands of children, often in schools with "no gun" policies.

Because of many of the abuses documented herein, the U.S. has come under fire from the UN's Committee on the Rights of the Child regarding adherence to the Optional Protocol on the Involvement of Children in Armed Conflict (OPAC). In short, the treaty calls for criminalizing the recruitment and use of children in armed conflict under the age of 18. The Committee notes that approximately 10% of recruits enrolled in the U.S. armed forces are under 18 years of age.

The military recruitment quota system undermines the safeguards contained in the Optional Protocol regarding the voluntary nature of the recruitment of children. The Committee notes that schools are required to provide military recruiters access to secondary school students' names, addresses, and telephone listings, and parents are not always informed of their right to request not to release such information.

Despite herculean efforts by a handful of activists to publicize U.N. concerns, the issue has been largely ignored by the mainstream American media.

Resistance

Effectively challenging militarism in the high schools requires legislative and policy-based remedies. This is not meant to detract from the important work being done by hundreds of community activists who regularly visit their local high schools to provide counter-arguments to military recruiters. They've reached thousands of children, and they have a right to be in the schools. The courts recognize that the subject of military service is political in nature. If a school has created a forum for advocates of military service, it must allow a presentation of the other side.

This approach to countering recruitment, however, is considerably outmatched by the Pentagon. Some schools are visited more than a hundred times a year by recruiters while thousands of schools have JROTC programs and most encourage a staggering array of military programs. Visits once or twice a year by relatively small numbers of peace activists resonate in small circles, but they're dwarfed by the DOD's multi-billion-dollar recruiting budget that supports the constant presence of well-funded programs, recruiters, civilian employees, and pro-military school officials in schools across the country.

The most effective way to counter militarism in the schools is to appeal to moderate and progressive school board members and state legislators regarding these issues:

- The school's adherence to the specifics of the "Opt-Out" leg-

islation codified in ESSA Sec. 8025;
- The access to students enjoyed by military recruiters vis-à-vis college recruiters;
- The access enjoyed by counter-recruiters to students;
- The circumvention of FERPA by the military in its administration of the ASVAB in the nation's high schools and the resulting violation of student privacy;
- The content of the textbooks, the professionalism of the instructors, the existence of marksmanship programs, and the health hazards posed by lead particulate matter in classrooms and gyms – all associated with the JROTC program.

There's plenty in this book to begin researching these avenues of resistance.

Generally, resistance to military recruitment seems to be clustered in areas where the access military recruiters enjoy to high school students is the most regulated. An examination of the location of several dozen active "counter-recruitment" groups across the country shows that many are clustered in the northeast, the west, and in urban areas throughout the country. Whether this resistance simply mirrors local community distrust toward military recruiting or it has actually played a role in regulating the movement is a question that deserves additional study. There is data to suggest that at least in the realm of ASVAB testing, sustained community involvement translates to fewer numbers taking the test and greater regulation of military testing in the high schools.

It appears there are five distinct groups that make up the c-r movement across the country: parents, veterans and their families, religious pacifists, radical anti-imperialists, and high school students. Membership of these groups overlaps somewhat.

Often, parents are concerned their children may be put in danger by getting too close to military recruiters while at school, and their fears are justified. News reports routinely document cases of sexual misconduct, falsification of records, and inappropriate behaviors by recruiters toward youth.

Youth may enlist to exert their independence from parents. Sometimes, they sign up in angry defiance. It can be extraordinarily painful to witness. Recruiters get between rebellious teens and their disapproving parents, and these parents feel powerless, leading them to consult with counter-recruitment groups or legal counsel. There's nothing parents can do if a child has turned 18, other than attempting to convince them not to report to basic training.

There is a basic misconception among many parents when they discover their child has enlisted in the armed forces. Almost always, youths enlist in the Delayed Entry/Enlistment Program (DEP). The agreement is not binding. GI Rights counselors and attorneys trained in military law advise parents to do everything possible to talk their child out of reporting to basic training. If a recruit fails to show up, the Enlistment Agreement is void.

To repeat: Enrolled in the DEP? Having second thoughts? Don't go. Nothing will happen.

A second distinct group of counter-recruiters is made up of Vietnam, Gulf War, Iraq War and Afghanistan War veterans who may or may not be opposed to war and military service in general, but share a burning desire to tell their story and convince youth to think deeply about any decision regarding enlistment. Some veterans are conscientious objectors, and some are not. Some hold extreme political views, and some are moderates. They share a desire to counter the Top Gun - shoot-'em-up-hero myth of modern warfare. "There's no replay button in combat," they explain.

A third segment of the c-r community is comprised of disciples of the pacifist message rooted in the Gospel of Jesus Christ, who said, "Love your enemies and pray for those who persecute you." All human life is sacred; they point out. God causes his sun to rise on the evil and the good, and sends rain on the righteous and the unrighteous. It follows that we shouldn't be launching drone strikes into residential areas and glorifying war the way it is presented to our youth. Christian counter-recruiters point to a host of Biblical excerpts, like the "Parable of the Weeds," which is cited by these disciples as a clear prohibition of killing in wars:

> The kingdom of heaven is like a man who sowed good seed in his field. But while everyone was sleeping, his enemy came and sowed weeds among the wheat, and went away. When the wheat sprouted and formed heads, then the weeds also appeared.
>
> The owner's servants came to him and said, "Sir, didn't you sow good seed in your field? Where then did the weeds come from?" "An enemy did this," he replied. "The servants asked him, "Do you want us to go and pull them up?"' "No,' he answered, "because while you are pulling the weeds, you may uproot the wheat with them. Let both grow together until the harvest. At that time I will

tell the harvesters: First collect the weeds and tie them in bundles to be burned; then gather the wheat and bring it into my barn."

Catholic Workers, Presbyterian Peace Fellowship, Pax Christi, Quakers, Mennonites, Church of the Brethren draw strength from these lines. They're increasingly involved in the counter-recruitment movement.

The fourth group is comprised of passionate, youthful, anti-imperialists (for lack of a better label) who carry a visceral anti-war, anti-American message. These activists have managed to close more high school doors than they've opened. It's painful to elucidate, but they may have oddly colored hair, wear revolutionary T-shirts and bandanas. They're sometimes unruly and show disrespect toward men and women in uniform. They're justifiably angry about the crimes committed by the U.S. government, but this should never enter into the policy debate regarding military access to children. It is counter-productive counter-recruitment, and it won't work in the schoolhouse, in front of the school board, or in the legislature. These views spring from pragmatic socio-cultural considerations rather than any cultural prejudice.

Our last group of resisters is made up of high school activists who are in the front lines in this struggle. They should follow this advice:

What High School Students Can Do to De-militarize Their Schools
(Adapted - and amended - from Project YANO's list)
1. Be courteous and respectful of school and municipal authorities. You'll lose all credibility if you lose your cool.
2. Know your First Amendment rights. See the New York Civil Liberty Union's page on Youth and Student Rights.
3. Get counter-recruitment information into your schools. Make sure everything you propose is factually correct. Ask that literature racks and posters with alternative information be placed in school wherever military recruitment information is on display. Check out Project YANO's page on Literature and Resources.
4. Present Counter-Recruitment Information during career fairs: Ask career counselors to invite a group to counter the military's message or see if you can set up your own information table with reliable information from Project YANO, NNOMY, the National Coalition to Protect Student Privacy, The Committee Opposed to Militarism and the Draft, (COMD) and the American Friends Service Committee, (AFSC).

5. Keep your contact information from recruiters and help others to do the same. Let your school and your parents know that you do not want your name, address and number released to recruiters and that you want to opt out at the beginning of the school year before the lists are released. Your school should have a military recruiter opt-out form. If not, you can download one from www.projectyano.org. Educate other students and parents about the right to opt out.

6. If the ASVAB is to be given at your school, insist that the test is voluntary and that student information is not released to recruiters. The ASVAB is the military's aptitude test and is given in half of the high schools in the country so that recruiters can obtain test data and personal information on students. In order to prevent the information from automatically being given to recruiters, your school must tell the military in advance that "ASVAB Release Option 8" must be used for ALL the students who are tested. (The school decides whether student information will be shared with recruiters – not kids or parents! Most schools release information to recruiters.)

7. Counter visits from recruiters: This is when activism takes guts. It's helpful to have your parents' support:

- Stand next to recruiters and hand out truthful literature.

- Express symbolic opposition by having a student stand silently next to the recruiters dressed as the grim reaper.

- Demand recruiters are never allowed to be with students while unsupervised.

- Surround military recruiters when they sit for lunch in the cafeteria. Let them know their presence is not welcome. Are military recruiters allowed to have lunch with children in the cafeteria during lunch while college recruiters are required to meet with students by appointment in the Guidance Office? Federal law calls for military and college recruiters to have equal access to children. Complain to your principal and school board.

- Call other schools and the school board to determine recruitment policies.

- Organize a campaign for the school district to adopt a policy to regulate all recruiting activities, like the one adopted in 2010 by San

Diego Unified.

8. Investigate JROTC:

- Find out if marksmanship training is given and, if so, whether shooting ranges are present in schools.

- If shooting ranges are present, determine if the school is adhering to the stringent, "Guide to Lead Management for Air Gun Shooting" published by the Civilian Marksmanship Program.

- Find out if students are ever placed in JROTC classes without requesting it.

- Request the JROTC enrollment statistics for each school. If any units have fallen below a total of 100 students two years in a row, agitate to remove them as required by federal law.

- Research the teaching credentials of JROTC instructors. Do they at least hold college degrees and are they certified?

- Compare JROTC history textbooks to the normal history textbooks. Are the facts correct in the JROTC textbook? If not, make a list and present it to the principal and your school board.

Counter-recruitment activists of all stripes have compelling facts and moral justification on their side, and they should use them judiciously. Teams of mature activists managed to pass ASVAB legislation in Maryland and New Hampshire, and they did it without bashing the military or the nation. In fact, they passed bills that some Republicans supported. School boards have been prevailed upon by soft-spoken middle-aged activists who stick to a carefully crafted script concerning "opt-out" forms, ASVAB release options, and the access granted to recruiters, among other issues. They're effective because they use carefully crafted words:

- We're not trying to starve the military of recruits. We're seeking a balanced message concerning military enlistment.

- We're not against the military. There are many honorable men and women who serve.

- We're not trying to drive recruiters from the schools - we acknowledge and respect the law that gives them the right to be there.

- We don't think most recruiters lie all the time. Instead, it's well documented that recruiters, working to fill quotas, can be overzealous.

- We're not outraged by a military testing program in the schools, predicated on lies, that recruits cannon fodder for an imperial machine. Instead, we understand that many counselors appreciate the ASVAB Career Exploration program; however, we think parents should be allowed to give consent before their child's information is sent to the Pentagon.

- We don't say the JROTC Marksmanship Program creates killers. Instead, we're concerned children may receive a mixed message in a school with a "no guns" policy.

NNOMY (National Network Opposing the Militarization of Youth) is a national networking body that brings together national, regional and local organizations to oppose the growing intrusion of the military in young people's lives. This essential organization promotes communication and sharing of organizing skills and resources across the country. NNOMY's website acts as a hub of resistance to American military recruitment and provides visitors with information on military programs operating in the schools and proven strategies to counter them.

The organization fields questions from citizens across the country who are concerned with the rapid militarization of youth, particularly in the nation's schools. NNOMY hosts an invaluable Yahoo "Counter-Recruitment" list-serve with 600 members across the country. The group has been in existence since 2000 and has logged nearly 20,000 posts. The searchable archive holds a treasure trove of information on the topic of American militarization. It has become an indispensable stopping point for research on militarism.

The NNOMY Reader, available online, is a useful primer to learn about the realities of military recruitment. The collection of articles represents a historical overview of the counter-recruitment movement's strategies to inform and intervene in schools and the community about the Pentagon's multi-billion-dollar programs to recruit America's youth into escalating wars.

Further Research

American Friends Service Committee (AFSC)
http://afsc.org/program/youth-and-militarism-program

Committee Opposed to Militarism and the Draft
http://www.comdsd.org/

Draft Resistance News
https://hasbrouck.org/draft/index.html

National Coalition to Protect Student Privacy
www.studentprivacy.org

National Network Opposing the Militarization of Youth (NNOMY)
http://nnomy.org/

Project on Youth & Non-Military Opportunities (YANO)*
http://www.projectyano.org/

Quaker House
https://www.quakerhouse.org/

Stop Recruiting Kids
http://srkcampaign.org/

War Resisters League
https://www.warresisters.org/counter-recruitment-0

World Beyond War
http://worldbeyondwar.org/

Youth Activist-Youth Allies (YAYA) Network
http://www.yayanetwork.org/

* Start here

Veterans' Groups:

Courage to Resist	http://www.couragetoresist.org/
GI Rights Hotline	http://www.girightshotline.org/
	877-447-4487
Iraq Veterans Against the War	http://ivaw.org/
Military Families Speak Out	http://www.militaryfamiliesspeakout.com/
Veterans for Peace	http://www.veteransforpeace.org/

Acknowledgments

Two wonderful women have helped me write this book. I couldn't have written it without the loving support of Nell, my dear wife. Nell designed this book. I know it's been tough for her at times. This goes out to all the partners who live with strung-out obsessive-compulsive, nonviolent political junkies like me.

I *could* have written it without the help of Mary Liston Liepold, but it wouldn't have been very good! Mary meticulously edited this manuscript, cleaning up my grammatical bombshells. Mary is a secular Franciscan, mother, grandmother, reader, writer, editor, and activist. Actively retired from a career in child care and nonprofit communications, she currently chairs the Metro DC-Baltimore Region of Pax Christi USA.

Finally, I owe of debt of gratitude to Rick Jahnkow of the Project on Youth & Non-Military Opportunities, (Project YANO). Rick possesses a kind of encyclopedic mind on U.S. military recruitment and he has always been willing to field my questions and offer compelling insight, much of which is reflected in this book.

About the Author

Pat Elder is the Director of the National Coalition to Protect Student Privacy, an organization that works to counter the alarming militarization of America's high schools. Elder was a co-founder of the DC Antiwar Network and a longtime member of the Steering Committee of the National Network Opposing the Militarization of Youth. His articles have appeared in *Truth Out, Common Dreams, Alternet, L.A. Progressive, Sojourner's Magazine*, and *U.S. Catholic Magazine*. Elder's work has also been covered by *NPR, USA Today, The Washington Post, Aljazeera, Russia Today*, and *Education Week*.

Pat Elder has crafted bills and helped to pass legislation in Maryland and New Hampshire to curtail recruiter access to student data. He has been instrumental in helping to convince more than a thousand schools to take steps to protect student data from recruiters. Elder helped to organize a successful series of demonstrations to shut down the Army Experience Center, a first-person shooter video arcade in a Philadelphia suburb.

Elder worked to lead the UN's Committee on the Rights of the Child to call on the Obama Administration to adhere to the Optional Protocol to the Convention on the Rights of the Child on the Involvement of Children in Armed Conflict regarding military recruiting practices in the schools.

Elder holds a Master's in Government from the University of Maryland and Maryland high school teacher certification. He lives with his wife, Nell on the St. Mary's River in St. Mary's City, Maryland. •

INDEX

1 Peter 3:13-16, 67
1st Recruiting Brigade, 59
3rd Recruiting Brigade, 59, 69
Abrams, Floyd, 84
Accuplacer, 189
Afghanistan, 11, 21, 30, 55, 82, 90-92, 122, 238, 244
Air Force, U.S., 24, 45, 47, 59, 79-80, 96-97, 135-36, 138, 153, 190, 205, 207, 232
Alabama, 58, 105, 125, 131, 207
Aljazeera, 82
Alexander, David, CT Rep., 198
Allende, Salvador, 217
America's Army 104, 116, 118-20, 123, 127, 240
America's Army Comics, 104
America's Sea Power Van, 97
American Academy of Pediatrics, 118, 148
American Civil Liberties Union, 162-63, 170, 195
American Friends Service Committee (AFSC), 31, 45-46, 245, 248
American Journal of Public Health, 34
American Legion Magazine, 41
American Psychological Association (APA), 123
American Public Health Association, (APHA), 34, 238
American School Counselor Association (ASCA), 57
Armed Forces Qualification Test (AFQT), 19, 36, 56
Armed Services Vocational Aptitude Battery (ASVAB), 54, 59, 69-70, 161-162, 166, 169, 175-199
Army Accessions Support Brigade, 96
Army Anti-Bullying Campaign, 48
Army Chopper, 99-100
Army Doctrine Publication 6-22, 50
Army Experience Center, 120, 127
Army Extreme Truck, 97, 98
Army Field Manual, 68, 239
Army Marketing and Research Group (AMRG), 106, 108
Army Recruiter Handbook, 29, 37, 43, 47, 162, 166, 181
Army Recruiting Command, 35, 43, 53, 158, 181
Army STEM Van, 96
Army Strong Zone, 101-2
Army War College, 50
Army, U.S., 17, 20, 35, 49, 51, 53, 100-5, 109, 119-20, 126
Armystrongstories.com, 167, 170
ASVAB Counselor Guide 177
Athy, Sgt. 1st Class Jeremy, 48
Aviation Recruiting Van, 96
Batschelet, Maj. Gen. Allen, 18-19, 35-6, 191
Benedictine College Preparatory, 65-68
Benjamin, Medea, 16
Best Practices for ASVAB-CEP Administration, 177-78
Beveridge, Lt. Col. Christopher, 196
Bloomfield H.S., CT, 46
Boca Ciega High School, FL, 209
Boot Camp, 20, 29, 31, 86, 239
Box, Col. John, 53-55
Boxer, Barbara, U.S. Senator, 23, 153
Bowie HS, MD, 57-58
Boykin, Lt. Gen. Jerry, 37
Brewer, Mike, 90
Brower, Elaine, 121

Buckley Amendment, 170
Buncombe County Board of Education, NC, 49
Bureau of Labor Statistics, 35, 39
Bush, President George W., 199, 237
Bushman, Brad, 122
Cadet Command Regulation 145-2, 208, 220
California, 23, 84, 96, 98, 126, 134, 138, 152, 168-169, 194-195, 210, 212, 220
Cardin, Sen. Ben, 153
Carson, Brad, 36-37
Carvers Bay High School, SC, 208
Catechism of the Catholic Church, 72
Catholic Church, 240
Cedar Ridge High School, NC, 183
Center on Conscience & War, 4, 164
Central Catholic High School in Greensburg, PA, 70
Chaminade Catholic High School, 69
Channel One News, 108-9
Chemerinsky, Irwin, 84
Child Soldiers International, 228, 261
Church of the Brethren, 70, 240, 245
Citizens Commission on Human Rights, 22
Civilian Marksmanship Program, 59, 131-58
Clancy, Tom, 83
Classical Magnet School, CT, 47
Coast Guard, U.S., 24
Code of Canon Law, 73
Coleman, Lt. Col. Michael D., 197
Commandant of the Marine Corps General James F. Amos, 23
Committee on the Rights of the Child, 227-28, 231
Congress, 13, 15-16, 28, 35, 39-40, 50, 82, 102-3, 131, 153, 159, 163, 165, 190, 205-7, 238, 240
Connecticut, 58, 122, 197
Connecticut News Junkie, 198
Consumer Product Safety Commission (CPSC), 133
Convention on the Rights of the Child, 13, 72, 230, 250
Corporation for the Promotion of Rifle Practice and Firearm Safety, Inc., 131
Courage to Resist, 249
Counter-Recruitment and the Campaign to Demilitarize Public Schools, 44
Court of Appeals for the Ninth Circuit, 28
Crosby HS, CT, 46
DD Form 4, 27, 238
Defense Activity for Non-Traditional Education Support (DANTES), 50
Defense Data Manpower Center Personnel Testing Center, 189
Defense Department, (DOD), 4, 24, 79, 81, 165, 167, 171, 175, 182, 199, 214, 241
Defense Industry Daily, 107
Inspector General, Department of Defense, (DOD IG), 87, 186
Delayed Entry Program, 30-31
Dillard, Major Larry, 122
Discovery Channel, 90-91
DoD Branding and Trademark Licensing Program, 102
Doom Video Game, 122-25
Dowd, Alan, 41
Durango HS, CO, 183
Duval HS, MD, 57-58
Eagleville High School, TN, 209

Earnhardt, Dale Jr., 102
Education Department, 4, 50, 193-94, 209, 212
Education Week, 179, 250
Eisenhower, President Dwight D., 240
Elementary and Secondary Education Act (ESEA), 40, 47, 69, 193
Enlistment/Reenlistment Document, 27-29, 32, 209-10, 238
Entry Level Performance and Conduct Discharge, 31
Equifax, 169
Evans, Gary, 122
Every Student Succeeds Act (ESSA), 44, 47, 110, 159, 242
Fairfax County, VA, 143-45
Family Educational Rights and Privacy Act (FERPA), 110, 159, 177, 194, 241, 243
Family Research Council, 37
Fitchburg High School, 44
Flake, Senator Jeff (R-AZ), 105-6
Flint, MI, 150
Florida, 50, 58, 134, 183, 188, 209
Flynn, Lance Corporal David, 57
Fordham University, 71
Forrest Gump, 85-87
Fort Knox, Kentucky, 35, 43, 59, 69
Freedom of Information Act request, (FOIA) 44, 79, 81, 88, 179
Future of Privacy Forum, 168
Gabbard, David A., 52
Gallup Poll, 11, 15, 217
GED, 220
Georgia, 52, 58, 98, 183
GI Rights Hotline, 4, 30, 249
Gillibrand, Sen. Kirsten (D-N.Y), 23, 49-50

Goebbels, Joseph, 96
Government Accountability Office (GAO), 232
Grapes, Jesse, A., 65-66
Griffith, D.W., 84
Grossman, Lt. Col. Dave, 117-18, 124-25
Guardian Newspaper, 126
Guide to Lead Management for Air Gun Shooting, 137, 140-41, 143, 148, 153, 241, 247
Gulf War, 21
Gumbleton, Bishop Thomas, 72
Hauck, Staff Sgt. Michael, 57
Harris, Barbara, 3, 199
Hartforn Public HS, CT, 46
Hawaii, 30, 151, 194
Health & Environmental Technology LLC (HET), 140
Hezbollah, 127
Hiroshima, 73, 215
Hollywood, 79, 82-88, 240
Holt, Kathryn Anne, 210
Homeland Security Department, 261
Houston Independent School District (ISD), 51
Hudson, Rep. Richard (NC-08), 102
Hurt Locker., The, 88
Iraq Veterans Against the War, 249
Iraq War, 38, 65, 82, 244
Jahnkow, Rick, 19, 61, 134, 213, 221
Job Corps, 165
Joint Advertising Market Research and Studies Recruiting Database (JAMRS), 160, 162
JROTC School of Cadet Command, 205, 207-8, 212, 220
Junior Reserve Officers Training Corps (JROTC), 52, 59-60, 71, 119, 131, 134, 166, 204-5

Justice Department, 163
Just War Doctrine, 73, 240
Kentucky, 35, 43, 59, 69-70, 117, 170, 184, 192
Kershner, Seth, 44, 199
King, Dr. Martin Luther, 111
Leadership, Education, and Training (LET) textbooks, 215-16
Lockheed Martin, 52
March 2 Success, 109
Marcus, William, 147
Marine Corps, 18, 24, 56-58, 60, 66, 68, 83, 87, 103, 106, 124, 135-36, 151, 167, 187, 208, 217, 233
Marine Corps News, 57
Maryland, 3, 57-59, 69, 100, 120, 143, 146, 148, 153, 169, 182, 194-96, 250
Massachusetts, 44-46, 58, 98, 118, 134, 137, 199
Matthew 18:6, 67
Matthew 5:33-34, 73
McCain, Senator John (R-AZ), 23, 105-6
McCann Worldgroup, 106-8
McCarthy, Colman, 71
McCaskill, Sen. Claire (D-Mo.), 102
McConville, Lt. Gen. James C., 19
Mehay, Stephen, 212
Mello Yello Drag Racing Series, 100
Mennonites, 70, 245
Mercury, Karen, 16
Miami, FL, 188
Military Entrance Processing Command (USMEPCOM), 38, 69-70, 109, 169, 178, 180, 182, 188, 191, 195, 229
Military Entrance Processing Stations, 19
Military Justice Improvement Act, 23
Military Occupational Specialties, (MOS), 18-20, 190
Military Recruitment in Western Massachusetts High Schools, 45-46
Military Sexual Trauma (MST), 23
Minnesota Department of Education, 191
Mirror Online, 84
Mission Bay High School, 222
Missouri Department of Elementary and Secondary Education, 193
Mississippi, 40, 192, 211
Monster.com, 56
Montgomery County, Maryland, 143-44, 195
Mortal Kombat, 118
My Future.com, 168
Nagasaki, 215
NASCAR, 102
National Academy of Science, 153
National Air Rifle Championships, 132
National Catholic Education Association, 69-70
National Catholic Reporter, 67-68
National Coalition to Protect Student Privacy, 228-29, 245, 248, 250
National Defense Authorization Act (NDAA), 213
National Football League, 11, 105-6
National Guard, 60, 102, 106
National Hot Rod Association (NHRA), 100-1
National Institute for Occupational Safety and Health (NIOSH), 147
National Institute of Health, 147
National Museum of American History, 112
National Network Opposing the Militarization of Youth (NNOMY),

248, 250
National Parent Teacher Association, 160
National Research Council of the National Academies, 193
National Rifle Association (NRA), 12, 151-52
National Security Agency (NSA), 126-27
NATO, 16, 99
Navy, U.S., 18, 24, 36, 45, 47, 60, 79, 85, 87, 97, 135, 146, 150, 190, 204-8, 213, 218-19, 240
Nebraska, 59, 69, 151, 182, 187
New Chevron, The, 65
New Mexico Public Education Department, 192
New York Civil Liberties Union, 163, 245
New York Coalition to Protect Student Privacy, 3, 199
New York Times, 38, 83-84,
Niebuhr, Reinhold, 72
Nielsen Claritas, 160
Nindl, Dr. Bradley, 20
No Child Left Behind Act, 34, 41, 47, 94, 159-60, 182-83, 198, 228, 233-34
North Hardin High School, KY, 184
North Salem High School, OR, 184
Nuclear Power Van, 97
Obama, President Barack, 169-70, 186, 227-228
Occupational Safety and Health Administration (OSHA), 136
Office of the Army Surgeon General (OTSG), 89
Office of the Assistant to the Secretary of Defense for Public Affairs (OATSD-PA), 81

Ohio, 71, 122, 132, 166
Omaha, Nebraska, 151
Optional Protocol on the Involvement of Children in Armed Conflict (OPAC), 72, 227, 230-34, 242, 250
Opt-out provision of the No Child left Behind Act, 159, 163, 169, 182, 190-91, 196, 198, 230, 233, 242, 246-47
Orwell, George, 16
Palm Center, 40, 41
Panetta, Leon, 87
Paramount Pictures, 83, 85-86
Partnership for Assessment of Readiness for College and Careers (PARCC), 189-191
Peacock Productions, 92
Pema, Elda, 212
Pennsylvania, 70, 134
Pepperell High School, GA, 183
Philadelphia Inquirer, 120
Planning for Life Program, 57
Pledge of Allegiance, 48, 73
Policy Memorandum 50, U.S. Army Cadet Command, 212
Pope Francis, 73
Post-traumatic stress disorder (PTSD), 13, 21, 23, 34, 238
Project YANO, 19, 61, 134, 213, 221, 245-46, 248
PSAT, 194
Quakers, 58, 70, 240, 245
RAND Corporation, 35, 233
Raptor Trailer, 97
Reed, Col. George, 50
Reporters Without Borders, 82
Rhode Island, 58, 98
Robb, David, 84, 92
Robert E. Lee High School, Staunton, Virginia, 47

Rodosevich, Robert, 140-41
Roger L. Putnam Vocational Technical Academy, 44, 46
ROTC Vitalization Act, 207
Saltman, Kenneth J., 52
San Diego CARD v. Grossmont Union H.S. District, 1986, 61
San Diego Unified School District, 134, 221, 246
Sanger, California, 151
SAT, 19, 166, 187, 189-90, 192
Schwarzenegger, Gov. Arnold, 195
Secker, Tom, 79, 81, 88
Selective Service System, 13, 161-65
Senate Armed Services Committee, 24, 39, 213
Senate Intelligence Committee, 88
Sergeant Lacroix, 104-5
Sexual assault, 11, 23, 50, 238
Sheyboygan, Wisconsin, 152
SkoolLive, 1 09-11
Slovik, Eddie, 16-17
Soldier's Creed, 52, 71
South Carolina, 58, 98, 208
Spellman, Cardinal Francis, 72
Springfield Central High School, 44-46,
St. Augustine, 73
St. Pius X High School, Lincoln, Nebraska, 69
St. Mary Catholic High School, OK, 70
St. Thomas Aquinas, 73
Stop-Loss, 28, 30
Student Digital Privacy Act, 168-69
Student Privacy Pledge, 168, 170
Student Racing Challenge, 101
Suicide, 11, 13, 15, 22-23, 34, 48, 50

Supreme Court, U.S., 61, 84, 177
Suwannee High School, FL, 183
Swanson, David, 9, 112
Tailored Adaptive Personality Assessment System, TAPAS, 19
Tampa Tribune, 40
Tanana Valley Alaska, 152
Ten80 Education Student Racing Challenge, 60, 101-2
Tennessee, 111, 188, 209-210
Texas, 50-51, 101, 123, 184, 199
Texas Education Agency, 51
Texas Examination of Education Standards (TExES), 51
Todaysmilitary.com, 167
Top Gun, 85-86, 244
Troops to Teachers, 50-52
Tzu, Sun, 55
U.S. Army Chief of Public Affairs, Los Angeles, (OCPA-LA), 79-80, 87, 92
U.S. Army Institute of Public Health, 20
U.S. Central Command's Public Affairs Office (USCENTCOM PA), 90-91
United States Conference of Catholic Bishops (USCCB), 73-74
US Department of Housing and Urban Development, 146
USA Today, 21, 88, 102, 196, 250
USMEPCOM Regulation 601-4, 169, 178, 180, 182, 229
Vatican, 72
Vermont, 58, 209
Veterans Department, 15-16, 21-22, 238
Veterans for Peace, 249
Vietnam War, 13, 23, 72-73, 83-84, 86

Vitter, Rep. David (R-LA), 40, 237
Waimea, Hawaii, 151
Wallace v. Chafee, 28
War Resisters League, 249
Washington Post, 103, 145, 196, 250
Wayland Baptist University, TX, 51
Weld County School District, CO, 159
Western New York Maritime Charter School, NY, 219
Wood, Diane, 199
World Beyond War, 249
Wright, Jessica, Acting Undersecretary of Defense for Personnel and Readiness, 39
Yahoo Groups counter-recruitment list serve, 248
Young Marines, 136, 240
Youth & Education Services (Y.E.S.), 100
Youth Activist-Youth Allies (YAYA) Network, 249
Zarembo, Alan, 22
Zero Dark Thirty, 87-88
Zinn, Howard, 82

Made in the USA
Lexington, KY
14 February 2017